GW01316192

The T

Vernon Coleman

'In times of universal deceit, telling the truth is a
revolutionary act.'
George Orwell

Bestselling author Vernon Coleman has written over 100 books which have been translated into 24 languages and have sold over 2 million copies in the UK alone. His novel Mrs Caldicot's Cabbage War was turned into an award winning movie. His series of seven books about the village of Bilbury are Amazon bestsellers. For a list of available books please see either the Vernon Coleman author page on Amazon or www.vernoncoleman.com

Dedicated to my beautiful wife, Donna Antoinette.

CONTENTS

Chapter 1

I stood on the porch outside the surgery and heard the two voices becoming louder and louder. They were both shouting and I really didn't want to be there. I always find other people's rows deeply embarrassing. I suspect most folk do. I was standing in the porch, as far away from the argument as I could get without going outside. It had been raining all day and now it was raining heavier than ever. The skies were black, the rain was bouncing off the few cars left in the car park and the atmosphere was undoubtedly packed to the edges with invigorating negative ions. The pellets of rain, hitting the thin metal of the cars, sounded like distant machine gun fire. Puddles had already developed on the badly laid tarmacadam and the usual small stream had formed down one side of the car park. We should have made the contractor come back and deal with it but we'd never got round to chasing him and now it's far too late. I could see my raincoat. It was safe and dry, draped uselessly over the front passenger seat of my rather boring BMW. My brown fishing hat was in there somewhere. I'm one of the few people on the planet who still wears a hat. I still believe the old theory that in cold weather nine tenths of the body's heat is lost through the head. I wear the thing in summer too, since the brim is just wide enough to provide a little screening from whatever sunshine might manage to struggle through the traditional English summer clouds. The car, the raincoat and the hat were no more than a dozen yards away. But I knew I would be soaked before I could reach any of them. I have another couple of decades to go before I'm officially entitled to retire but I'm desperately out of condition and already have arthritis in my knees and hips. I have patients twenty or thirty years older than me who could beat me in a race for a bus. Damp and cold just make the pain and stiffness worse, of course. I put my black drug bag down beside me and decided to wait a few minutes more.

There were just the three of us left in the surgery. The last patient had gone twenty minutes earlier and Daisy, the evening receptionist, had hurried away moments later.

`I've put the phones through to your mobile number,' she'd told me as she'd left, grabbing her bag and her coat and rushing to get home before the rain started. 'I hope you have a quiet night.' She was the oldest and the kindest of the receptionists and the only one I've ever got on with. To be honest she is the only one whose name I can regularly remember. There are eight or nine others, mostly working part-time, and they are as vaguely recognisable, and as indistinguishable, as the staff at the bank or the post-office. They are all women and mostly in their forties or older. No employer with functioning brain tissue hires women of childbearing age and Jock, who is in charge of hiring our employees does have a modest quantity of brain. He has many faults but he's not going to hire someone who is going to disappear for a year or more to breastfeed her State supported offspring. And so Daisy, like the rest of the staff, is of an age to be unlikely to demand endless maternity sabbaticals guaranteed by the bureaucrats of Brussels to be funded at someone else's expense.

I'd been standing in the reception area, dictating referral letters for three patients who needed to see hospital consultants, and I had thanked her and wished her a good weekend. I always feel guilty when I send patients to hospital these days. I know damned well that the appointments they send out are merely times at which patients have to be available so that a nurse can lie and tell them that the consultant hasn't turned up because of an emergency. He isn't really dealing with an emergency, of course. Senior hospital doctors don't deal with emergencies. He's at his private rooms charging £200 for twenty minutes and another £250 for an X-ray.

I hate being on call; constantly waiting for the telephone to ring. I put my hand into my jacket pocket, pulled out my phone and checked that it was switched on. The battery was low and I realised that I would have to put it on charge as soon as I got home. When I started in general practice I was tied to the landline telephone when I was on call; never daring to go out of earshot of a handset plugged into a socket in the wall. If I went out anywhere I either had to switch the phones through to that number or tell someone where I'd gone. No one could reach me when I was in the car or at a patient's house. When I was on call for the weekend I didn't even dare go out into the garden in case the telephone rang and I missed a call. The mobile telephone has made life infinitely easier though, I confess, the most joyful words known to the doctor who is a mobile telephone owner must surely be 'network search'. I can spend all weekend in the bar at The Bell and no one knows where I am. At nights and at weekends I switch the landline calls to my mobile phone and I can be on call anywhere. Thinking of home made me think of dinner and I decided that if I called into The Bell I could eat at the bar and have something with chips. Thinking of food reminded me that I'd intended to buy some bread but had forgotten. The stuff I'd used for toast had penicillin growing on it.

Minutes after Daisy had left, the two of them started shouting instead of just raising their voices; they were both almost screaming. I really didn't want to be there or to know what the argument was about.

The male voice belonged to Jock Cohen. He's a few years older than me and since the practice was originally started by his late father he is now the senior partner. He owns the building we practice in. It was built as a house in the late 19th century and for as long as I can remember Jock has been promising to make some basic improvements to the layout in order to make it more suitable for use as a medical centre. The patients sit in what used to be the dining room, the reception staff squeeze into an uncomfortable, partitioned area in the hallway and the doctors ply their trade in what used to be the bedrooms. My consulting room has an old Victorian fireplace and a ceiling that is so high that even with a stepladder none of us can replace the bulb in the ceiling light fitting. For the last seven years I have relied on standing lamps for light. I sometimes think this gives the room a rather unnaturally intimate atmosphere, although there is the advantage that the poor lighting means that the flaking paint is not so noticeable. All of us who work there would be thrilled if Jock organised a lick of paint here and there but there is about as much chance of that as there is of me becoming a world class athlete. Jock's only concession to the modern world has been to rename the building `The Jock Cohen Health Centre'. His father, now a permanent resident at the local cemetery, was also called Jock and our noble senior partner claims that the building is named after him but no one believes this.

Jock senior was humourless, puritanical and unforgiving. He was pompous and self-important and reminded me of George Abbot, an early Archbishop of Canterbury, who in 1605 sent one hundred and forty undergraduates to prison for sitting with their hats on in his presence. He liked to think of himself as a general, leading the forces of health and fitness against our arch enemies: disease and death. The trouble was that Jock senior, like his son, wasn't a terribly good leader. General Baron Kurt von Hammerstein-Equord, Commander in Chief of the German Reichswehr between 1930 and 1934, and an ardent critic of Adolf Hitler, once claimed that all his officers exhibited just two qualities from the following list of four: cleverness, industriousness, laziness and stupidity. The problem with Jock senior was that although he would have doubtless described himself as being clever and industrious his real qualities were stupidity and industriousness – the most worthless pairing of all.

If I were asked to sum up our Jock, Jock junior, in a single phrase I would have to choose the words `careful with his money'. There isn't much else to say about him, though being of Scottish origin he is, of course, a rabid racist, full to the brim with loathing for anyone who doesn't own a travelling rug in the clan tartan. His mother is South African and I assume that she must have been the primary source of his wonderful sense of humour for she is quite typical of the endless hearty wits who hail from Johannesburg and Cape Town. His father, as Scottish as sewn up pockets, made Scottish Nationalist and former Prime Minister Gordon Brown look like one of the rampaging Marx Brothers.

The only thing Jock and I have in common is that as white, male, middle aged citizens we are both members of an oppressed ethnic minority. He's married with two grown up children (neither of whom followed him into medicine) and plays golf with the earnest caution of a man whose Sunday is ruined if he loses a tee, let alone a ball. In the winter months he always wears a blue blazer with gilt buttons and a white shirt with a small crest on the breast pocket. The whole outfit is made ever more glorious by the addition of a tartan waistcoat designed to celebrate his Scottish ancestry and made, presumably, in the Cohen colours. In the summer he wears white trousers with turn-ups and blue deck shoes with white piping and looks like a refugee from the South of France. When he stands he puts his right hand in his jacket pocket, with the thumb hanging outside.

Superficially Jock often seems mean and vindictive (which he is) but somehow he always manages to give the impression that underneath he is kind and generous. `Do people hate me because I'm Jewish?' he asked me once. `Are you mean because you're Jewish?'

I asked him. 'Of course not!' he replied indignantly. 'Then people don't hate you because you're Jewish,' I replied. 'They just hate you because you're mean.'

Jock lives a completely stress free life because he never really worries about anything. Most of us become increasingly sad, anxious, angry, bitter and resentful as we become increasingly aware of life's general injustices, and as life fails to live up to our many expectations. Not Jock. He only ever worries about potential injustices which affect him personally, and those he deals with dispassionately and efficiently. He will probably live to enjoy several birthdays in his 90s though you'd have to wonder why he'd bother.

I believe that medicine is a complex mixture of wisdom (learning from experience), science, art, black magic and intuition. Of all these, intuition, which enables us to access wisdom and experience from our subconscious, is perhaps the most valuable of them all. Jock believes that medicine is a matter of listening to the blandishments of the drug company representative, choosing the most expensive wine at a drug company sponsored dinner, and then prescribing the latest wonder drug without pause or question. I believe that a doctor who is not also a cynic is a dangerous fool. Jock believes that it is not a doctor's place to think.

Most of us drift through life, missing opportunities, accumulating regrets and travelling from crisis to crisis, buffeted by fate and her whimsical family. Jock Cohen travels serenely through life, like a swan on a lake but with the big difference that with him the serenity is as real under the water as it is above it. He still lives in the house where he was born and probably still has the silver spoon that was found in his mouth when he was a baby. I doubt if he has ever even had a parking ticket. Fate would not dare be so cruel. It would be a thrill for us all if one of the receptionists walked into his surgery and found him making wild love to one of the nurses, or even a patient damnit, but Jock's life is dedicated to the accumulation of money and that's really all there is to him. He has devised a number of ways to hasten this process. He does trials for drug companies, provides second opinions for cash and accepts chunky kickbacks from the consultants to whom he refers patients requiring private treatment.

Jock has a considerable cash income from these various activities. He doesn't bother declaring any of this to the rest of us, the practice accountant or Her Majesty's Revenue and Customs but every month he takes the train to London where he visits a stamp shop in the Strand and uses the month's accumulation of cash to buy rare stamps. I once asked him how he'd explain the collection if the taxman ever discovered it and he told me that he'd simply say that it was a collection he'd been given as a child and that he'd found it in a drawer when clearing out an old piece of furniture. Since the stamps are all old it's difficult to see how anyone could prove otherwise.

After a rare dinner at his home he once showed me his collection but instead of being able to tell me the history of the individual stamps (as other collectors are usually able to do) all he could do was tell me the prices. I think I've only been to the house that one time. His wife turned out to be very mousy and subservient; treating him more like an employer than a husband. We had one of those frozen meals that the supermarkets advertise on television and a single bottle of cheap Spanish red wine. I suspect that more important guests are better fed and better wined.

The other half of the argument, the female voice, belonged to Molly Tranter, our trainee doctor, aka our general medical dogsbody. Molly looks after all the new patients, the mother and baby clinics, the life insurance medicals and the difficult patients who take up too much time for Jock to bother seeing them. She and I also shared the out of hours duty. Jock insisted that we provide a 24 hour a day, 365 day a year, service and said that he insisted on this because it is best for the patients. He was right, of course, but he didn't share in providing the cover he insisted we provided. He said that at his age he'd done his stint and that it was up to the younger members of the practice to provide cover at nights, weekends and bank holidays.

Our other doctor, Dr Deidre Canterbury, was younger than me but she had two small daughters and said that it wouldn't be fair to them if she worked at nights or weekends. As a partner, I received a small, extra annual payment from the practice for providing this service. (It was, inevitably, much less than the 6% extra the practice received, and so both Jock and Deidre made money from the out of hours commitment.) Molly, who was salaried, didn't receive a penny extra. No one ever mentioned it but the practice did well out of Molly and myself covering the out of hours work. Back in 2004, the

Government rewrote the GP's contract and allowed family doctors to stop providing out of hours cover in return for a 6% cut in salary. I cannot imagine what sort of political idiot thought that the extra work was worth just 6% of a doctor's income. The result, inevitably, was that the vast majority of practices leapt at the chance to give up working at nights and at weekends and happily took the modest drop in pre-tax income. Today, politicians and doctors all seem genuinely surprised that there has been a dramatic increase in the number of patients turning up at Accident and Emergency Departments outside normal working hours. No one seems to suspect that there might be a link between the increase in the number of people dying from routine but serious health problems and the fact that doctors no longer provide 24 hour cover for their patients.

The one advantage of having just two of us look after the nights and weekends was that it was fairly easy to work out the rota. And if one of us needed to change a weekend or a night it didn't involve a great deal of negotiating. I know a doctor who works in an eight doctor practice in Lancashire. They too have agreed to provide their patients with 24 hour cover. They all share their on call rota equally and they've had to have special software designed to enable them to organise their commitments. One of their practice secretaries spends half her life keeping the rota up-to-date and there are constant arguments about the number of bank holidays, Christmases and evenings worked. Molly and I usually managed to work things out pretty amicably.

As I stood in the porch, sheltering from the rain, I cleaned out and lit my pipe and tried to remember why we'd hire Molly Tranter as our trainee. There had been two dozen candidates and she hadn't been the best qualified in any respect although she had certainly been the smallest. Only the thickness of an envelope more than five feet tall if she stood on tiptoe, Molly was the daughter of a couple who ran a greengrocery business in Wolverhampton. She got the job as our trainee as a compromise. Jock Cohen had wanted to appoint a young rugby playing doctor whose father was a consultant neurologist somewhere in the Home Counties. But the rugby player was a cocky bastard and I think even Jock realised that he would have been a disaster. He'd turned up in a Porsche which he'd left sprawled across three spaces in the car park. I had thought him too far aloof and arrogant for our practice and to my relief Deidre

Canterbury, a woman who talks a good deal but usually says very little, and who does not regard tact or diplomacy as having any part to play in her job description, had summarily, and not at all unfairly, dismissed him as a 'smarmy little git with far too high an opinion of himself'. The young pretender didn't help his chances by mistaking Deidre for one of the receptionists, handing her his Burberry and telling her to hang it up 'but make sure you put it on a hanger'. This was a big mistake. Deidre is scarier than Andy Murray's mother.

The discussion about whom to appoint had gone on for over a week, though I had kept it out of it all as much as I possibly could. I'm pretty sure that Molly had been the only one none of us disliked enough to veto. In a way this was surprising since Jock has a strong dislike of women doctors. He said that having Deidre working in the practice was more than enough of a nod towards feminine supremacy. When there were no women within hearing distance he used to be fond of quoting Noel Coward who apparently once said that women should be beaten regularly, like gongs. Jock stopped quoting Coward when a midwife overheard him and, instead of accusing him of political incorrectness, laughed at him for quoting an 'old poofter'.

Suddenly, a door burst open and I heard it slam into the wall. We used to have those little rubber door stopper things to prevent the doors hitting the walls but over the years marauding, thieving children have unscrewed them and stolen them so now when a door is thrown open with enthusiasm the doorknob tends to crunch into the plaster. The voices were much louder now and half of the row, the feminine half, was heading in my direction. I had just decided that the rain was the lesser of two evils when Molly Tranter joined me in the porch. Her cheeks were red with anger and she was shaking. She looked out of the door and up at the sky and swore quietly.

I said something banal about the rain looking set in for the night and Molly agreed with me. Quite unexpectedly she then burst into tears. She was still in her twenties and I remember thinking that she looked too young and inexperienced to be a student nurse, let alone a doctor. She always dressed casually, never wore make-up and wore her hair in a short page-boy cut. She was so skinny she looked as if she needed nailing down on windy days.

I've been told I have a reputation among our less discerning patients as a kind and sympathetic listener, but I've never been good with women who aren't showing me lumps and rashes or describing their symptoms. I muttered something intended to be soothing. Molly pulled a packet of tissues out of her pocket, took one out and blew her nose. She then took out another tissue and dabbed at her eyes. `Life's all about money to him,' she said, clearly having taken my calming murmur as an invitation to confide in me and share her pain. `He's a mean, grasping, thieving crook. He doesn't give a damn about the patients.' She paused. `I told him all that,' she said defiantly.

`He has to look after the practice,' I said, feeling I had to offer a half-hearted defence of Jock who is, after all, our senior partner. `Expenses are constantly going up. Staff costs. Stationery. Health and safety. Heating bills.'

`Oh bugger you!' Molly cried. `Why do you always have to be so damned reasonable and sensible? This isn't about making enough money to pay the gas bill, this is about making enough money to pay for his farmhouse in the Dordogne and the third car and the boat in Dartmouth.' She was right about that. Jock still believes that having good time means spending money he doesn't have on stuff he doesn't need and probably doesn't even really want. He hasn't yet worked out, and probably never will, that real luxury is space, light, peace and quiet.

Molly started crying again. `I hate crying,' she said. `I'm only crying because I'm so damned angry.' She blew her nose. `Why do you put up with him? Why do you defend him?'

`I'm too tired to fight anyone,' I told her, too weary to feel embarrassed by this admission. `I'm just worn down by daily rubbish. The last time I filled in a form where they asked for my occupation I put: `Filling in forms and dealing with crap'.' The truth was that I didn't know where it had gone, or when it had disappeared, but all the righteous passion I'd had as a young man had faded away. `Without cowards and failures like me there would be no courageous, successful people and the courageous, successful people would have no one to look down on. How can I end that sentence without a preposition?' Molly looked at me but said nothing for a while. I pulled out my pipe and puffed at it even though it had gone out long ago.

A pipe is a very useful toy. I always puff on it when I don't have anything apt or witty to say and so I puff on it a good deal. In fact, although I'd never admit this to anyone, I don't smoke because I enjoy the taste of the tobacco but because I rather like the process and the paraphernalia. Like most pipe smokers I have quite a collection of pipes, stored on a rather fine mahogany rack at home. Nearly all of them are really large, with huge bowls, because I never inhale the smoke and am perfectly happy for it to float up into the air around me. It may not be politically correct but my idea of political correctness is putting a cross in the right place on a ballot form and I rather like wandering around in my own private cloud of blue smoke. One of the receptionists, the stout, middle-aged one who has an undiagnosed thyroid condition that I have never found the courage to mention and who spends so much time on her sunbed that she must surely be a dead cert for multiple basal cell carcinomas, once said that I live in my own piece of foggy, Victorian London. I think it was meant as an insult, but I took it as a compliment. My pockets are full of pipe smoking stuff: a leather tobacco pouch, a three in one silver gadget for poking and cleaning pipes and a packet of old fashioned pipe cleaners with which I sometimes make small animals to entertain fractious child patients. Their mums think I do this because I love children but I'm afraid I do it because I hate children crying. And besides you can't examine a child who's screaming. If it takes a small giraffe to shut him up then I'll sacrifice a pipe cleaner and make a small giraffe. I once told Jock, in mock seriousness, that the practice should pay for my pipe cleaners and that they ought to be tax deductible. He can never tell when he is being teased. He said that I ought to take it up with the accountant and ask him to consult our local tax inspector.

`Do you think he'll fire me? I don't care if he does. He's even got personalised number plates on both his cars. How vulgar can you get? They're the middle class equivalent of having your name tattooed on your arm.'

`They aren't very good personalised number plates.'

`How can a personalised number plate not be very good?' she demanded.

`It took me three months to realise that the letters and numbers were anything other than an ordinary number plate,' I explained. `I had to squint at it and use my imagination to realise that it sort of made up a dyslexic version of his name. There's a number 4 making up the last letter of `Jock'! '

Molly smiled and sort of nearly laughed and stuffed her used tissues into her coat pocket. She looked terrible. `I'll buy you a drink,' I told her. `You aren't fit to drive so we'll go in my car. I'll bring you back here to pick up yours afterwards.'

`I don't drink much,' she replied. `Hardly at all. Hardly ever. It makes me too tiddly and gives me a sort of hot flush.'

`You have to drink something or your kidneys will pack up,' I told her. `I'll buy you a glass of water. You can have it with or without bubbles but I suggest you live dangerously and have it with bubbles.'

Twenty minutes later, soaked from the short run to my car, we were sitting at the bar in The Bell Hotel. To save time, and to avoid the town's impenetrable one way system, designed by a maniacal pedestrian with a hatred of motorists or some sort of deal with the oil companies, I'd taken the `short' route which involves heading out of town onto the motorway, slaloming between the cones and warnings put there to give the authorities an excuse to make oodles of money out of enforcing speed limits, and then driving back in again at the next junction. This had the added advantage of enabling me to purchase a few gallons of petrol for the car. The stuff they sell on the motorway is expensive but at least it is available. Most of the petrol stations in the town centre have been converted into `Hand Car Wash And Valeting Centres' manned by hard working and enthusiastic East Europeans who must make a fortune out of their polishing and buffing. I wonder how much of it is passed onto the Chancellor of the Exchequer. We will all be in real trouble when the motorway service stations have been taken over by the red fingered men with plastic buckets and sponges.

Even though Molly and I had travelled no more than a couple of miles on the motorway we still drove past two broken down vehicles. Now that people can't afford to have their cars serviced this happens more and more often. The stranded motorists, including one mother holding a young baby, were standing on the grass behind their cars. It was still bucketing down and they must have been drenched to the skin. The idiots who answer emergency calls always tell people to get out of their cars. I bet more motorists die of pneumonia than die of being squashed in their parked cars. It's the same with aeroplanes and airports. They are staffed almost exclusively with leering, bullying layabouts who have a collective IQ lower than a ballerina's shoe size and who would never notice if a team of terrorists with tea towels draped over their heads went past them carrying sacks full of Semtex. No one dares complain because they're frightened of being arrested for aiding and abetting terrorism. The Nazi storm-troopers at airports take nail clippers off octogenarians in order to prevent hijackings but the aeroplane owners recycle dirty air to save money and, as a result, far more people die of infectious diseases caught on aeroplanes than have ever died because of terrorist attacks. I haven't been on an aeroplane for years and with any luck I'll manage to keep off them in whatever years I have left until the Good Lord gives me wings or a toasting fork.

Chapter 2

The Bell is invariably deserted on Friday evenings. No one goes there for a romantic, dirty or any other sort of weekend. Commercial travellers stay there from Monday to Thursday. There are weddings on Saturdays. And upwardly mobile locals enjoy a popular fixed price carvery on Sundays. It looks and smells of decay and is one of those typically English establishments; once glorious, now faded.

'We don't see you in here very often, Dr Tranter,' said Harry the barman, who had poured out a large Laphroaig the minute he'd seen the two of us approaching the bar. He makes sure they always keep a supply of my favourite 18-year-old single malt. If I were sent to a desert island I would not know whether to choose the single malt or my pipe as my luxury. 'What can I get you?' Harry is the barman's professional name and to prove his skills there are certificates in frames hanging behind the bottles on the glass shelf behind him. There are two diplomas registering his cocktail mixing skills and three attesting to his health and safety prowess. His real name is Leonard. He is a nervous, jittery fellow who always reminds me of the snooker player Alex Higgins in that he is never able to keep still for more than a few seconds at a time. He is constantly twitching and has a thousand different tics. He has a compassionate attitude towards rules and regulations and when the bar is quiet, as it was that evening, he does not object to my smoking my pipe. He once told me that when I have left he sprays the area with a can of furniture polish – far less offensive than air freshener. I am one of the few people he gets on with. He is a sensitive and easily offended soul and the scattered debris of a hundred former friendships lie as uneasy and troubled testament both to the ease with which he can take offence and the longevity of his hurt. The owners of The Bell don't visit the establishment often or they would know that Harry has scared away most of the former regulars and that if I ever stop drinking there the takings will have to appear in the accounts under the heading 'petty cash'. I like Harry. We get on well. We understand each other.

'I'll have one of those,' Molly said, pointing at the glass which Harry had placed on the bar counter. I nobly pushed the drink in her direction and waited for a duplicate to be poured. `Are you eating?' I asked.

She shook her head. `Larry said he'd order a pizza when I got home.' Larry, Dr Tranter's boyfriend, was an unemployed geologist who was trying to carve out a career as a stand-up comedian. A pot holing accident had left him as a paraplegic and life hadn't been going well. He had, so Molly had told me, a burning desire to be too famous to shop in supermarkets.

`One steak and kidney pudding with chips,' I said to Harry.

`How can you eat kidneys?' demanded Dr Tranter, who like all vegetarians rarely wasted an opportunity to warn people of the hazards of eating meat.

`What were you and Jock arguing about?' I asked her, hoping that this would distract her from a lecture on the general benefits of vegetarianism and the specific perils of eating a steak and kidney pudding. `I'm surprised the neighbours didn't ring the police and report a domestic altercation.' I didn't really want to know but I knew I had to ask sometime.

`We had a row about vaccination,' said Dr Tranter. She picked up the glass of Laphroaig, took a mouthful as though she were drinking from a glass of wine and immediately started coughing. `What the hell is that?' she demanded, holding the glass at arm's length and staring at it as though it had tried to bite her.

`It's a food product,' I told her. `The ingredients are impeccable, though I'm sorry that the presentation isn't to your liking.' Laphroaig is a single malt from Islay. It has an exceptionally peaty flavour and is probably the most robust malt whisky of them all. Even determined drinkers of blended whisky can be taken aback when they take a sip – or even a sniff. I took her glass from her, poured the contents into my own and, having asked her what she wanted as a replacement, ordered a diet cola. It seemed marginally more exciting than water but not likely to do much more for her spirit.

`Aren't you on call this evening?' Molly asked, looking at the enhanced contents of my glass.

`My steak and kidney pudding will soak this up,' I told her. I felt a twinge of guilt and was, for a moment, cross with her. She could be annoyingly sanctimonious. I knew as well as she did that I shouldn't drink when I was on call and that I shouldn't drink when I was driving.

`I saw Mrs Jackson this morning. Michael, her little boy, reacted badly to his last vaccination and she wanted to know if he could miss the next series of jabs. He was screaming for hours after he was vaccinated. I talked to her about the side effects and the dangers and told her that she and her husband must make the decision.'

`But you loaded the dice a bit?'

Molly blushed. `I didn't tell her what to do. I didn't tell her not to have her child vaccinated. I just told her the truth.' She managed to sound defensive and defiant at the same time.

`And as a result, Mr and Mrs Jackson decided not to have Jackson minor vaccinated?'

Molly nodded. `And she also wrote to Jock telling him why she wasn't having him done.'

`People don't want to know the truth about contentious subjects like vaccination,' I told her.

`That's patronising!'

`Maybe it is. But they don't want to know because learning is hard work, understanding is harder work and knowing is the hardest work of all. And so they trust us to tell them the truth.'

`But that's exactly the point. We tell people bits of the truth but mainly we lie to them.'

`How can you say that?' I demanded, staring at her aghast.

`We tell patients a little bit of the truth but a scrap of truth is no truth at all. It's absolutely no good to anyone. If we tell people half the truth but don't tell them which half of the things we're telling them are true and which half are lies they won't know which is which. And so everything we tell them might as well be a lie because it is no more use than a lie.'

I was, to be honest, wearying of this. I have, over the years, had too many arguments with individuals who are passionate about the fluoridation of water supplies, the awfulness of vivisection and the hazards of genetic engineering. Being a doctor seems to make me fair game for everyone with a bee in their bonnet. I was tired, I wanted to eat and drink and forget the practice and the real world for a while. But Molly was getting under my skin.

'Why do you keep on saying that we tell people untruths?' I demanded. 'We tell them what we're told by the Government.'

'Exactly! And who tells the Government what to tell us?'

I thought about this. 'I don't know. Experts I suppose.'

Molly shook her head. 'The drug companies tell them what to tell us; or so-called experts working for the drug companies. And they tell them to tell us stuff that will sell vaccines.'

'Oh, I can't believe that!' I protested.

'It's true!' insisted Molly. 'Patients don't ask us questions because they believe that we're telling them the truth. And, they want to believe us. They want to believe in vaccination because it's such a lovely idea. Have your kids jabbed and they won't fall ill. It's as comforting as the idea that there's no need to look after your body because doctors have access to magic pills that will cure everything. And doctors don't ask questions because we desperately want to believe that the Government is telling us the truth when they tell us that vaccines save lives. It's convenient, it's profitable and we think it's a lovely idea too. The people working for the Government believe what they're told by the drug company people because it's convenient and easier than not believing. It's certainly much easier than asking questions. No one actually does any research. No one tries to find out whether vaccines are good or bad or a mixture of the two. The drug companies create a vaccine and it's in their interests to sell as much of it as they can. So their experts tell the people working for the Government that the new vaccine is brilliant and will save lives and save money and the civil servants write leaflets telling doctors and nurses and patients and journalists that vaccines are wonderful. But no one really knows the truth because no one has ever bothered to ask the questions that should have been asked.'

'But you can't just launch a new vaccine without proving that it works!'

'Of course you can! All you have to prove is that it doesn't kill zillions of mice or guinea pigs or rabbits and that when you give it to a few dozen people it doesn't kill too many of them in the first fortnight. And then when you've proved that you can give it to millions of people and make a fortune.'

'But they have to do tests!' I insisted.

'They rely a lot on animal experiments,' said Molly, who was now on a roll. 'If the animals develop cancer or have heart attacks they say the results are irrelevant because animals are different to people. Everyone nods wisely and agrees. But if the animals are fine the vaccine is given the all clear. It's the same with a new drug. They test it on animals and a few people and if it doesn't produce pretty sudden and obvious problems they dish it out by the lorry load.' I nodded and hoped that this wasn't going to go on for too long. 'The problem is that some dangerous side effects aren't immediately obvious. And some may only affect, say, one in every ten thousand patients. They test the new drug on a thousand patients and there are no dramatic side effects so everyone says 'whizzo' and the drug gets a licence. Within no time at all the drug is on the market and GPs around the world are prescribing the drug for ten million patients. Two years later a thousand people have died because they've developed brain cancer.'

Harry brought her diet cola, a glass and a little paper doily. He looked disappointed that someone in his bar was drinking a non-alcoholic beverage. Molly thanked him and sipped her new drink.

'You told Mr and Mrs Jackson some of this?'

'Some of it. Just a bit of it. They asked me for my opinion so I had to give them some of the facts to show why I don't believe in vaccination. People tend to reject things they don't want to hear – especially if they're frightened or they don't understand.'

'And then went to Jock and told him what you'd said?'

'Yes, I'm afraid so.'

'Giving you the credit?'

Molly blushed. 'Mrs Jackson said that I was the only person who'd been honest with her.'

'Jock wouldn't like that.'

'No, I don't think he did. But it was the money we lose out on that really upset him. He went on and on about it. He explained in great detail that it's not just the fee for vaccinating the child, and the profit on the vaccine we bulk buy from the drug company that makes it so profitable but that we also lose our bonus if not enough of the practice patients are vaccinated.'

'All that disgusting loot helps pay your salary.' The truth is that the fees we receive from vaccinating patients add up to a very decent sum at the end of the year. Jock reckons we make a quarter of our gross income giving vaccinations (or, more accurately, telling a nurse to give them). Our vaccination income is the cream on top of an admittedly rich cake. Jock can't remember much but he knows to the penny how much profit there is in a vaccination.

'Oh, not you as well,' said Molly, sounding exasperated. 'That was Jock's argument. I told him that being honest with patients is more important than making money out of vaccinations. We're none of us exactly starving are we?'

'I bet that went down well.' I took a sip of my Laphroaig. The distillers who make the stuff really should be given a couple of Nobel Prizes.

'He then gave me the official spiel about vaccinations having saved the world from infectious diseases, and being directly responsible for saving millions of lives and being totally safe and all that stuff. And I said that if he believed all that guff he probably also believed that vaccines protected us from terrorism, money laundering and global warming. And I asked him if he still believed in the Tooth Fairy and Father Christmas. He then said that even if vaccination was dangerous it wasn't my place to go round banging my drum and scaring the patients.'

I told her that she had to agree that Jock had a point and that she could hardly deny that vaccines were one of the great medical inventions. I asked her what she was suggesting. Did she want to ban all vaccinations or just some of them?

She said she didn't want to ban anything but that she did want patients to be told the truth so that they could make up their own minds. 'The whole issue is more contentious than anyone admits,' she claimed. 'We tell patients that vaccines are safe and effective because that's what we are told. But who tells us that? The bloody drug companies and the Government! And if it's not my job to say something about a medical practice I believe to be wrong then what is my job? Was I trained to obediently give vaccinations that don't do any good but which might kill the people I give them to?'

'You don't think the Government is telling us the truth?'

Molly looked at me and raised an eyebrow.

'Sorry,' I said. 'Stupid thing to say. I know they exaggerate and smooth things over but generally speaking what they say about vaccines is surely fair.'

'That's the whole point,' Molly replied angrily. 'What they say isn't fair. They lie about everything. If you believe that vaccines are safe and effective you must have willed yourself to suppress the doubts you know you should feel and the questions you should be asking. Haven't you read my article in the *British Clinical Journal?*'

I confessed that I didn't even know she'd written an article anywhere.

'I'll e-mail you a copy.'

I looked at her.

She laughed. 'Sorry, I forgot you don't like e-mail. I'll print it out and give you a copy. I've got some copies the journal sent me in lieu of a fee. I'll give you one of those.'

Harry brought my steak and kidney pudding and chips and put it down on the bar in front of me with a flourish. The Bell might be on its last legs as a hotel but the chef, who is well past retirement age and a fellow arthritis sufferer, knows how to make good old-fashioned English fare. He doesn't do wonderful things with sweetbreads and lime marmalade, or serve up tiny portions of braised duck's buttock swimming in a raspberry coulis, but he makes damned good pies and puddings and his chips are as good as any I've ever eaten out of newspaper which is, when you think about it, a considerable tribute. He produces excellent beef, reliable ham and succulent pork and never gets upset when his customers ask for mustard, horseradish or apple sauce. He may work in a hotel but he's an old-fashioned English pub chef. For puddings he serves spotted dick, roly-poly and treacle sponge rather than profiteroles and other modern inevitabilities.

'I cannot sit here and watch you eat that,' said Molly, staring at the plate Harry had placed before me. She stood up and picked up her coat.

'You can't go until I've finished,' I told her.

'Why not?'

'Because your car is still parked at the surgery and you can't get back there until I've finished my dinner.'

Molly sat down again.

'Don't say a word about my meal,' I told her, picking up and unwrapping the cutlery which Harry had laid down beside my plate. I laid the linen napkin across my lap. There may be holes in the carpets and draughts in the bedrooms but even in the bar they still have linen napkins at The Bell. And they starch them nicely too.

For the next twenty minutes or so we talked about nothing of consequence. `Do you always play that crappy music in your car?' she asked. `That was La Boheme,' I told her, aggrieved. `I know what it was. I just can't get into the idea of two rich, fat, middle aged millionaires pretending to be impoverished, starving students and singing across the body of an overweight diva who is alleged to be dying of tuberculosis but somehow manages to find the energy and the breath to sing back at them.'

`What do you like?' I asked her.

`Have you heard the latest from the `Bald and Tattooed Bastards'?' I said I hadn't. She said they were fantastic and that the lead singer had eighteen earrings in just one ear. I told her I'd trust her judgement.

I took Molly back to the surgery and waited while she picked up her car. It's a glum neighbourhood and we get hoodies hanging around outside in the evenings. I have given up telling them to clear off. On one notable occasion a young man wearing an anorak and baggy trousers asked me if I'd had my arse sewn up and then, without waiting for a reply, told me that he thought this to be the case because in his opinion I was full of shit. He laughed a lot at his joke and I confess I smiled too because it was funnier than the usual abuse. Jock did put up a sign warning trespassers that they would be prosecuted but it did about as much good as you'd expect.

Before she drove away Molly gave me a copy of the article she'd mentioned. She had several tucked into a manila folder in the boot of her car. I popped the article into my drug bag.

It was a Friday evening and I was on call for the whole of the weekend. I think I assumed that by Monday morning the argument would have been put to one side, if not forgotten, and that Molly and Jock would have resumed their rather brittle working relationship.

Looking back that was obviously wishful thinking. Molly wasn't about to abandon what she saw as a morally defensible position. And Jock was never going to change his mind. As author Upton Sinclair once wrote: `It is difficult to get a man to understand something if his salary depends on his not understanding it.'

Chapter 3

I had a surprisingly quiet and professionally uneventful weekend.

I was woken only once on Friday night to visit an asthmatic. He thought he needed intravenous steroids but he recovered with two squirts of an inhaler he'd never seen before, a good deal of reassurance and, possibly, the knowledge that the injection was in my bag three feet away from him if he didn't recover.

The telephone didn't ring at all on Saturday morning but during the afternoon I had a number of calls, none of which involved anything that wouldn't have waited until Monday.

An unmarried woman in her early twenties demanded infertility treatment so that she could have a baby and a council flat, and a gamine girl of 16 wanted breast enlargement surgery so that she could become a topless model and, no doubt, a figure of great influence in the entertainment world. The teenager told me, with considerable pride, that she already had a tattoo of `someone called Van Dyke' on her pubic area. `He's got a real beard,' she added with a giggle and asked me if I wanted to see. `The tattooist said Van Dyke was a painter but I've never heard of him.' She giggled again. `I give him a trim every now and then.' I never fail to be amazed at the ingenuity of tattoo artists, though being given all that bare skin to despoil must be a delight to a lunatic with a needle and a palette of multi-coloured inks. But I do wonder how people find the patience and the time to sit still while it's all being done. And how will those tattoos look when the underlying skin is wrinkled and peppered with liver spots?

I told them both that I would help with their requests when all the nation's patients waiting for cancer surgery had been treated. The woman who had demanded infertility treatment threatened to report me, though she did not say to whom, and the teenage girl just sulked and said she'd take an overdose and I'd be sorry.

The minute I'd put some baked beans onto the stove a very shouty woman demanded that I go round right away and clip her toenails. When I demurred and asked why she'd telephoned me she said I was the chiropodist wasn't I? I said I wasn't the chiropodist and then for reasons which I cannot explain I adopted a Welsh accent and told her that God would bless her feet and that she would walk through the valleys of righteousness and light. She said I was mad, which may well be a more accurate diagnosis than she realised, and hung up the telephone on me which saved me hanging it up on her.

On Saturday evening I had five calls, one after the other, and there were two more calls during the long, dark hours of the night. The evening calls weren't particularly dramatic. Three were to patients with colds and two were to men who'd hurt themselves playing football and needed to be told how brave they were and that they really didn't need to have their bruises X-rayed. But both of the night calls took time. The first was to a boy of 12 who had appendicitis and needed to be admitted to hospital and the second was to a man of 36 who had decided to kill himself by cutting his throat. He'd missed the artery and had cut only the jugular vein but he had made a mess of every room in the house as he'd wandered around wailing and showing everyone what he'd done. He too needed a trip to the local hospital and when the ambulance had taken him away I stayed for half an hour to help his unfortunate wife clean up some of the blood he'd spilt. A small amount of blood goes a long way when dripped onto furniture and carpets. A sympathetic neighbour looked after the two children who were strangely, and rather worryingly, accustomed to Daddy's odd behaviour.

Sunday was more of the same, but quieter.

There are two main varieties of patient who call out the doctor at the weekend.

The first group of people are apologetic about being a nuisance on a Saturday or a Sunday. They often call about something which has been troubling them for weeks; a problem which they've left for too long and which has finally become unbearable in some way. Some of the patients in this group genuinely don't want to be any trouble. They would rather suffer than be considered a bother, and sometimes, actually not infrequently, they die for their kindness. A few of the patients in this category are nice to me not because they like me, or because they are nice to people in general, but because I am their doctor and they hope that one day, if they are in pain, I will give them enough morphine to make life bearable and that until then I won't follow the evil footsteps of the much missed Dr Shipman and give them a large dose of morphine which they don't need.

The second group know their rights and aim to get their money's worth (even though most of them have never paid any taxes at all). They don't give a fig whether it's three o'clock in the morning or three o'clock in the afternoon when they call the doctor. Their attitude is that they are entitled to see a doctor when they want to see one and that's that. Most practices no longer cater to the patients in this category. The modern on-call doctor who is responsible for looking after 500,000 or more patients, spread over a huge area, won't visit anyone. There are plenty of health care bureaucrats around, hospitals are awash with them and health centres are stuffed with them, but most people, and I'm delighted to say that this includes the bureaucrats, of course, won't ever be able to find a doctor outside banking hours.

But our practice does do night and weekend calls, of course.

The selfish bugger who rang me at 3.30 am on Monday morning, and who demanded an immediate home visit, fell into this second, demanding category. He turned out to want nothing more urgent than a repeat prescription of contraceptive pills for his girlfriend who was, he told me, in the bathroom and unavailable. He had one of those haircuts that look as though the owner has just got out of bed but I rather suspected that he had spent hours teasing every single hair into the right position. The whole confection was covered in a thick layer of perfumed gel. He probably thought he looked good enough to eat. 'We're going to Majorca this morning,' he told me. 'But she hasn't got enough of her pills.' When I told him that I couldn't do what he wanted (making the excuse that I needed to check the girl's medical records) he became quite belligerent. When he grabbed my lapels and threatened to knock my teeth down my throat I told him that he needed to find a new doctor. Curiously, he seemed to be surprised by this. He then told me that if his girlfriend became pregnant he would blame me. I told him that I would demand a DNA test and suggested that if he didn't want his girlfriend to get pregnant he should either find some alternative form of contraception or remain continent for a week. He said this would ruin his holiday and that he would sue me.

'You're past it,' he snarled.

'At least I got past 40,' I told him. 'You'll be lucky to reach 25.'

He repeated his threat to sue me and I asked if he intended to do this before or after he had knocked my teeth down my throat. When he didn't answer I said I very much looked forward to appearing in court and drove back home.

The phone went just as I climbed out of the car and I had to drive back to within a quarter of the mile of the man who'd wanted to knock my teeth down my throat. This time I had to give some anti-histamine tablets to a woman in her forties who'd developed a rash in all those places where women routinely spray their perfume. She admitted that she'd tried a new product, given to her by her husband, and thought I was brilliant in knowing what had caused the irritation. I told her to give or throw away what was left of the perfume and also gave her a prescription for a few more anti-histamine tablets.

`Shall I lose this or will you?' asked her husband accepting the prescription. `Oh you're much better at that sort of thing,' said the woman quite seriously.

Half an hour after arriving back home and switching on the kettle I had a call from a Mr Parrott who said his wife was in terrible pain. When I got there I found them both watching television. I still find it slightly shocking that people watch television at a time when most sensible folk are asleep. The woman said she had backache. When I said I'd better examine her she turned off the television set with some reluctance and headed out of the room and to the stairs. Her husband followed. As she climbed the stairs, without any obvious discomfort, the husband said, quite loudly: `Nice bum hasn't she, doctor?' She was wearing jeans, which were stretched to their limit, and there was no doubt that whatever the quality of the contents might have been the quantity was at the top of the range. The proud husband's strange remark reminded me for some reason of Sir Thomas More, the man for all seasons. When his prospective father-in-law invited More to pick one of his daughters the Utopian had difficulty in choosing. To make things easier the father had the girls undress and lie together under a sheet in their bedroom. More was then taken into the room and the father pulled back the sheet. `Now make your choice,' said the proud father. More examined the girls for a few moments and then asked for them to turn onto their faces. He then looked at them for a few more minutes and then smacked one on the bottom. `I'll have that one,' he said, as though choosing a side of beef at the butchers.

I did not mention Sir Thomas to the Parrots.

I examined Mrs Parrott with her husband peering over my shoulder and watching my every move and could find little of any significance. She had no sign of any pathology and her legs seemed to move in all the usually acceptable directions without causing her any pain. I gave her a few analgesic tablets out of my bag and pointed out that the easy chair in which she'd been slumped looked as if its springs had had better days. I suggested that she try sitting on a hard chair for a day or two. She looked less than pleased with this advice. In the bad old days, when doctors were respected, patients used to obey their GP's instructions to the letter. Today, patients only follow the instructions which they like the sound of. Tell a patient to stay off work for a fortnight and he'll stick to the instruction like a religious zealot. Tell him to keep off the beer and he'll forget the advice in seconds.

By the time I got back home there didn't seem any point in going back to bed so I made myself a cup of tea and a marmalade sandwich. Once I'd drunk the tea and eaten the sandwich I looked around for some silly chore to pass the time and decided to clear out and refill my drug bag. A few of the packets of drugs were past their use-by date and inevitably I found used glass ampoules rolling around at the bottom. I threw out the rubbish and replaced the old medicines with new ones from my store cupboard. While I was doing all this I found Molly's article. I lit a pipe and sat down to read it.

And then the telephone rang.

I stuffed the article into my pocket and rushed off to see a patient of Deidre's who had gone into labour a week early. Deidre is always encouraging her patients to choose to have their baby at home because she gets paid more when they do. Sadly, however, she is never there to help with the delivering. I doubt if she's seen a baby born since her own last daughter popped out. `We need boiling water,' I said to the father-to-be, the moment I'd seen his wife. The young man looked terrified. It was his first child but his wife's third. `Are you going to operate?' he asked. `No,' I told him with a smile. `We all need a nice cup of tea.' Something seemed unusual and suddenly I realised what it was. He was white and she was black.

Nothing odd about that in itself but I have noticed that in films, television shows and advertisements mixed marriages are always the other way round. And the woman is nearly always blonde.

I spent the rest of the night helping a 26-year-old mother of two empty her womb and turn an expectation into a hope and inspiration. Her husband and her mother boiled water and provided fresh towels by the armful and none of us even dreamt of calling an ambulance or troubling the local maternity ward. Under firm instructions from the mother-to-be the husband, a jittery soul with nerves of frayed cotton, stayed downstairs, filling saucepans, boiling water and drinking cheap blended whisky while his mother-in-law provided encouragement and damp flannels. The new father was not allowed into the bedroom until his wife and new son were arranged just so; mother with hair brushed and lipstick on, son washed and wrapped in a shawl. I didn't get back home until the streets were full of people going to work. The dawn chorus had long since closed beaks and settled down for a snooze. Those GPs who no longer do night visits miss that glorious feeling of fulfilment which comes from doing something all by yourself; without nurses, without equipment other than the stuff that can be carried in a black bag and, most of all, without bloody forms and administrators.

Many of the calls which come in out of hours are, to be frank, little more than a nuisance. More than three quarters of emergency visits are unnecessary and more than half of the unnecessary callers know damned well that their call isn't really necessary but those rare moments when I can make a difference, by myself, keep me going and make the work worthwhile.

In the car I listened to a CD of HMS Pinafore performed by the D'Oyly Carte company and when I arrived back home I cooked myself bacon, sausage and two eggs, toasted four slices of bread, found a jar of my favourite whisky flavoured marmalade and made myself a pot of strong coffee. It was the biggest, and best, meal I'd cooked in quite a while. Everything was a bit overdone but I've always liked crispy bacon and I hate eggs with runny yokes.

The postman called while I ate breakfast.

I used to enjoy the postman's visits. He used to bring letters and greeting cards and occasionally parcels that were welcome and exciting to open. These days he brings me mysterious letters and statements from my bank (which I cannot understand), mysterious statements from the energy company (which I cannot understand) and threatening letters from a wide variety of government departments and international corporations. He also brings a huge pile of unsolicited, unaddressed leaflets, booklets and pamphlets advertising sofas, pizzas and colleges offering courses in subjects such as hairdressing and nail varnishing. It's a good day when the postman brings mail which appears to be little more than superficial crap, rather than stuff which is terminally disruptive.

Today the scurrying bastard brought me seven pieces of unaddressed junk mail and the usual reminder letter from the television licensing people. No one sends me as many letters as they do. I don't blame them. In the bad old days people used to buy stamps in little booklets. Today, they buy them one at a time and pay with a credit card. The cost of sending mail has soared in recent years and the quality of the service provided has deteriorated by much the same figure.

I amused myself as I ate by writing rude remarks all over the letter from the television licensing people. When I'd finished I stuffed the letter back into the envelope and wrote `Gone Away. Return To Sender' on the outside. The BBC's heavies are always threatening to call round to see whether or not I am watching television. But they never do, of course. And if they do turn up they won't get very far because I never answer the door to unexpected visitors.

I was now late for morning surgery but I was past caring. I sipped my coffee, opened my copy of the *British Medical Journal* and turned to the back to look at the situations vacant. It must be twenty years since I've done that. One advertisement caught my eye. It was for a job on a small Scottish island. The local health authority needed a full-time solo GP to look after just 200 islanders. No partners, no receptionists, no nurses and very few night or weekend calls. I tore out the advertisement and stuffed it into the paperback copy of a book of short stories by H.E.Bates that I was reading.

Then I went to the surgery to attend to the morning's patients.

Chapter 4

A few days later, it was actually the following Wednesday, I was sitting in my consulting room working my way through a huge pile of repeat prescriptions, and trying hard not to allow the noise made by builders on a nearby property drive me to murder or suicide (all builders seem to buy special radios which are set to a permanently high volume and pre-tuned to a special 'builders'' radio station which plays only the cheesiest and most unpleasant music) when Molly telephoned me on the intercom to ask if I could see her for a few minutes. I told her I was free and two minutes later she waltzed in looking flushed and rather excited. After making the usual fuss about the cloud of pipe smoke hanging over my desk she asked me if I would like to go with her to see her boyfriend working. Larry had got a gig at the Red Lion in the centre of the town and Molly said they were both very excited by it. I admired her enthusiasm and was reminded of the good Cobbett who was, it was said, always as generous with his enthusiasms as he was forthright with his criticisms. I reminded her that it was my turn to be on call for the practice but promised that if things were quiet I would be there.

'Tickets are £5,' she told me. 'But to save you having to queue at the door I've got one you can have.' She rummaged in her handbag and produced a medium sized brown envelope. From the envelope she took a small handful of bits of paper that looked like raffle tickets. They had the name of the pub stamped across the top in red ink.

'Is that it?' I asked, taking one of the tickets from her and examining it rather critically. 'I've seen more impressive bus tickets.'

'They don't want to waste money printing expensive tickets,' she said. 'That'll be £5 please. Do you want to bring her? I've got plenty of tickets. I can let you have two for £10.'

'Her?'

'That woman you're seeing.'

'Her name is Enid.'

'I know. Wonderful isn't it? Serves her right. You're not going to marry her, are you?'

`Are you always this direct?'

`You're not are you?'

`Not as far as I know.'

`Thank heavens for that! Have you ever been married?'

`Yes. Once.'

`What happened?'

`She fell out of love with me and into love with someone else.'

`I'm sorry.'

`It was a long time ago. We were both very young.'

`Did you love her?'

`I thought I did at the time.'

`Did she love you?'

`I thought she did.'

`When did you realise that she didn't?'

`It's a boring story.'

`I don't care. Tell me. Anyway, it won't be boring.'

`You're very nosey aren't you?'

`Yes. I like knowing about people.'

`We were on a train in Spain; travelling on a long journey from Madrid to somewhere. I can't remember where we were heading. We were in a one of those old-fashioned little compartments which seat six people; three on one seat and three facing them.'

`I used to like those compartments. They were cosy.'

`There were three other people in the compartment. Two of them were an elderly Spanish couple who had brought with them a huge basket of food: bread, meats, cheeses, fruits. They ate constantly. The funny thing was that they were both as skinny as rakes. But they never stopped eating.'

`And the other one?'

`A young Spaniard. He was in his twenties and, I suppose, good looking in a bull fighter sort of way. We'd been travelling for about half an hour when he lit up a cigarette. It was one of those cheap Spanish things that smell of wet carpet. I asked him to put it out and pointed to the No Smoking sign. I'd specifically asked for a 'No Smoking' compartment because in those days I didn't smoke and I hated cigarette smoke. He just shrugged, laughed and blew out a huge cloud of smoke. When I repeated my request he looked at me and sneered. He then took out his cigarette packet, turned to my wife gave her the big smile treatment and offered her one.'

`She didn't take one?'

`She did. He lit it for her. And they blew out clouds of foul smelling smoke. She coughed a bit at first. But she persevered. And they started giggling together like a pair of young lovers. He didn't speak a word of English and she didn't speak a word of Spanish but they seemed to get on well enough.' I stopped and remembered. `It was our honeymoon.'

`What did you do?'

`I sat there like a lemon and fumed. I felt like an old cuckold watching his wife flirting with a young lover.' I paused, remembering. `The funny thing was that she didn't smoke. She hated cigarette smoke even more than I did.'

`And that was the end of the marriage?'

`It was the moment when I realised she didn't love me. She enjoyed humiliating me too much to love me. It was the beginning of the end. Then a few months after we got back she met someone else at the hospital where she worked.'

Molly didn't say anything. She looked at me and then looked away again, as though embarrassed by my long-ago shame.

`Why don't you like Enid?' I asked her.

`Whatever gave you the impression that I don't like her?'

`Why don't you like her?'

`She's not right for you. She's too cold and efficient. She reminds me of a concentration camp guard only considerably more frightening.'

I should have defended Enid more vigorously but I couldn't think of anything suitable to say. `I doubt if she'll want to come I'm afraid. She goes to her drama society on Wednesday evenings and it's an unbreakable date. They're doing something by Chekov next.'

`Not Macbeth?'

`Why Macbeth?'

`She'd make a marvellous witch if they got her to tone down the cackling a little.'

`I'll ignore that. She doesn't cackle. She just makes a rather funny noise when she laughs. It's probably something to do with her sinuses. And why do I have to pay you £5? I thought I was being invited.'

`You are. But you still have to pay.'

I took out my wallet and handed her the £5.' Have you invited Jock?'

She raised an eyebrow as though this were a silly question. 'Just you,' she said. 'Jock wouldn't go anywhere unless there was a free meal paid for by a drug company. He's not speaking to me, by the way. He's downstairs in the reception closet studying the accounts. Have you noticed that when he reads he puts his finger under the words? I'll swear he's only just managed to stop himself moving his lips. I realised today that he reminds me of someone.'

'Who?'

'Hitler. But without the brains, the charm and the sense of right and wrong.'

I ignored this. 'Have you invited Deidre?'

Molly shuddered. 'It's going to be a fun evening,' she said. 'We want to have a good time.'

I could understand this. Deidre is not known for her joie de vivre. 'Her highlight of the week is the arrival of the *British Medical Journal.* I've seen her tearing open the wrapper with her teeth to get at the latest editorials.' And another thing that annoys me is her way of saying: 'You get what you deserve in this life'. This is patently untrue since most people do not remotely get what they deserve. Millions of people work hard, do their best and deserve much but their lives are, nevertheless, a disappointment. Just think how many artists, singers and writers work their socks off and try their hardest at what they do. They all deserve to succeed but, inevitably, the vast majority do not.'

I didn't say anything but I agreed with Molly's dislike of Deidre. Our only female partner is an unpleasant woman. She makes small sacrifices for people, objects and causes but only when doing so does not affect her in any way. She does this in order to maintain a reputation for magnanimity that she cultivates but does not deserve. 'Petty unselfishness,' E.M.Forster called it. The other thing about Deidre is that whenever something bad happens to someone you can pretty well guarantee that something worse will have happened to her. If you're ill, she will have been sicker. If something bad happens to a friend of yours, something far, far worse will have happened to a friend of hers. She has, it seems, an inexhaustible supply of unfortunate friends. If you've had a run of bad luck, she will have had a much longer run of bad luck and each unhappy event will have been far worse than any of yours. Patients who tell her their symptoms invariably have to put up with a recital of her own similar problems. It's well known among the patients that she has had every disease going except for those involving the male genital organs and the prostate gland and she'll probably have those symptoms soon.

Deidre isn't as mean as Jock but her interest in her work is inspired by one thing only: money. She needs the money because she firmly believes that no home can have enough bed cushions and scented candles.

'There's something I want to tell you after the show,' said Molly.

'That's very intriguing.'

She smiled and pointed at my pipe. 'Don't forget you can't light that thing. The Red Lion is a decent, law-abiding establishment. You can't bribe the barman to let you light up.'

'I never bribe barmen to let me light up!'

'Yes you do. You give outrageous tips to the barman at The Bell so that he'll turn a blind eye when you smoke that thing. And put your mobile phone on vibrate so that it doesn't start ringing in the middle of Larry's best joke.'

'What do you want to tell me? I hate mysteries. You're not pregnant are you?'

She shook her head.

'Getting married?'

Another shake.

'You're not leaving the practice?'

A laugh and another shake of the head and she left.

I got stuck into the paperwork again and was moving through the stuff quite quickly when Jock walked in.

'May I ask why you're removing this patient from our list?' he asked. He always manages to sound like a headmaster talking to an errant junior teacher.

I looked at the form he was holding. The patient was the one who'd threatened to remove my teeth. I explained what had happened.

'His family has been with the practice for some years,' said Jock. 'He has a lot of relatives with the practice.'

I shrugged. `You can keep him if you like,' I told him. `But you'll have to give him your home number for emergency calls. I refuse to treat patients who threaten me.'

Jock looked at me. `But you and Molly do all the night and weekend calls,' he said. `That's the agreement.'

`Not for patients who threaten physical violence,' I told him. `He's lucky I didn't report him to the police.'

We continued like this for a while and eventually Jock gave in. He then pulled a couple of photographs out of his inner jacket pocket and showed them to me. The photographs were of a large, local hotel.

`What do you think?'

`I don't understand.' I said. `Are you inviting me to go away with you for the weekend? To this hotel?'

Jock blushed and looked embarrassed. `No, no, of course not,' he said quickly. `I'm thinking of buying it.' Whatever Jock does he always does it in the first person. He never includes his wife in his thoughts or, indeed, in many of his actions.

`You're going into the hotel business?'

`No, of course not. It's going bust. It's just been put on the market. I thought I'd make a pre-emptive bid and get it cheap. The vendors are in a lot of financial trouble. The agent, who is a patient of mine, thinks they'll take a low offer if its cash and quick. I've had a word with the bank and they're prepared to lend me the money.'

`But what are you going to do with it?'

`Live in it. Knock it about a bit and turn it into a house! There are some marvellous ceilings, the gardens are magnificent and the views are out of this world.'

`Will they let you do that? The local planners don't like people converting hotels into houses. I think they've worked out that it reduces the amount of local employment and damages the tourist trade.'

`I've thought of a way round that,' said Jock slyly. `I'll simply put up the prices.'

`I don't understand.'

`Officially it will still be a hotel but I'll charge £2,000 for a room and £500 for breakfast. Something like that. So no one will want to stay there.'

`Can you do that?'

`My lawyer says I can. I'll still be running it as a hotel.' He put the photographs back into his pocket. `The council can insist that I keep running the place as a hotel but they can't tell me what I can charge.'

`Very clever.'

`I thought so,' agreed Jock rather smugly.

`What are you going to do with all those rooms?' I asked him, looking again at the brochure. For no good reason that I could think of I was suddenly reminded of an old Frenchman I met when on a train in Northern France. I was a student, travelling alone and very broke. `I have learned four things,' the old man told me. `Bien manger, bien boire, bien baiser, bien dormer.' He waved a hand as though dismissing everything else anyone could think of. He leant forward across the compartment. `The man who enjoys these four things will have a happy and contented life.' We shared a baguette and a cheap bottle of wine he had brought with him and he then fell asleep for the remainder of the journey. Jock, who dreams only of bigger and better and of creating envy among his neighbours, would have thought the old man quite mad.

I wasn't surprised by Jock's plan but one thing did worry me. I'd already seen an advertisement for the hotel. And it was priced at £1,500,000. Even if Jock managed to buy it with a huge discount he would still be taking on a massive loan. I couldn't help wondering what this might mean for the practice. Where was he going to find that sort of money?

Chapter 5

I signed the remainder of the repeat prescriptions, read a dozen letters, threw away a binful of advertising material and unwanted magazines and returned three telephone calls. One of the receptionists (the stout, middle aged one with the untreated thyroid condition) then brought me another pile of mail and one of those cardboard carrier bags which people fill with presents which are too difficult to wrap. Inside the bag I found a bottle of Laphroaig, a packet of my favourite tobacco and a thank you note, signed by both the mother and the father of the new addition to the town's population who I had helped bring into the world. I made some trivial, light-hearted remark to the receptionist but the note brought tears to my eyes. I looked up and noticed that the receptionist who'd brought the gift was still standing there. She's Oriental in origin and like most of her compatriots is rather on the small size. I've often wondered why Orientals are so small. Perhaps it has something to do with the fact that they are produced in such huge quantities. Come to think of it the mass production process also means that there is also surprisingly little variation in style or format. Since I did not want to get arrested I did not mention any of these thoughts.

`The community social worker wants to know if you've had any ideas for her patient groups,' she said. I looked at her, puzzled. We are besieged by social workers of various types who, since they don't have any real work to do, spend their days thinking up bizarre ways to make themselves seem important. These schemes invariably involve those of us who have plenty of things to do in being invited to meetings where much coffee is drunk and many biscuits are eaten. It has been reported, doubtless by some Quango which keeps a record of these things, that the average office worker spends (and largely wastes) 16 hours a week attending meetings. My bet is that social workers manage double that figure. A few years ago a radical Dutch town planner did away with traffic lights and found that road safety improved dramatically. Someone should try doing the same with meetings. Far more useful work would get done if meetings were banned completely. I usually manage to find a convenient emergency which enables me to avoid turning up to any of them. I remember our community social worker only because his name is Wasir. Obviously, I call him Kilroy but like most social workers he had any sense of humour removed at birth and since the nickname is based on an English cultural icon he doesn't understand it at all. He is one of those sanctimonious do-gooders who is always keen to be generous with other people's money. He wears an old army jacket with retro T-shirts underneath it. The T-shirts always advertise long forgotten rock groups whose members became labourers, shop assistants and van drivers long before he was born.

`He says he's spoken to you about it several times. He wants to put up notices inviting patients with specific diseases to attend monthly groups where they can make what he calls `social interface contact' with other sufferers. Do you have any ideas for themes?' The receptionist stood waiting, a notepad in one hand and a pen in the other.

`Let's have a curry club for the irritable bowel syndrome sufferers,' I suggested. `And a darts club for the patients with Parkinson's Disease.'

The receptionist thanked me and wrote these down.

`And special meetings for men suffering from premature ejaculation,' I added. `But let's make sure the meetings always start ten minutes earlier than advertised so that everyone who turns up thinks they've got there late.'

The receptionist looked at me and raised an eyebrow. `Do you want me to write that one down?'

`No,' I said. `You can forget that one.'

`The parents want to name their new baby after you,' she said. Puzzled, I looked at her. `The parents who left you the present,' she explained. `They rang up to ask what type of drink you like. That's how they came to buy you the Laphroaig.'

`That's nice,' I said, not knowing what else to say.

`The father is a huge fan of cowboy films so they're going to call the baby `Hopalong'.'

I looked at her but she wasn't smiling.

`Is that a joke?'

`No. I don't think so. Of course I'm too old to remember but I gather there used to be a cowboy called Hopalong Cassidy.' She paused. `Actually, I think you've probably done the kid a favour. They were going to call it Money.'

`Why on earth would you call a child Money?'

`Something they're both very fond of, I suppose. Why would you call a baby Apple or Rainbow? What are these parents thinking of? What if their baby grows up to be a judge or to marry a prince? You can't have a Judge Apple can you? Or a Princess Rainbow.'

I sighed, shook my head and carried on filling my waste paper bin. Most of the mail seemed to be either from people telling me things I didn't want to know, or warning me about the terrible things that were about to happen to me because I hadn't done things I'd been told to do and hadn't. There were three letters from various people with important sounding titles advising me that I had been seen smoking in places where smoking is forbidden and warning me of the consequences. I sometimes think that I have wandered into the wrong life. Somewhere there is probably someone who would like my life. Or maybe I just turned up for it a hundred years too late. I know the lower orders had a rough time of it but life at the end of the 19th century would have been much more fun for someone with a little initiative and a top hat with a stethoscope in it.

When I'd finished ploughing my way through all the crap I did three of the five home visits that were listed on the slip of paper one of the receptionists had handed me before I'd done an Elvis and left the building. (It was the fairly young one with surprisingly bad varicose veins and red streaks in her hair who always wears a turtle neck sweater because she has a tattoo of a dotted line around her neck. Jock only agreed to hire her on condition that she always wore something that covered up the tattoo. I don't know her name and she doesn't seem to know mine though on her good days she seems to recognise that I am one of the doctors employing her. She has a string of boyfriends and seems obsessed with sex. I once heard her tell one of the other receptionists that she was thinking of giving up her job and selling her body for a living. `Unlimited sex with enthusiastic partners and I get paid for it! That's something I could get used to. Maybe I ought to start now before it's too late. Or maybe I should just practice a bit more.')

The first visit was to a woman who claims she is allergic to everything on the planet and that because of this she cannot possibly leave her luxury flat and travel to the surgery. She also has a self-diagnosed addiction to chocolate (to which she is apparently not allergic) and, as a result, weighs about twice as much as a pregnant rhinoceros with the dropsy. She wanted a prescription for something to help her sleep. I told her that I feared that she would doubtless be allergic to all the pills I could give her and that instead I recommended that she tune into something soporific on the BBC. She has the biggest television set I've ever seen and spends her days watching ten hanky movies.

The second visit was to a lovely old fellow who had twisted his knee while digging his neighbour's garden. He is 94-years-old and was terribly apologetic about calling me out. His family are forever trying to enlist my help in persuading him to retire but I always tell them what he tells me – that if he retires he won't have a reason for living and so he will die.

The third visit was to a 62-year-old woman who lives with, and cares for, her 86-year-old mother who is physically fit but who has Alzheimer's disease and who doesn't know who she is, where she is or what she's doing. Many people who develop Alzheimer's tell themselves that they'll kill themselves when things get too bad but they never do, of course, because the disease develops slowly, getting worse bit by bit, and they always think they can hang on a bit longer and cope and then suddenly it's too late because they can no longer remember what they were going to do or why. The 62-year-old daughter, who is called Zahlia, looked exhausted. Her mother had taken to wandering around at night and twice the police had found her mooching around the town in her nightdress. I gave Zahlia some sleeping tablets to give her mother and promised that one capsule would knock her out for eight hours. I wrote out a prescription for another thirty and to be honest I wouldn't blame her for a second if she gave her mother the lot in one go. I told Zahlia to make sure that I visited at least once a fortnight. I didn't tell her that if I did this I would be able to write out a death certificate without troubling the coroner.

After the third of these visits I realised that my journey to the fourth would take me past the bookshop Enid runs. I parked on a single yellow line, put my *Doctor Visiting* card on the dashboard and walked fifty yards to the shop. There are some who say that our small town has deteriorated in recent years but the High Street seems to be thriving. We have two fast food restaurants, a chemist, a nail parlour, a sandwich bar, three pawn shops, three phone shops, seven charity shops, two tattoo parlours and three estate agents. Since the shops we get must be the shops the customers want the local population is clearly richly served. Less than a third of the shops available are empty and available to let. Enid, half hidden behind the counter, was sternly completing a transaction with a customer who was buying a cheap paperback. He had silver rings dangling from his ears, nose and lips and looked like an African tribal chief dressed up for a night out on the town. There was so much metal hanging from his nose that he jingle-jangled when he moved his head. I stood back, well out of the way, and waited for Mr Jingle to leave. It occurred to me, as I waited, that Enid reminded me very much of a school teacher I'd once had who had absolutely terrified me.

Within days of our having met, Enid had told me, with great certainty, that she intended to make something of me. I did not have to courage to point out that, since my next birthday would take me perilously close to my half century, she was rapidly running out of time. She was processing the man's transaction with all the enthusiasm and levity of a border guard examining passports. She was wearing a tweed skirt and a matching jacket with a white polo necked sweater with a large and hideous brooch pinned to the front of it. I looked around her shop. It was full of television tie-in publications. Grinning reality TV performers were lined up alongside grinning television chefs, grinning television gardeners and grinning newsreaders. It occurred to me that just every damned book on display had a picture of the author on the front cover. The only fiction on the shelves was either the miserable, pretentious guff that no one ever reads but which always wins all the prizes, or the special variety written for bored housewives looking for something mildly titillating. There was nothing by Greene, Doyle or Wodehouse. There was nothing by Shakespeare either, though most female authors were well represented. (Last Christmas Enid gave me half a set of paperbacks by Jane Austen. She promised me the other half of the set for my birthday.) Enid succeeds by supplying the local schools and colleges with all their literary needs. I suspect that she is helped in this by her friendship with a woman called Hazel Thickett who is the Senior Information Resource Purchasing Officer for whatever the local education authority calls itself these days. Hazel is an actress manque, active in the local dramatic society, and although she is in her fifties and neither a good looking woman nor a great thespian, is usually the first choice for the female juvenile lead.

There have, I believe, been murmurings of favouritism and since Enid is the company's casting director some of these murmurings have been directed towards her. Fortunately, Enid's position as supplier of all things bright and readable to the local would-be intelligentsia is not widely known and the secret of her shop's commercial success seems safe for the time being.

As I looked round at all the hideously perfect faces grinning at me from their respective book jackets it occurred to me that no proper book ever has a picture of the author on the front. When did a publisher last put a picture of a grinning Evelyn Waugh, John Buchan or H.G.Wells on the front jacket of one of their books?

Enid and I first met at a tobacconist where I was buying a packet of Gawith Hoggarth Ready Rubbed to put in my pipe. I usually smoke a rather peculiar blend of Cuban leaf tobacco which is the same stuff that Mark Twain loved. The chap who runs the shop gets it in especially for me. He is in his eighties, though he looks older, and when he is called to the great humidor in the sky I expect that sixty years of tobacco selling history will be closed down overnight and the tobacconist turned into a shop selling mobile telephones. For some reason, which he explained at length but which I didn't begin to understand, the Cuban leaf was unobtainable and the old man had recommended that I be daring and try the Gawith Hoggarth. Enid was buying a box of matches with which to light her gas fire. It was bucketing down with rain and I offered to share my umbrella with her. It always seems to be raining these days. If it isn't raining then it's either just stopped raining or it's about to start raining. If I had any money I'd put it into a firm making sou'westers and umbrellas. On the way to her car she told me that she knew who I was, that she was a widow with no children, that she was a councillor and that she ran a bookshop. Since the journey was no more than a hundred yards I thought that was pretty impressive.

No one could describe Enid as pretty or having any physical charms but no one would deny that she had a strong character, and if Playboy chose playmates according to the size and power of their personalities she would be the first in line to be Miss January. She told me that she did a lot for what she calls `the community' and said that people who knew her usually described her as energetic and hard-working. She handed me a discount card for her shop and told me that they had a special offer on all cookery tie in books that was

45

being extended for another month in response to overwhelming public demand. While I waited for her to open her car she asked me if I'd seen the latest production by the local dramatic society and when I said I hadn't she'd told me that she was performing and her enquiry as to whether I would like to go one evening had not been one which had invited any answer other than an enthusiastic `yes'. Three days later I'd spent the evening watching a performance *of The Importance of Being Earnest* and at the end of the evening's entertainment Lady Bracknell took me by the arm and introduced me to the rest of the cast and the production team as her new partner. It seemed rude to offer any dissent and so I said nothing. Not for the last time Enid had taken charge of my life.

The following day we attended the wedding of two young amateur thespians and I was stung for £50 as my contribution to our wedding gift. I can still remember that wedding. The best man, a bank clerk and leading man in the dramatic society, gave a long speech in which he talked endlessly and exclusively about a young stage manager who had died six months earlier in a motor cycle accident. `He would have so loved to have been here,' said the best man, after finishing what seemed more like a funereal eulogy than a wedding speech. By the time he'd finished the guests were all in tears and much mascara was running on both male and female cheeks. The best man made, I remember, just one reference to the bride. `She is no virgin, of course,' he remarked. `But in the bedroom as in the theatre, experience is invaluable.' No one except me seemed to be embarrassed by what I thought was a rather tactless remark.

`Why don't people use cash anymore?' demanded Enid when I stepped forward and said hello. `That man who was just here bought a £3.99 paperback and paid with a credit card. Most of my profit will have gone to the credit card company. Why don't people carry money? And please don't smoke that awful pipe in the shop. It's illegal to smoke in here.' She looked at me, as though she were looking at a painting or a piece of curtain material. `Why don't you grow a beard?' she asked.

`It's not lit. A bookshop should welcome pipe smokers. Sherlock Holmes smoked a pipe as did Mark Twain, Bertrand Russell, J.R.R.Tolkien, Ernest Hemingway, William Faulkner and Jean-Paul Sartre. Twain once said that he wouldn't go to heaven if they didn't let him smoke his pipe there. I don't know why you don't just refuse to accept plastic. There are two banks less than a hundred yards away from you. Your customers could easily take out some cash.'

I thought I was being supportive and offering constructive advice. But I was wrong.

Enid glared at me. `I don't care whether it's lit or not. It's still illegal and it still smells. You public service employees don't understand how the real world works, do you?' We often had conversations which involved two or more topics at a time.

`Am I?' I asked. I put my pipe away in my jacket pocket. I didn't see how having an unlit pipe in my pocket was any less illegal than having it clamped between my teeth but I didn't want to have that argument again with Enid. She made no secret of the fact that she hated my pipe. She said that men who smoked pipes remind her of babies sucking dummies.

`Are you what?'

`A public service employee?'

`Who pays your salary?'

`I'm self-employed.'

`Technically, maybe. But who pays you the money you use for clothes, food and petrol.'

`By some mysterious means money is paid into my account from the practice account.'

`And how does the practice get money?'

`The Government sends the stuff along, by the same mysterious process.'

`Exactly!' said Enid. `You're paid by the Government. You're a public employee. You're another civil servant. And none of you people has any idea how the real world works. I can't stop taking credit cards because if I did my customers would simply buy their books elsewhere.'

I listened to this tirade, which seemed a trifle unfair, without defending myself. I have learned not to defend myself when Enid climbs onto one of her soapboxes. In much the same way that I don't throw stones at angry looking dogs, or poke sticks into wasps' nests, so I have learned to keep quiet when she is on the rampage.

When I was younger I imagined myself to be something of a revolutionary anarchist with humanitarian overtones. I was naïve enough to believe in freedom and democracy. These days I know that I'm an overweight, middle aged pudding and I expect to be bullied by Enid and people like her. (It terrifies me that there are people like Enid.) Accidental glances in the mirror fixed to the wardrobe in Enid's bedroom have not spared me the truth about my shape, and my heart tells me that weariness and fear have sucked all the fight out of me. The odd thing is that I'm not sure why I feel so weary or where the fear came from. All I know is that civilisation seemed to me to come to an end when the police started arresting old ladies for feeding the birds in our parks and that history, far being an accumulation of facts, is merely an aggregation of politically acceptable truths; dependent upon attitude and interpretation. A patient of mine once said that if the Germans had won World War II the holocaust would now be regarded as a great human achievement, up there with the Pyramids and the Hanging Gardens of Babylon, and the frightening thing is that I think he was probably right. These days most of life is 30 to 1 against unless you're a member of the Royal Family or an EU commissioner.

`Why would I want to grow a beard?' I asked her.

`Rodney Stoke has a beard.'

`Yes, I know. But that's not a great reason for growing a beard.'

`Fidel Castro said that he saved ten days a year by not shaving. That's two extra working weeks every year!'

`I don't want to do any more work than I do already.'

`You could spend the ten days doing something else. Learning to play the saxophone or learning German.'

`I don't want to play the saxophone or speak German. Maybe if not shaving meant that I had two weeks holiday sitting in a nice hotel by the side of one of the Italian lakes I might consider it.'

Suddenly Enid abandoned the subject of beards. `Do you know what happened this morning?'

Although the question was clearly rhetorical I decided I ought to take my part in the proceedings and so I confessed that I did not.

`A woman came in and spent nearly an hour browsing. She took out dozens of books and put them all back in the wrong places. But she didn't buy one book. Not one. She sat on the chair in the children's section, which I put in for weary parents, and she ordered book after book on her mobile phone. When she left she gave me a big smile and said that even with the postage costs it was cheaper for her to buy her books from Amazon. '

'Not a good sign,' I agreed.

Enid glowered at me as though it were all my fault.

'I popped in to see if you'd like a quick bite of lunch,' I said. 'We could drive to The Bell or pop along to the King's Head.'

'Look around,' snapped Enid whose manner can appear a little sharp at times.

I looked around. The shop contained a lot of books but no people. Boring, dull books; but a lot of them. They were all new. I don't know why this should be but I have always found second hand books more interesting than new ones. And, on the whole, I have always found hardback second hand books, the ones without dust jackets, far more fun than paperbacks. I have no idea why this should be.

'How many people can you see?'

'None. Except you.'

'Exactly. Simon has gone for his lunch. I can't go to mine until he gets back.' Simon was Enid's only assistant. He was on some sort of trainee scheme, sponsored by the Government, and he was very knowledgeable about his statutory rights as an employee. On the morning he had started work he had given Enid a list of the breaks to which he was legally entitled. Twenty minutes for a morning coffee break. One hour for luncheon. Twenty minutes for an afternoon tea break. When Enid had told him the shop's opening hours he had responded by telling her his working hours. The shop was open from 9.00 am until 6.00 pm except Fridays and Saturdays when it remained open until 7.00 pm. Simon, however, started at 9.00 am and finished at 5.00 pm and didn't work on Saturdays. The truth is that, speaking objectively, he's an obnoxious pantywaister and I wouldn't hire him to knock the dottle out of a cold pipe. He always wears brown corduroy trousers, a dark shirt and a hideous, striped tie that looks as if it were designed by a blind man. In cold weather he wears a Fair Isle sweater with red reindeer on a green background (though, last January he insisted on going home when the temperature in the shop fell below the legal minimum). He invariably carries a grey nylon shoulder bag which he puts over his head so that the strap is on his left shoulder while the bag rests against his right hip. I don't know why but I've always felt uncomfortable around people who carry shoulder bags in this undoubtedly sensible way. If Chekhov was correct when he wrote that we are what we want then Simon is a life lived strictly by the rules; a life regulated and organised and entirely without passion or commitment.

`I could pop out and fetch us a couple of sandwiches and two coffees,' I suggested. There was a shop just two doors away which sold sandwiches and coffee to office workers. This was a sure sign of my desperate, pathetic need to please and to squeeze some warmth from this woman. I never usually buy sandwiches. Most cases of food poisoning are a result of people preparing food with hands which have not been properly washed and the average sandwich maker has fingers which are alive with bacteria. People think that wrapped sandwiches are safe and sterile but they're not, of course. The bugs are all safely wrapped up inside, merrily building up their strength and breeding on the roast beef, ham or cheddar cheese. It's not surprising that vomiting and diarrhoea are endemic these days. There is, at least, a chance that piping hot food won't have been fondled by coli laden digits.

`That's probably the only way I'll get anything to eat. Get me a beef and lettuce on wholemeal bread and a latte.' This was the warmth for which I was prepared to sacrifice so much.

`Any second choice for the sandwich?'

Enid thought for a moment. `No. Just the beef and lettuce on wholemeal. No mustard. You know I hate mustard.'

I was about to join the queue which started outside the sandwich shop when I noticed a traffic warden hovering next to my car. I hurried over to see if I could talk him out of giving me a ticket. Like most GPs working in our town I collect parking tickets the way other middle aged men collect stamps, train numbers or beer mats.

`Ah, it's you, Doctor Cassidy,' said the traffic warden. `I thought I recognised the car.' He was a fat man, in his forties, and he had either put on weight since being measured or else the people providing the Gestapo style uniforms with which they equip traffic wardens these days had a wicked sense of humour. The buttons down the front of his tunic were straining to burst through the button holes. If there had been anyone around with whom to have a bet I'd have put money on the button which was second from the top escaping first. As I looked at him I couldn't help thinking that a few decades ago he would have been working in a circus or a travelling fair. Today, our politically correct world does not allow obese people to earn a living out of their greed. And, besides, with a quarter of the population fat enough to merit a place in any travelling fair the competition for employment would be fierce. It won't be long before anyone who isn't two stones overweight will be officially considered skeletal, dragged off to hospital and force-fed burgers and chips.

Apart from him obviously being a traffic warden I didn't have the foggiest idea who he was though from the way he greeted me he was obviously a patient of ours and possibly even one of mine. I have learned always to say hello to people who seem to know me even though I don't know who they are. Early in my career as a GP I popped into a branch of WHSmith, the newsagent, and met a patient who had been lying naked on my couch just a few hours earlier. I didn't have the foggiest idea who he was because I'd spent more time with my finger up his bum than I had spent looking at his face. My innocent explanation that I didn't recognise him with his clothes on drew very strange looks from other shoppers.

`Oh hello!' I said cheerily. `How are you? How are things? You're looking well! How is everyone?' I find that if I ask these generic questions quickly, without allowing time for a reply, I can usually get away without confessing my ignorance, and, more importantly, without having to listen to too many boring answers. `Am I OK for another few minutes?' I added.

`Are you visiting a patient?' he asked with all the pompous self-importance of a State employee in a uniform. `Is it an emergency?'

`In a terrible rush,' I said, evading the question.

`Just time to get a sandwich, though?' The smarty pants bastard had clearly seen me about to join the sandwich bar queue and wasn't about to make things easy for me.

I abandoned fancy evasion and opted for straightforward, old-fashioned deceit. `Diabetic emergency. Patient needs food urgently. Chocolate bar, gooey cake, that sort of thing.' Telling lies to traffic wardens doesn't seem like telling proper lies and these came out easily. When Robert Peel invented policemen the plan was that they would defend the people. These days our policemen and their ungodly spawn have risen far above such old-fashioned nonsenses and their professional aim is not to protect the people but to protect the law and, in my view, those are very different things. So I've grown up. When I was a kid I was taught to respect the police and always to tell them the truth. These days I trust them as much as I trust estate agents and income tax inspectors and I tell them the truth only if I think it's good for me or that there is a chance that they will find it out for themselves.

`Ah.' He nodded, as though understanding. `Can you spare a moment to scribble me a prescription before you rush off?'

`A prescription?'

`For my blood pressure tablets.'

`Oh right!' I smiled. I took out the prescription pad I always keep in my jacket pocket. My jackets are crammed so full with pens, bits of paper, medical records, prescription pads, sick note pads, unanswered letters and the paraphernalia I need to keep my pipe happy that they bulge. Enid is for ever telling me to put all my stuff into a bag instead of into my pockets. Last Christmas she bought me a blue leather man-bag with a shoulder strap and a little brass clasp and clearly expected me to use the bloody thing. I hate bags and I love pockets. The first thing I do when I buy a new jacket (which is about once every ten or fifteen years) is to make sure that it has enough pockets. Within days they will have lost their shape and within weeks they will be terminally baggy. There is no doubt that this does make me look rather scruffy but what is a pocket for if not to keep things in? A few months ago I stood in the street clutching an empty waxed paper cup and staring into space trying to remember what it was that I had forgotten to do when a fellow in a cheap suit dropped something into the cup as he walked past. I looked into the cup and saw seventy pence in metal lying in a quarter of an inch of cold coffee. I made the mistake of telling Enid about this. She immediately used this dubious piece of evidence to support her contention that I am scruffier than most tramps and all *Big Issue* sellers.

`Remind me which tablets you have.'

`They're blue and triangular. Very pretty little things they are. They look a bit like sweets'

`Angipax?' I suggested. Jock Cohen prescribes Angipax a good deal. It is very expensive and in my view one of the most dangerous drugs on the market. The list of side effects is longer than the tax code. But Jock likes prescribing new and complicated drugs, which he much prefers to simple, safe, effective products. He claims Angipax is the drug of choice for heart disease, high blood pressure, nervous problems and a whole host of unconnected problems and he can, when pressed, quote a whole host of research papers (all conducted by or for the drug company which sells it) which prove the efficacy of the damned stuff. He has a mutually profitable association with the international company which makes this universal panacea and invariably has lunch with the regional sales manager once a week.

`That's the one!'

I wrote out a prescription for thirty tablets. Rock stars and actors sign autographs in the street. I sign prescriptions. As I scribbled the traffic warden peered. `Don't suppose you could make it sixty, could you? Now that the price of prescriptions has gone up…'

I tore up the prescription and wrote out a replacement. `Remind me of your address?'

He told me and I managed to add `Chez Guevara', 27 Grimsdyke Avenue to the prescription without a blink. Thankfully, he then told me his name and how to spell it. I finished the prescription and handed it to him. He folded it neatly into four and placed it in one of his tunic pockets. I looked around, saw a bin attached to a nearby lamppost, and got rid of the torn up prescription.

`I'll just take this up the chemist,' he said. `Then I'll be back down here in twenty minutes. Will that be long enough for you to deal with the diabetic emergency?' He said it in such a way that I knew that he knew that there was no diabetic emergency.

`Oh, plenty of time.'

I waited until the loathsome traffic warden had strolled off in the direction of the nearest pharmacy, and then hurried back to join the queue in the sandwich shop. I comforted myself with the thought that Angipax invariably causes a variety of unpleasant side effects including impotence and persistent itching around the anal area.

`We don't have any more beef,' said the assistant, a sour faced woman who looked as though she'd spent her entire life testing lemons by sucking them. `Just tuna on white and ham and mustard on brown.'

`I'd better have one of each,' I said. `And a latte and a black coffee. All to take out.'

The woman grabbed two ready wrapped sandwiches and slammed them down on the counter in front of me as though she hated them. Her hands were filthy and her nails looked as though she'd spent the morning servicing a couple of coal lorries. Looking at her grime encrusted fingers and thumbs I couldn't help wondering who'd made the sandwiches. Hygiene in most eateries is appalling and it really isn't any wonder that half the nation is vomiting while the other half is sitting down wondering where all the diarrhoea comes from. The woman with the grubby hands shouted the coffee order to her accomplice, an equally cheerless looking harridan who was presumably stone deaf since she was standing no more than three feet away. She, after a good deal of banging and clattering and some mean-spirited abuse of an expensive looking piece of machinery, managed to fill two cardboard containers with something hot which I daringly took on trust to be coffee. I then had to wait in another small queue in order to pay for my purchases. A fat woman in front of me paid her bill and then, instead of simply slipping her change into her purse, proceeded to reorganise her apartment sized handbag. Why do women always spend so much time putting away their change in shops? I was tempted to nudge her along but the last time I tried that the nudgee accused me of accosting her and threatened to call the police so I contented myself with coughing and making loud comments about my sandwiches going stale and my coffees going cold. Eventually, the fat woman shuffled away and I paid a third assistant, who was every bit as much a harridan as the first two. This third harridan, whose malodorous body reminded me of the stench of rotting fish, accepted my ten pound note only after holding it up to the light, subjecting it to a rigorous pseudo-scientific test with a curious pen shaped device and crinkling it and pulling it so hard between her fingers that I thought it must surely tear. I wondered if the owner of the shop had a policy of only hiring menopausal women with attitude problems or if things had simply turned out that way by chance. Maybe the advertisements for new staff members made it clear that only women who had failed the Post Office charm school course would be considered for employment.

    Outside it had started raining. I stood in the sandwich shop doorway for a moment and waited while a large, rabid looking hound bounded along while a fat, red-faced fellow in a pale blue jogging suit hurried along behind him. It wasn't difficult to decide which of the two was the alpha dog in that pack. I cheered myself up with the thought that although I would get wet the traffic warden would soon be soaked. It is a sad but true fact that these days my life is given purpose by simple thoughts such as this.

`How long have we been together?' demanded Enid when I arrived back at her bookshop with my spoils. This unexpected interrogation threw me for a moment but I was saved the embarrassment of having to produce an undoubtedly incorrect answer by the fact that the absence of any pause in what was clearly destined to be a monologue made it obvious that no answer was expected or required. `You know I don't like mustard. I can't stand mustard. I told you I don't like mustard. And I can't eat tuna. It brings me out in a rash and besides there's the dolphins to think about.'

`The dolphins? They don't do dolphin sandwiches do they?'

`The Japanese fishermen catch them when they catch the tuna.' Enid can sometimes give a good impression of being slow witted. `The dolphins get stuck in the nets and die,' she continued. `It's awful. The Japanese don't care. They're like the Spanish. They have no feelings for animals. I can't eat either of these. You have them.' She wrinkled up her nose in a theatrical expression of distaste and pushed the two sandwiches back across her counter as though they were mildly radioactive.

`I got the coffee,' I said trying to salvage at least one brownie point from this minor shopping disaster.

She took the lids off the two cardboard coffee containers.

`They're both black,' she said with an audible sigh. `I asked for a latte.'

`I don't seem to have done very well,' I said. How much would it have hurt the damned woman to drink a black coffee for a change?

She sighed again; putting more effort into it this time. My scary schoolteacher used to sigh a lot too. `I'll pop out when Simon gets back, if he ever does.' She looked up at the clock. I looked too. It was ten past two and there was still no sign of her assistant. He had probably discovered an obscure piece of employment legislation which entitled him to an extra ten minutes lunch break on days when it was raining.

`I'll have to go,' I said. `There's a traffic warden coming back in a few minutes.'

`Take all this with you,' said Enid, waving a hand at the sandwiches and the two coffees. `I don't want it filling up my rubbish bin. The council only allows me to fill one small bin a week. And that costs me a fortune. Do you have any idea how much I have to pay to have my rubbish taken away? You wouldn't believe the number of people who leave their rubbish in my shop. Some even have the nerve to ask if they can put their sweet wrappers and cigarette packets into my bin.'

`When shall I see you next?' I asked, more out of a bizarrely misplaced sense of duty than anything else.

`Are you off duty this weekend?'

`Yes.' And I realised as I said it that'd I'd rather spend the weekend on call than the weekend with Enid.

`That's a nice change. I was beginning to think that girl you hired did no work at all. Friday evening I thought we'd go and see the new film showing at the Regal. It's about a family of Polish miners. Apparently the director shot it in black and white to give it a grainy, gritty look. The man in the Guardian liked it very much and said it will probably win an award somewhere. I can't remember where, though not an Oscar I suspect. And on Saturday evening we've been invited to dinner with the Stokes.'

`We're not throwing our keyrings into the fruit bowl and swapping wives again, are we?'

`I wish you'd stop talking like that. I know you're joking but one of these days people will think you're serious. You can come back to my place afterwards. But you'll have to go home on Sunday morning because I have the drama society committee coming round for brunch.' Whenever Enid and I spent time together it was always at her place. When I first took the job with Jock, the bank and I went into partnership and bought a small detached house on the outskirts of the town. To start with I hired a woman to come in and do cleaning, ironing and cooking for me and an old bloke to cut the grass and dig out some of the weeds. But after about five years the woman decided to retire and I decided not to replace her. To be honest I'd become something of a loner and I found it uncomfortable to have a stranger in the house. The advent of the mobile telephone enabled me to eat out. I cleaned the house whenever the dust became noticeable and I sent my shirts to a local laundry which, to my surprise, turned out to be not much more expensive than having a woman come in and iron them. When, a few years later, the gardener decided to emigrate to Spain I didn't replace him either. The lawn at the front of my house is cut by a neighbour who does it because he says he can't bear to see it looking unkempt. If it pleases him I see no reason to stop him. His own house has been for sale for seven years (a process encouraged, I believe, by the bank, the rightful owners) and I suspect he fears that my dandelions could cause terminal dismay and seizure of the wallet among potential buyers. My other neighbours all believe that I am rather odd and perhaps a little unhinged and I do nothing whatsoever to disappoint them. When leaving the house I occasionally sing or recite poetry. The grass at the back of the house is now about three feet tall. I keep hoping that the back garden will somehow turn itself into a wild flower meadow but unfortunately not even the dandelions seem able to survive in a thicket of hogweed, ground elder and a particular energetic variety of bramble which grows rapidly but never seems to produce any fruit. Occasionally, I get rid of some of the thickest of the scrub by having a bonfire. I usually have these on warm summer days when the neighbours are holding barbecues for their posh friends. I always keep a boxful of carpet remnants and white polystyrene packing material to give my fires added zest. Enid came to my house once but steadfastly refused to return. She complained that the place reeks of old books and stale pipe smoke. I sympathised with her loathing of the stale pipe smoke but I thought it worrying that a bookshop owner should dislike the smell of old books. She complains about my car too. She once told me that it looks as if it has never been cleaned. I told her that in this case looks were not deceiving. When she moaned a bit more I told her that I kept the car dirty as a road safety measure. `Cars that shine can dazzle other motorists,' I explained. `Having a dirty car helps reduce road accidents.' I'm pretty sure she didn't know whether or not I was being serious.

I loathe the Stokes. He does something indefinably tedious for the Regional Health Authority. Every time we meet he tells me about his exercise programme. And when he tells me how many beats a minute he can get out of his heart I tell him that making the human heart work faster in an attempt to make it fitter and stronger is like driving a car faster and hoping that it will, as a result, last longer. I don't really believe this, of course, but it annoys him and so I repeat it as convincingly as I can. His wife works as an accountant for the council and is a raging feminist. I don't have anything against feminists as a breed (the ones who shave their legs can sometimes be quite cute) but I'll swear Ms April Stoke waxes her moustache. (Her maiden name was Spring and her parents clearly had a bizarre sense of humour. She has two sisters called March and May. May Spring married a boy called Geoffrey Summer and presumably regarded her marriage as some sort of promotion.)

The Stokes, April and her husband Rodney, are without a shadow of a doubt the most boring people I've ever met although I confess that it has never been my misfortune to meet that ageing pop bimbo Simon Cowell, the self-appointed king and queen of nerdsville. I hate all dinner parties but the ones Chez Stokes are the most tedious I've ever attended. (Their cottage is called Chez Stokes. It was once quite a pretty looking little residence but when the roof needed re-thatching they had it covered in asbestos tiles and then rented out the space to a solar panel company. The local `green energy' lobby having clearly overruled, or taken precedence over, the local `preserve our outstandingly beautiful buildings' lobby the result was that the Stokes got cheap electricity at the price of turning a traditional English cottage into a fairground attraction.)

The Stokes are the sort of people who have learned great chunks of Arthur Rimbaud's scribbling and who quote it at the drop of a hat. They believe that pipe-smoking Jean Paul Sartre was the greatest philosopher who ever tossed a cobble stone and they claim to enjoy the films of Cocteau and Godard. They are, in short, the sort of blinkered idiots who would have heaped unending praise on the Emperor's new clothes. The Stokes duo always serves prawn cocktails as a starter with chicken as the main course, followed by a slice of ice cream cake served straight from the freezer. Rodney, who thinks of himself as a wine buff, serves Retsina, a red wine from Greece which is probably brewed in metal tanks. They go there on holiday every year and bring back several bottles (doubtless tightly wrapped among her one piece bathing suits with attached little skirts designed to disguise the size of her bum and his tartan patterned Bermuda shorts), and praise it extravagantly even though the stuff was undrinkable before it had to travel. If it now has a use at all then that must include either dirty ovens or machine parts. Mr Stoke once spilt a little on his shirt and seemed startled when it burnt a neat hole in the material. 'Oh all red wine does that,' said Ms Stoke with her usual air of quiet and determined certainty. When I dine with them I always ask for water and in sympathetic voices they always ask if I am a recovering alcoholic. When I tell them that I am not they ignore my protestation, as they invariably ignore everything else I say, and ask me if it makes me feel uncomfortable if they drink in my presence. 'You must think us very wicked,' says Ms Stoke with admirable predictability.

Every meal with them is like a dull wedding reception. When we have dinner with them I always eat beforehand so that I can pick and choose from the predictable culinary horrors Ms Stoke serves up. If you dropped the chicken it would bounce.

I wasn't too keen on Enid's planned Friday evening entertainment either. I rarely watch films recommended by critics. They never seem to know anything of (or take any account of) the audiences for which the film was made. The same idiot critic reviews films made for horror addicts and cowboy film aficionados. How can one person be a sound judge of musicals, romantic comedies and cartoons for children? As far as I'm aware literary editors don't expect the same reviewers to report on modern poetry, environmental concerns and the latest story about Bertie the Bumptious Bunnie. And the thought of spending an evening watching a film praised by a critic working for *The Guardian* made me nauseous. If they gave out awards for sanctimoniousness *The Guardian* would undoubtedly sweep the board. But I consoled myself with the thought that it could have been worse; it could have been a night at the ballet. For a large, cumbersome woman with bad feet Enid is surprisingly enthusiastic about ballet. I've never seen the attraction in watching tiny girls wearing horizontal skirts cavorting with men who appear to have a pound and a half of mixed fruit stuffed down the front of their tights. We once had a row about it. I said I didn't understand why they didn't employ taller dancers so that the girls didn't have to wander round all the time on tip toes. Enid was furious at this mild attempt at a joke. She doesn't like jokes very much at all.

We once spent an evening with two social worker friends of hers. They were both enthusiastic members of the Amateur Dramatic society. They were also tedious would-be revolutionaries. Halfway through the evening I told them that all revolutionaries crave normality. `Che Guevera was a huge fan of a radio series called Mrs Dale's Diary,' I told them. `He used to have the programmes recorded on seven inch reels of tape by a friend at the Russian Embassy in London and then have the tapes flown out to him every week in the diplomatic bag. And Lenin, of course, would never go to bed without a copy of one of P.G.Wodehouse's school stories on his bedside table.' The two ersatz revolutionaries were astonished by these revelations but apparently delighted that I had shared them. The one with the biggest beard said that he was going to put the information in his blog and his next twitter message so that it could be shared with all the comrades around the world.

`I was amazed by what you had to say about Che and Lenin,' said Enid in the car afterwards. `I didn't know any of that. Where did you read these things?' I looked at her and raised an eyebrow. `Don't tell me you made it all up!' she said, horrified.

`OK.' I said.

`What do you mean?'

`I mean, OK I won't tell you I made it all up.'

Enid was furious and appalled and when we arrived at her home she didn't even invite me in for coffee. The small stock of contraceptives in her bedside drawer remained untouched that night and I should, I suppose, have learned that humour was not destined to play a large part in our relationship.

`And call in at the chemist and buy another pack of thingies if you want to do any you know what afterwards,' said Enid as I left the shop. `I checked the bedside cabinet and we're out.' Enid never found it easy to talk about sexual matters and invariably managed to work her way around the straightforward. Our sex life had never risen above or beyond a strictly by numbers regime that even a Scottish Presbyterian might have found unimaginative. And whatever we do we always do it in the dark. I had never seen Enid without clothes and her nighties, which she has never removed in my presence, are all knee length and doubtless sensible enough to be approved by the Liberal Democrats. She wears them over a bulletproof black corselette which, as far as I am aware, she never removes. She probably bathes in the damned thing as protection against peeping window cleaners. She once told me that she wore it because when her husband was dying she had sworn that she would always wear black in his memory. 'But I thought something out of sight would be a more subtle way to show respect.'

'The last time I bought the thingies the girl said they do them in different flavours now. Do you fancy strawberry for a change? Or you could have blackcurrant.'

Enid bent her head forward and looked at me over her glasses. She didn't say anything but just looked at me and in a way that made me feel about six years old.

I decided there and then not to bother buying a pack of thingies. Experience told me that the effort of finding a chemist where I'm not known and where the girl behind the counter wouldn't almost die giggling at the sight of the doctor buying rubber johnnies was more than the result could possibly be worth. Without the condom I would not be expected to perform because Enid lived in a world where eyes must be kept tightly shut at all times, nighties pulled up only just as far as is strictly necessary and penises covered up for the same reason that the Victorians dressed their piano legs in little frocks. Most people assume that condoms are used to prevent pregnancy or the spread of infection. Enid's view is that an undressed penis is, quite simply, indecent and as much in need of covering up as a Victorian piano leg.

After Enid had ignored my merry quip about the strawberry flavoured condoms (known, in her parallel world only as 'thingies') I packed the sandwiches and coffees back into the small paper bag in which the shop assistant had first placed them, waved goodbye and left. I had for some time been searching for a way to end a relationship which seemed to have about as much point to it as a water bed in a nunnery and was beginning to get the happy feeling that maybe I wasn't going to get the other half of the Jane Austen collection after all.

Outside, on my way back to my car, I handed the bag of food to a particularly seedy looking tramp in a shop doorway. He stank and clearly hadn't bathed for at least a decade. He looked at me and it most suspiciously.

'What is it?' he demanded as he reluctantly took the bag from me. I told him there was one tuna sandwich and one beef.

'The beef hasn't got mustard on has it?' I confessed it had. 'I won't eat mustard,' he said. 'Can't abide the stuff. And I'm not terribly keen on tuna. Haven't you got any money you can give me?'

61

As I looked at him I realised he was much younger than I'd originally thought. He probably wasn't more than 35 or so.

I hurried away before the damned tramp could hand me back the unwanted sandwiches and then loudly cursed a heather touting gypsy who stopped me, tried to insert a sprig of tinfoil wrapped heather up my nose and accompanied the action with the stony faced threat of what would happen to me if I failed to fill her palm with something better than silver. In my annoyance I managed to curse with such venom that the wretched witch turned, crossed herself and darted away as though pursued by the hounds of hell.

I then drove to the King's Head where there is a decent sized car park and no traffic wardens. Trying to avoid one pothole I hit another and the car's damned warning lights all came on as a result. Modern BMWs are crammed from bumper to bumper with gizmos and toys I never use and which cause me nothing but confusion (I've had the car for two years and still haven't found out how to switch on the fog lights) but the system in my car seems so sensitive that if I drive over a sleeping policeman, or into a shallow pothole, the electronics have some sort of major fit and about fifty different warning lights come on. Since most roads now have more potholes than tarmacadam this is a constant problem. I hate all these silly warning lights. I never know what they mean. Some German idiot who fancies himself an expert in hieroglyphics has created a whole range of incomprehensible symbols. And there even seems to be a warning sign which comes on occasionally to tell me that nothing is wrong. The first time I saw that one light up on the dashboard I stopped and spent twenty minutes thumbing through the darned handbook in order to find out what it meant.

I ignored the warning lights, parked the car and tottered into the pub where I was greeted by a tall, pencil thin barman who was either dressed to enter a fancy dress competition or the owner of a peculiar taste in clothing. He wore a pink evening dress shirt, bullfighter tight trousers and brown cowboy boots.

`Would you like to try our tripe pie?' he asked, when I asked what bar food they had to offer.

`No thanks,' I replied. `I hate tripe. I can't imagine how awful it must be in a pie.'

`We serve it with fresh radishes and onion sauce.'

`No thanks. Do you have anything with chips?'

`The chef won't do chips. He says they're too common. Why don't you try the tripe pie? You might like it. It's on special today.'

`I hate tripe. Have you tried the tripe pie?'

He shuddered. `I tried it once,' he admitted.

`Did you like it?'

`No. It was awful.'

I had one pint of flat beer and a pork pie. The pork pie tasted a little stale but it contained no tripe and as far as I am aware no dolphins had died in its preparation. While I ate I deleted a string of annoying texts sent to me by Vodafone. I have been trying to stop them doing this since I bought the damned phone but they take no notice. I then smoked my pipe and read the paper for ten minutes. I learned that we had once more declared war on a country which hadn't done anything to threaten us and which will, no doubt, prove to be packed to the borders with skilled guerrilla fighters who will gradually learn to hate us. I don't know why we don't declare war on Germany again. We've always done well against them. And I read about a politician who claimed to be in close contact with aliens from another planet. The journalist who had written the story had forgotten to say which party the politician represented but I assumed that he was either a Liberal Democrat or a member of the Monster Raving Loony Party. Once I'd finished reading all this exciting news I left the pub, finished the home visits and returning to the Jock Cohen Health Centre just as patients with appointments for the evening surgery were arriving. Patients come early these days so that they can pick out the best magazines and the most comfortable chairs in the waiting room.

I had to walk past the waiting room to get to the staircase to my consulting room and, as I looked in, it occurred to me that many of the people sitting there were such regular visitors that the Jack Cohen Health Centre probably ought to be their registered addresses. None of the people I saw was a patient of mine and I had no idea whom they saw or why they came to the surgery so often. Maybe they called in simply to read Deidre's old copies of *Country Life, Horse and Hound* and *Dressing Up And Killing Animals For Fun Weekly*. Because she and her husband live with their daughters in a large house, and rent a field for a pony, Deidre regards herself as 'landed gentry". The house was designed by a prize winning architect and is, therefore, ugly, pretentious and poorly designed for human habitation. I once flicked through one of her discarded copies of *Country Life* and found that half a dozen of the advertisements for country mansions and stately homes had little comments written across the corners. There were notes like: 'This one's worth a look'. 'Probably not enough land but worth getting the brochure'.

Half a dozen uncontrolled, and probably uncontrollable, children were racing around throwing things at one another and terrorising the pensioners. Though they looked to me to be nothing more than badly behaved little bastards, straight out of *Lord of the Flies,* I had no doubt that they had all been diagnosed as being 'hyperactive' or 'autistic'. These days every parent believes that their new child is above average, a genius, the next Shakespeare or Milton, or maybe, cross your fingers and wish hard, even the next Jordan or Rooney. If the child hasn't been on the cover of *Hello!* magazine, or had a trial for Manchester United by the age of two, there must be some clinical explanation that can be treated with expensive drugs. Side effects don't matter. Everyone knows that a drug can't be doing any good unless it produces plenty of nasty side effects. A few of the poor little sods had probably been labelled as suffering from attention deficit disease or Asperger's syndrome; the modern, universal excuses for the child who is a constant disappointment to ambitious parents who are discontented with their lot in the same way that the rest of us feel discontented when we pull a Christmas cracker and find ourselves clutching a plastic shoe horn, an ugly egg cup or nail clippers. Around the room, broken and grey-faced mothers sat on Jock's hard chairs and watched but made no attempt to control their demonic, under-achieving offspring. They had doubtless been told that their badly behaved children were ill and not responsible for their exhibitionistic hooliganism. The undeniable clinical truth is that most of the little bastards simply needed a good thumping rather than pills and sympathy.

These days most parents seem simply unable to control the results of their couplings. I have long thought that the Government should introduce legislation allowing parents to have their children to be put down if their behaviour is consistently unacceptable. Maybe the legislation could be designed to give all parents the opportunity to opt for the euthanasia option on each child's 5th, 10th and 15th birthdays. 'Wayne's not going to improve dear, is he?' 'No,

I'm afraid he isn't. It's time to put us out of his misery. I'll take him along to the *Harold Shipman Euthanasia Centre* on Tuesday.'

Chapter 6

The Red Lion used to be a proper pub; a serious drinking establishment where serious drinkers met to consume significant quantities of beer without wasting time or energy on conversation or laughter. It wasn't a place where spirits were drunk or raised. There was a dart board but no one ever played darts (and not just because there were no darts). There was a cribbage board, some greasy playing cards and a few dead match sticks on one windowsill and a dying rubber plant on the other. No one took any interest in these items. The regulars sat around on uncomfortable, wooden chairs and rarely spoke to one another, though they muttered to themselves from time to time. The barman was taciturn and irredeemably irritable. The only heat came from a two bar electric fire which was turned on from the beginning of November to the end of March and anyone who felt hungry ate crisps or pork scratchings and would have been confused if the crisps had been anything other than salt and vinegar. But that was a few years ago, when I first took a job with Jock Cohen. In those now apparently far off days there were standards and there was some consistency in the world; enough, at least, for the unexpected to be a source of occasional joy.

Today, the bar staff at the Red Lion serve cocktails and spritzers and the only beer they sell comes in bottles and is called lager. During the daytime loudspeakers pump out stuff that is probably described as music by the people who make it, if not by those who sell it. It costs a small fortune to get even mildly inebriated there. At night local bands and comedians perform on a small stage at one end of the pub while evening diners select their choices from a blackboard which lists two dozen starters, meals and puddings. All of these culinary selections arrive at the pub ready-made, cocooned in plastic wrappers and are stored in the freezer until required. The chef's job is to pick out the items that have been ordered, put them into the microwave, snip the plastic and pour the contents onto a plate. Sometimes the chef, who wears a white smock and a white hat but whose entire training consisted of a twenty minute long introductory talk from the pub manager, has to snip the plastic, or use a fork to stab holes in it, before putting the chosen item into the microwave. The instructions are always written on the packets.

The writing on the blackboard appears to be in chalk and phrases such as 'Chef's Special' and 'Dish of the Day' suggest that these selected items are chosen according to the seasons or the chef's whims. In reality, however, the 170 pubs in the chain all have the same blackboards on their walls and the identical menus are printed on the boards at a factory on an industrial estate in Northampton. The 'Dish of the Day' is the dish of every day.

I was late finishing my surgery that evening. This was partly because there had been a small flood of panicking patients, all inspired to seek help and drug therapy by an advertising campaign paid for by the manufacturer of one of the biggest asthma drug remedies, but mainly because a patient who had been stung by a bee while sitting in the local park demanded that I take photographs and full written notes. She told me that she intended to sue the town council for having bees in the park. When I pointed out that bees tend to gather where there are flowers she said she would sue the council for planting the flowers. I suspect that, if she goes ahead, the council's insurers may well insist that the park's managers do away with all the flowerbeds in an effort to avoid any future problems. I do not envy the next generation, or, if there is one, the generation after that.

The pub was crowded when I finally arrived and it took me several minutes to spot Molly and quite a few minutes more to force my way through the crowd to reach her. Fortunately, she had managed to reserve a small table for two. Larry's on in two minutes,' she told me. She looked excited. I asked if I had time to get to the bar to buy drinks but she said not. It seemed odd to sit in a pub without a drink in front of me.

Larry was good and the crowd enjoyed his act. Two of the bar staff had to lift his wheelchair onto the platform, turn him to face the audience and hand him a microphone. The two youths who did the lifting both wore those three quarter length trousers which were much in fashion during the 1980's but which went out of fashion as soon as the people wearing them sobered up, caught sight of themselves in mirrors and realised how daft they looked.

'I've always wanted to be a stand-up comedian,' began Larry. If I could tell jokes I'd be half way there. Actually, I don't really need this wheelchair. I only use it so that people who don't like the jokes won't throw things. If I can't get laughs, I'll accept pity. You're not sure whether it's OK to laugh or not are you?'

He was right. The part of his audience that was listening to him wasn't laughing. Molly reached across the table and held my hand. `I hope he's going to be OK.'

`A friend of mine heard that the best way to deal with stress is to make sure you finish everything you've started. So he went home, opened his drinks cabinet and spent the evening emptying half a bottle of whisky, two thirds of a bottle of sherry, a quarter of a bottle of rum and two thirds of a bottle of vodka.'

This produced a few polite chuckles.

Larry grabbed the arms of his wheelchair and shook them. `You're not sure whether or not I need this chair, are you? You're wondering if it's just a prop.' He paused and looked around. `Well, you'll never know the truth unless the building catches fire.'

That gag enabled Larry to break-through the audience's reserve and embarrassment and from then on, although it would have been an exaggeration to say that he held them in the palm of his hand the risk of his being stoned to death was considerably reduced. The rest of his gig went surprisingly well.

Afterwards, the three of us went to an Italian restaurant to celebrate Larry's success. The waiter was a patient of Molly's. He gave us a quiet table and a complimentary bottle of Chianti and left the Parmesan cheese dispenser on our table which was pretty good of him because I always feel peeved when they take it away and won't bring it back. When Molly and I had finished congratulating Larry, I reminded her that she had something to tell me.

`I'm going to be on television,' she told me. `A chap Larry knows works as a researcher for Newsnight. Larry gave him a copy of my article in the *British Clinical Journal* and he spoke to the editor. They've arranged for me to be interviewed on tomorrow night's programme.'

`You're obviously going to be talking about vaccination.'

`Yes. They think that the viewers will be interested to hear an alternative view from a practising family doctor.'

`Have you told Jock?'

`Of course not! He wouldn't approve.'

'I think you could be right about that.' Jock was unlikely to approve of anything which didn't result in money appearing in his bank account.

'It's a tremendous opportunity to put the record straight,' said Larry. He wore jeans, a plain white T-shirt and one of those huge wristwatches which can also function as a stopwatch and which have loads of little buttons enabling the wearer to measure lap times and the distance to the moon. He was also wearing quite a lot of stage make up. 'It's something we both feel very strongly about. My sister is vaccine damaged. She had a bad reaction to the whooping cough vaccination when she was a baby.'

'I'm sorry,' I said. 'I didn't know.' I suspected that the existence of this hitherto unknown relative probably explained Molly's interest in vaccination. In my experience patients and their relatives often have more knowledge of, and more trenchant opinions about, the disease they know best than even the most experienced of specialists. And relatives whose loved ones have been damaged by medicine always know a good deal about what went wrong. Who can possibly blame them? We would doubtless all be the same.

'The doctors all deny that her damage had anything to do with the vaccine,' said Larry 'And though the Government gave my parents some compensation they made them sign documents promising not to tell anyone about it.'

'They'll have someone in the studio to say you're talking rubbish,' I warned Molly. 'A specialist in infectious diseases or a medical officer from the Department of Health. They won't be gentle with you.'

'That's OK,' said Molly. 'I've done a lot of reading. I can look after myself. Honestly.'

'All ideas which threaten the establishment are regarded as lunatic or even criminal,' said Larry. 'And original thinkers have always been regarded as a threat to society. Look at what society did to Cobbett, Paine, Tyler, Wilkes and Lilburne.' I could vaguely remember reading about the first four but I was struggling with Lilburne. I didn't like to ask. 'All great ideas,' he continued, 'go through the same three stages. First they are ridiculed. Those who oppose the idea deny that it is relevant, true or of significance. A lot of sneering goes on. Second, there is discrimination against those who promote the idea. They are marginalised. And then, in the third stage, the idea is accepted and the people who opposed it most vociferously will be the ones who claim it as their idea. The anti-vaccination movement is still early on in the first stage.' He looked at me to check that I was still listening. I nodded to show that I was. I was thinking that he was right. Many great doctors were ridiculed because they questioned the accepted way of doing things. The Austrian physician Semmelweiss went mad because other doctors wouldn't listen when he argued that puerperal fever was caused by doctors and medical students not washing their hands. Dr John Snow, the doctor who took the handle off the Broad Street pump and `cured' an outbreak of cholera in London, was ridiculed. Later on in his career he was attacked when he introduced anaesthesia. On the other hand there have, over the years, been establishment doctors with some fairly strange ideas. A notable 16th century physician called Dr William Butler once cured a patient of the ague by throwing him into the Thames. And when faced with a dead parson he had a cow slit open and then put the vicar into the dead cow's belly. The parson came back to life. No one had a bad word to say about Dr Butler.

`We're going to do some rehearsing,' continued Larry who was still talking. I hoped I hadn't missed too much. `I'll be the interviewer, trying to catch Molly out. We'll do it in the car going down there after surgery tomorrow evening.'

`These are tough professionals,' I reminded them both. I turned to Molly. `Have you ever been on television before?'

`Once. When I was at medical school. We filled the fountains in the city centre with detergent and I was interviewed by the local station. They filmed me dancing around in the bubbles. I seem to remember that I was dressed as a Womble so I don't think anyone recognised me.'

`Not the ideal preparation,' I said drily.

`The Womble suit got soaked,' said Molly, remembering the moment. She giggled. I'd never heard her giggle before. `The Dean of the medical school gave us all a stern talking to because they had to flush out the fountains for two days to get rid of all the detergent. He wasn't a bad bloke though. The police wanted to arrest us but he talked them out of it.'

`It'll be fine,' said Larry, reassuring me. `She knows her stuff.'

`I need you to do something for me,' said Molly.

`OK. If I can I will.'

`Will you swap duties and cover me for tomorrow night? Do the emergency calls? We'll have to drive to London and I won't be back until two or three in the morning.'

`Of course I will,' I said.

It may have been the worst decision of my life. I should have said `No'. I would give everything I have to have said `No' and made it impossible for Molly to appear on that damned programme. Every decision has consequences. Every decision, even the ones which involve doing nothing, involves a risk and a financial, emotional or spiritual cost. Sometimes the cost of a decision is so great that we have to live with regret. Would things have really been different if I'd said `No.' and Molly hadn't appeared on that programme?

I'll never know.

Chapter 7

I was called out to visit a patient with an emergency skin rash when Newsnight was due to start but I managed to get back home just minutes after the programme had begun. When one of the presenters listed the forthcoming interviews I was pleased to see that I hadn't missed Molly's appearance. In the old days I would have recorded the programme on my video recorder but since I had to buy a DVD player I've been quite unable to work out how to record anything.

I turned the volume up loud so that I wouldn't miss the start of her screen debut and tottered into the kitchen to make myself a marmalade sandwich. The sandwich made, and the inevitable whisky poured, I settled down and waited for Molly to appear on my screen.

The editor or the producer or whoever arranges these things had put Molly up against a doctor representing the most pompous, cobweb ridden corner of the medical establishment. He was one of those bumptious, self-satisfied fellows who had spent most of life sitting safely behind a desk and shuffling pieces of paper from his in-tray to his out-tray. He probably hadn't seen a patient since antibiotics were first introduced. He had one of those horrible little toothbrush moustaches which, for obvious reasons, largely went out of fashion during the 1940's, and was wearing a smart pinstripe suit enlivened with a blue shirt and a club tie. He was unctuous and smug and before he had even opened his mouth I'd guessed that he would turn out to be hideously patronising.

The interviewer, an unpleasant woman called Dawn Brakes, who was new to the programme and keen to establish a reputation as an assassin, began with Molly.

I was delighted to see that our young trainee had scrubbed up nicely for the programme. She was wearing a two piece grey suit, a white blouse with a demur neckline and a string of pearls. I couldn't believe the string of pearls. Heaven knows where they came from. She'd done something fancy to her hair and she was wearing make-up. I'd never seen her wearing make-up before.

Right from the start the interviewer made it clear that she wasn't going to hold back – and nor was she going to disguise her partisanship. This, of course, was no surprise. BBC interviewers, fascist bastards to the last cell, and representing the Government's most efficient propaganda machine, always fall over themselves in their enthusiastic attempts to demonise anyone who dares to threaten the sanctity of any part of the fascist, EU dominated establishment which keeps them neatly wrapped in Italian suits and German sports cars. They aren't bright enough, and don't know enough history, to realise that when everybody thinks alike, everybody is likely to be wrong. Samuel Smiles, the Victorian author, wrote that the function of government is to be restrictive and negative, rather than positive and active. He certainly had that right.

`We have with us in the studio tonight a controversial young apprentice doctor who believes that vaccines are more dangerous than the medical profession admits.' The presenter shuffled in her seat as though even making the introduction made her feel uncomfortable. `Moreover, she claims that both the medical establishment and the Department of Health have misled the public about the safety and efficacy of vaccines. In the past, renegade doctors who have questioned the official line on vaccination have rightly been accused of endangering the health of millions by discouraging patients from accepting official medical advice on vaccination programmes. It is generally agreed by experts that when doctors question the validity of vaccination programmes they imperil the safety of millions – particularly the most vulnerable members of our society, small children and the elderly. Miss Tranter, who is still training to be a GP, has claimed that her more experienced professional colleagues are all wrong in their belief that vaccination plays an important part in preventing infectious disease. The BBC does not usually pander to publicity seeking individuals but in this case we believe that this doctor's bizarre views should be investigated fully and in public. We will be making a transcript of this interview available to the General Medical Council in the hope that the medical profession's legal watchdog will take whatever action it deems necessary.'

I found this more than slightly offensive. The truth, too often an alien commodity as far as our State broadcaster is concerned, is that there are no experts in medicine. There are people who call themselves experts and who may even be regarded by those around them as experts, but there are no real experts because medicine is a constantly changing, ever fluid world and today's knowledge can, all too quickly, become tomorrow's embarrassing memory.

Ms Brakes then turned to her other guest and gave him one of her best smiles. It was done rather reluctantly, as though she had a limited supply and had to eke them out over her life-time, but it was without doubt a smile.

`To defend the Government's vaccination programme we are delighted to welcome Professor Cedric Hailsham, a member of the Department of Health's advisory committee on vaccination programmes, advisory editor to several eminent journals and a senior faculty member at Oxford University. Dr Hailsham has written several widely respected papers on the value of vaccination programmes and is a regular broadcaster.'

Hailsham, who had started off looking as blank and as uninteresting as a Government sponsored website managed a small smile of false modesty which made him look as smug as a standard issue Liberal Democrat. I knew before he spoke that he would turn out to be a pompous windbag, as full of sense as a pound and a half of elephant flatus.

The interviewer turned to Molly. This time there was definitely no smile. `Miss Tranter, you claim that vaccinations are dangerous and ineffective. But you don't have any scientific evidence to support your claim, do you?'

Molly, who looked startled by the interviewer's monologue and, I have no doubt, by the threat to involve the General Medical Council, paused for a moment before answering. I could feel myself willing her to defend herself with vigour. I had never had much time for Molly's dissent, putting it down to the natural and healthy desire of a young person to kick against the established way of doing things, but I liked her, respected her enthusiasm and didn't like to see her being patronised and marginalised by a hired mouthpiece for the medical establishment. I had a sneaky feeling that the ordinary viewer might also find the interviewer's deliberately intimidating approach a trifle clumsy and crude.

`I'm afraid I do,' said Molly quietly. `There is plenty of evidence to show that vaccines are crude, unreliable and dangerous. They can, and do, cause brain damage and they kill people – particularly children. I don't honestly see why anyone should be surprised by this. If you inject potentially toxic substances into people then it shouldn't be much of a surprise when things go wrong. The brain, particularly that of a baby or young child is…'

'I really cannot allow this nonsense to continue,' said Dr Hailsham, interrupting. 'Miss Tranter is throwing around all sorts of unsubstantiated accusations which will terrify viewers. How, for example, can she possibly justify describing vaccines as 'potentially toxic'? That's the sort of absurd rhetoric one expects from the sort of lunatics who oppose all medical progress. It certainly isn't the sort of language one expects from someone who wants to be a doctor.' He then produced a whole pile of statistics which didn't seem to prove anything at all other than that he filled his head with a lot of statistics. The lies they tell, the truths they hide. As politicians and drug companies know only too well you can prove anything you like with statistics. I remember reading somewhere that 500,000 walkers die every year in England and Wales. This makes walking seem a pretty dangerous activity until you realise that the figure 500,000 covers all the deaths in those countries and the fact that they were all walkers is quite irrelevant.

'What do you say to that?' demanded the interviewer, turning to Molly. 'How can you defend your claim that vaccines are 'potentially toxic'?'

'First, can I say that I am a doctor already,' said Molly. 'I am qualified and registered and licensed and I work as a GP.'

'You are a trainee GP are you not?' said the interviewer.

'A trainee GP,' agreed Molly. 'But I see patients, I prescribe, I perform small operations, I go out on night calls…'

'Night calls?' said Dr Hailsham, with a snort. 'Really?' He looked straight at the camera and raised an eyebrow. I could understand his disbelief. These days most general practitioners work shorter hours than librarians. And most of the time they do spend working is spent dealing with paperwork and buttering up bureaucrats. Very few family doctors are prepared to climb out of their easy chairs, or out of their warm beds, to attend sick patients.

'Yes,' said Molly firmly. 'Our practice is one of the few in the country which still provides 24 hour cover for patients. But to get back to your question, I would like to point out that vaccines can and do cause a whole range of unpleasant and dangerous side effects. They can cause headaches, allergy reactions, itching, dizziness, nausea, fever, gastro-intestinal disturbances…'

`Yes, yes…', interrupted Hailsham irritably and impatiently. `But these are relatively trivial complaints. We have to remember that vaccines have eradicated smallpox and pretty well done the same for polio and a whole range of other diseases which kill people.'

`It's not true that vaccines have eradicated smallpox,' replied Molly. `And you mentioned polio but the available evidence in America shows clearly that the incidence of poliomyelitis rose after the vaccine was introduced. In reality, as with other infectious diseases, the number of people with polio fell as cleaner water and better sanitation were introduced in the later decades of the 19th century. And we must remember that millions of people who were given polio jabs when they were children may well now be at serious risk of developing cancer.'

`That's a very serious allegation,' said Ms Brakes, who looked rather startled. `Can you substantiate that?'

`Certainly,' replied Molly. `When the first practical polio vaccine was prepared in the 1950's the scientists involved used kidney tissue taken from monkeys. Unfortunately, those scientists didn't realise that one of the viruses commonly found in monkey kidney cells can cause bone, brain, liver and lung cancer in humans. As a result something like 17 million people who were given the polio vaccine in the 1950's and 1960's are now at risk of developing cancer as a result of the vaccinations they were given. The American Government was warned of this danger in 1956 but the authorities closed down the laboratory of the doctor who had issued the warning. Moreover, even though the risk had been identified the British Government continued using the stocks of vaccine until they'd run out. Only when they'd used up all the dangerous vaccine stocks did they start screening new vaccine stocks for the virus.'

`Can the people who were given this vaccine be identified?' asked Ms Brakes.

`Unfortunately not,' said Molly. `The official records which would have identified those who had received the contaminated vaccine were all destroyed by the Department of Health in 1987. Naturally, this means that anyone who develops cancer and thinks it may be a result of the vaccine they were given cannot take legal action.'

'I think it's important to put all this into perspective,' said Hailsham who now looked distinctly uncomfortable and clearly wanted to be somewhere else. Miss Tranter is talking about one specific vaccine and the incident to which she refers is something which happened a long time ago. Today's vaccines are extremely safe and very effective; they may cause small problems in a small number of people but nothing serious.'

'Would you not describe brain damage and death as serious problems?' demanded Molly, who instead of looking upset by this steady barrage of interruptions seemed to be growing in strength, and seemed to have forgotten that she was in a television studio being watched by millions of people. Dr Hailsham, on the other hand, now looked distinctly uncomfortable and well aware of where he was and what was happening. Beads of sweat were visible on his forehead.

I realised that although Molly may have had a good deal to lose personally, in terms of credibility, her opponents stood to lose a great deal more. It occurred to me for the first time that vaccination programmes are a billion pound a year industry, with drug companies and doctors all making a good deal of money out of them. Rather naively I hadn't really thought about this before.

'That's absolute nonsense,' said Hailsham, now unconsciously rubbing his hands together as though trying to wash them clean. 'Miss Tranter is inexperienced and ill- informed. There's no evidence that anyone has been brain damaged by a vaccination. That's pure scaremongering. Modern vaccines, such as the one we have used with such success in the battle against whooping cough, are extremely safe and effective and the companies which make them take great care, under Government supervision, to ensure that vaccines remain that way.' I suddenly realised that my telephone was ringing. I looked at the number which had appeared on the screen. It was Jock's number. I didn't take the call.

'The whooping cough vaccine, like most vaccines, is nowhere near as effective as the authorities say it is,' countered Molly. 'Dr Hailsham claims that I am ill-informed but everything I've said is proveably true. And since he has questioned my credibility I think it's valid to point out that Dr Hailsham is, in addition to his other work, a paid consultant for several of the companies which make vaccines. Viewers might like to take that fact into consideration when judging his evidence. The plain fact is that the introduction of the vaccine has had no effect on the number of children dying from whooping cough. The incidence of whooping cough had fallen dramatically long before the vaccine was introduced in 1957. And if you're right about that particular vaccine being safe then perhaps you can explain why the British Government has paid out millions of pounds in damages to the parents of children who were brain damaged by the whooping cough vaccine?' Molly paused and then hammered the nail home hard. `As you are undoubtedly aware, the Government has secretly paid out huge damages to the parents of hundreds of children who have been seriously brain damaged by the whooping cough vaccine.'

The interviewer, suddenly aware that if she wasn't careful she would be going down with Dr Hailsham's ship, turned to the man representing the medical establishment. `Is that correct, Dr Hailsham?'

`Well, I'd have to check the figures. We may have paid out small sums in compensation to the parents of some children.' There was a pause while Hailsham thought of some way to minimise the significance of this admission. `But we've never admitted liability.'

`The Government paid money to the parents of over 700 children,' said Molly.

`That's quite possible.'

`And secretly paid out millions of pounds of taxpayers' money to protect the drug company making vaccines.'

`I couldn't possibly comment on the sums involved. These were all confidential arrangements.'

The presenter, who hadn't spoken for a while, looked petrified. `All this will be very frightening for parents,' she said. She looked as if she'd rather be somewhere else. A war zone in the Middle East, perhaps.

`The Government still won't warn parents properly,' continued Molly. `But it has known about the risks of the whooping cough vaccine for years. Way back in 1985 the Journal of the American Medical Association published a major report showing that the whooping cough vaccine was linked to the development of serious brain damage.'

Throughout this interview it had not escaped my notice that the BBC interviewer used what I imagined were a number of standard tricks to demonise Molly. When she spoke to the man from the Ministry she smiled and bent forwards slightly but when she spoke to Molly she looked stern and bent backwards. I had noticed in the past that BBC staff, working after all for a State broadcaster, tend to do whatever they can to demonise anyone who dares even to think of threatening the establishment but I had never before quite appreciated how unfair and dangerous a practice this is. It occurred to me, for the first time, that the BBC never allows balanced debate when the establishment has taken a specific policy line. And so viewers never have a chance to see protagonists debating the merits, or demerits, of issues such as global warming or genetic engineering. The establishment view prevails because the broadcasters make sure that no other view is aired. The BBC doesn't have much sympathy with Mark Twain's view that: `whenever you find yourself on the side of the majority it is time to reform.'

`I'm sure this debate will continue,' said Ms Brakes. `But, Miss Tranter, I'm sure that not even you will argue that there is any link between vaccination and the development of autism. Do you at least agree with the medical profession that that particular bogey has now been laid to rest?' I couldn't help noticing that Ms Brakes had now managed to isolate Molly completely from the entire medical profession.

`No I certainly don't,' said Molly, much to my surprise and rather more to the surprise of the interviewer. `Some of the existing evidence for the link is admittedly circumstantial. For example, is it significant that the incidence of autism has rocketed as the number of vaccinations being given has also risen? I certainly think it is worth noting that in America a group of paediatricians who between them have 30,000 child patients, and who all refuse to give vaccinations, don't have any patients with autism. Is this significant? I certainly think it is something worth investigating.'

`I'm afraid we're running out of time,' said Ms Brakes suddenly. She had clearly received instructions in her earpiece from someone in authority. `We have to cut this item short because we've received breaking news on an important story. '

`Just one final thing about autism,' said Molly quickly. `I know that our Government still insists that there is no link between vaccines and autism but then they would, wouldn't they? They're pushing vaccines and they are legally liable. But other Governments have come to different conclusions. For example, the American Government has accepted that vaccines can cause autism. The US Health Department's National Vaccine Injury Compensation Programme has admitted that childhood vaccines kill and seriously injure 2,500 to 3,000 previously healthy children each year in America. The parents of those children receive official payouts totalling around £75 million a year in damages. And parents of children diagnosed as suffering from `autism' receive some of that money.'

`And that really is all we have time for,' said Ms Brakes who looked as if she was about to explode. She thanked Molly and the unfortunate Dr Hailsham, who now looked as if he had been repeatedly run over by a steam roller, and handed over to one of her colleagues who introduced an item dealing with a three day old rumour that a Member of Parliament was suspected of having an affair with one of his researchers.

The minute Molly disappeared from my television screen the telephone rang again. It was Jock.

`Have you been watching?'

I was tempted to tease him by pretending that I didn't know what he was talking about. But Jock didn't sound in a mood for teasing. I said I had. `She did brilliantly, didn't she?'

`You think she did brilliantly? It was a disaster. It was an absolute disgrace. We're going to have to get rid of her. We'll be the laughing stock of the profession. I've already had three telephone calls about her.'

`From your drug company pals?'

`One was,' admitted Jock defensively. `But the other two were from eminent members of the profession. Both high up in the British Medical Association.'

`Well, I thought she did brilliantly,' I said. I have never had much time for the British Medical Association or its enthusiastic members. The BMA is a trades union which exists to gouge better pay for its members out of taxpayers. As far as I'm aware it has never been known to do anything – anything - likely to further the interests of patients. If they could negotiate a one hour working week and a 100% pay rise they do it like a shot. `And I think you'll find that if we try to get rid of Molly we will find ourselves on the losing end of a massive lawsuit. You can't sack someone for appearing on television and telling the truth.' It occurred to me that doctors used to recommend smoking cigarettes as a way of staying healthy. Perhaps Molly was right. Perhaps the rest of us were wrong about vaccination. Could vaccines be even more dangerous than cigarettes?

'You're a fat lot of help!' snarled Jock, ending the connection.

I poured myself another whisky. When Molly rang me as she and Larry drove home I congratulated her on a brilliant performance.

'You've made even me think twice about some of the pro-vaccination arguments,' I told her. 'You're bound to have made other people think too.'

That was the problem, of course. Molly had made too many people think. She had been far too successful. It would have been much, much better for her if she'd made a fool of herself and Dr Hailsham had made mincemeat of her. And the idiots at the BBC hadn't helped. By making her own position clear, the interviewer had turned Molly into a victim and made the audience far more sympathetic and supportive than they might otherwise have been.

Chapter 8

I've heard of people becoming celebrities overnight but I've never before seen it happen.

When I arrived at the surgery the following morning there were half a dozen reporters and photographers standing around outside the entrance and a tired looking Molly, now dressed in a white blouse, a pink cardigan and a pair of beige trousers, was standing in the porch giving an impromptu press conference. Larry, her boyfriend, was in earnest conversation with a balding man in a sports coat. Moments later a television crew turned up and a smartly dressed man with plastic hair, whom I vaguely recognised, pushed himself to the front and started asking questions. Despite the morning chill a small crowd of patients collected when they saw him. A young mother with two small children looked as though she might be ready to swoon.

Inside, Jock was hopping from one foot to another like a frog on a hotplate. `This is outrageous!' he cried, when he saw me. I got the feeling that he was peeved that it was Molly the reporters wanted to speak to and not him. `Our telephones have been red hot with reporters wanting to speak to Molly. Patients won't be able to get through. People could be dying if this absurd state of affairs is allowed to continue!'

I suspected that our senior partner might be exaggerating a tad and this thought was confirmed when Sharon, one of the receptionists (the one who has psoriasis and a nasty looking mole on her upper lip) quietly whispered to me that there had been just three calls. Since the practice had four incoming lines and a squad of receptionists the three telephone calls for Molly hardly seemed likely to be a serious threat to the public at large.

The patients who had seen the programme were excited at being treated by a famous doctor. Most of the receptionists hadn't seen the programme but collectively they persuaded Jock, who had recorded Molly's appearance, to bring in the DVD so that they could watch it on one of the practice computers. Fortunately, Deidre was away in Austria visiting her sister and brother in law. (As an aside, it always seems to me that if people go to the trouble of travelling all that distance to get away from their family they probably prefer to be left alone. Moreover, I've always found Austria a deeply boring country. Everything there is dedicated to the memory of Mozart. If the Great Musician had really eaten in all his `favourite' cafés, and drunk in all his `favourite' bars, he must have eaten a thousand times a day and been drunk around the clock. Oddly, there is no mention anywhere in Austria of the country's most famous son of all. But then Hitler's paintings weren't as good as Mozart's music and `Adolf Hitler's favourite café' probably wouldn't attract too many tourists or go down well with the European Union's Commissioner for Political Correctness.)

At lunchtime, I took Molly and Larry to The Bell for a quiet luncheon. I wanted Molly to tell me about her experiences at the BBC (I was hoping, I suppose, that she might have seen someone famous while she was wandering around the studios) but Larry, who seemed to have appointed himself Molly's press agent, dominated the conversation. He told us that he had already arranged a series of interviews with selected reporters and feature writers. `At this stage we have to maximise our exposure and strengthen the brand positioning,' he explained, when I'd ordered some drinks and three bowls of vegetable hotpot. `Later on we'll be able to charge for interviews but at the moment I think we should do everything we can and do them all for free.' He had compiled a list of all the interviews he'd arranged. `Several reporters want to make it a joint interview with Molly and myself,' he said, with what I thought was rather feigned reluctance on his part. `A few reporters wanted to know if I'm a vaccine victim so I told them about my sister Pauline and they want me to talk about her too. It gives the story a personal interest; a bit of colour.' He hesitated. `One or two say they'll send photographers along to my next gig. There aren't many stand-up comedians sitting down in wheelchairs.'

It had never occurred to me that anyone, even a major celebrity, would ever charge for an interview and it had not occurred to me that Molly's sudden fame would be anything more than a one or two day phenomenon. I don't really know but I felt a little uncomfortable about the way Larry seemed to be taking over and I got the feeling that Molly wasn't entirely comfortable with it either. He seemed to be making sure that his career got as big a boost as possible from her moment in the limelight and I couldn't help feeling that this was rather more opportunistic than seemed entirely decent.

'Best of all Molly has been asked to write an article for the *Daily Mail*,' said Larry, his eyes now aglow with excitement. He'd clearly kept what he thought was the best for last. 'They want 1,500 words for tomorrow's paper and they'll pay us £1,000. They want a piece explaining why vaccination is bad for us. The woman on the features desk said they want Molly to concentrate on parents and children but also include a few paragraphs about the flu vaccine and old people. I suspect they'll probably print that as a box or a breakout. I told them they'd have the article emailed to them by 4.00pm.'

'A breakout?' asked Molly.

'One of those bits of text at the side of the main piece,' explained Larry as though he'd been dealing with newspapers all his life. 'They also want a photograph so I've emailed them the one I took of you in that blue dress.'

'Oh no!' cried Molly genuinely upset 'Not that one. I look half naked. Its strapless and got a plunge neck. I can't imagine why I ever bought that dress. I only ever wore it once.' She blushed.

'It's a great picture!' insisted Larry. 'You want readers to know you're not some frumpy vegetarian nutter who dresses like a hippy and has no figure. Quite a few of the reporters I spoke to were worried about that - worried that you'd turn out to be a bit of a health food fruitcake. Anyway, Imogen, the girl on the features desk at the *Mail*, said that if the piece turns out well they might want you to write regularly for the feature pages. They're always on the lookout for doctors who can be a bit controversial. And they want you to mention Pauline. Imogen said she'd pass my details to their show business desk and suggest that they might like to do a piece about my stage act. They wanted to know if you're VAT registered, by the way, so I said you're not. But if you write for them regularly then we'll probably have to consider it. Especially if we get you a regular spot on television and maybe a radio show of your own.'

'Wait a minute!' said Molly who seemed bewildered by what was going on. 'What's this about a spot on television and a radio show?'

'All sorts of things are possible,' said Larry. He looked at his watch. 'We'd better go. We've got to write this article and we've got a couple more interviews to do.' Neither he nor Molly had touched the soup I'd ordered for them. Molly had sipped at her Diet Coke but Larry hadn't taken a sip from the beer I'd ordered for him.

'I've still my calls to do!' said Molly, panicking.

Larry looked at me. 'Perhaps...'

'No, I couldn't,' said Molly. 'That wouldn't be fair.'

'How many have you got to do?' I asked, trying not to sound as weary as I felt. I was also concerned for Molly. I wondered if she knew what she was getting herself into. Controversial writers often seem to end in financial and emotional disarray. William Prynne, a 17th century author who upset the establishment, was fined £5,000 and pilloried before having both ears cut off and put in prison for the rest of his life. If the medical establishment, the drugs industry and the redtop tabloids got their teeth into Molly she would probably wish she was living back in the 17th century when the penalties for upsetting the establishment were still relatively light.

'Four or five,' said Molly. She took out the piece of paper on which the receptionists had written down her calls for the day and looked up at me. 'Five.'

I held out my hand for the paper.

'Are you sure?' asked Molly.

I nodded.

She reluctantly handed me the call sheet and mouthed the words 'thank you'. Then she and Larry hurried away. I sat in The Bell for a few minutes more and finished my whisky and soup. I was looking around for something to read when I remembered that I still hadn't read Molly's article. I took it out of my pocket, unfolded it and started to read. It was very impressive. It was only a couple of thousand words long but Molly had managed to produce a surprisingly exhaustive analysis of vaccination.

In a short introduction she had pointed out that Edward Jenner, the doctor recognised as the originator of all modern vaccination programmes, lost faith in vaccination after trying out the first smallpox vaccination on his own 10 month old son. Tragically, Jenner's young son remained mentally retarded until his death at the age of 21. Molly pointed out that as a result of this tragedy Jenner, now the revered hero of those in favour of vaccination, refused to have his second son vaccinated. And she added that the medical profession, which had originally rejected Jenner's discovery as far too dangerous, subsequently embraced it with great enthusiasm and few reservations only when it became clear there were huge profits to be made from the preparation and administration of vaccines.

Molly described the problems with each popular vaccine; going through them all one by one. She pointed out that the one significant trial done on the tuberculosis vaccine had shown that the vaccine offered no protection against the disease. Indeed, she said, the trial suggested that there was a link between the giving of the vaccine and the development of new outbreaks of the disease. Similarly, she pointed out that the number of deaths from poliomyelitis had fallen dramatically long before the vaccine was introduced and that the incidence of the disease rose again after the vaccine became popular. She claimed that, as with other infectious diseases the number of patients fell as better housing, cleaner drinking water, better food and better sanitation were introduced in the second half of the 19th century. It was, she claimed, social developments rather than vaccination which had increased human resistance to infectious diseases. It was powerful, carefully argued and convincing stuff.

Molly had then pointed out that there is little, if any, scientific evidence showing that vaccines do what they are claimed to do and no evidence at all showing that they are safe. She pointed out that, contrary to popular opinion, up to half the individuals who are vaccinated against a disease do not develop any resistance to that disease and therefore gain no benefit at all from the vaccination.

She'd ended by arguing that governments support and promote vaccination programmes for purely financial reasons, and that the medical profession and drug industry should be honest and admit that the aim of any vaccination programme is not to protect individuals but to benefit the community at large. She explained that bean-counting politicians like vaccination because if enough citizens are vaccinated then the incidence of a disease is likely to be lower than it otherwise would be. 'The Government believes that if a vaccination programme cuts the incidence of measles in half then the number of parents needing to have time off work will fall accordingly. Vaccination programmes ease the economic burden on the State. Vaccinations are given not to protect individuals but to protect the economy. There are considerable risks with vaccination but the risks are taken by individuals and the benefits accrue to society at large. In moral terms it's a bit like owning a house which stands in the way of a motorway development. The authorities compulsorily purchase your home so that they can knock it down. You don't benefit at all but the State can build its nice new road and motorists who use that road undoubtedly benefit considerably.'

Molly's argument was that public-spirited individuals (and parents) might well not object to risking their health (or the health of their children) for the State, but that they should not be lied to about the benefits. Her objections were twofold. First, the Government and the medical profession suppresses the truth and doesn't tell those being vaccinated that they are being vaccinated to protect the State. Second, the Government and the medical establishment suppresses the truth about the incidence of side effects because they know that the uptake of vaccines would fall still further if people knew just how dangerous they were.

When I'd finished the article I sat and thought about it for a while. It was the first time I'd ever seen anyone question the whole principle of vaccination. And Molly had done it very well. It suddenly occurred to me that the editors of Newsnight had probably not read Molly's article properly. They would never have allowed her within ten miles of a BBC studio if they'd known what she'd written. They had arrogantly and wrongly assumed that she was just a silly young doctor who would be easy to crush. They would make an example of her to silence other critics. And they'd have a bit of fun with her and create a lively few minutes of television. These are, after all, days not of learning and wisdom but of blunt opinions and blind prejudice. But it had all gone very badly wrong. I began, at last, to realise just how arrogant and ignorant her critics really were. I doubted if Dr Hailsham had even bothered to look at her article at all. I was reminded of Marcel Proust who wrote: `L'inexactitude, l'incompetence ne diminuent pas l'assurance. Au contraire.'

Au contraire, indeed.

I ordered a black coffee and took out a rather bedraggled pocket street map of the town and planned a route that would enable me to do my calls, and Molly's calls, without going over the same ground twice. Jock is forever trying to persuade me to use one of these satellite navigation systems but I hate technology with a passion. Molly uses one and seems to get on quite well with it, though she admits that it has on several occasions taken her to the wrong place, or got her stuck in dead end roads.

I've lived and worked in the same damned town for two decades and I still can't remember where all the streets, avenues and closes are in relation to one another. Life is, of course, constantly made more difficult by the enthusiasm of planners and builders for knocking down perfectly solid and sound old houses which don't fit new building regulations and building blocks of flimsy flats and maisonettes and then naming all the new roads and cul-de-sacs after egotistical local councillors. The demolition companies and the builders make a fortune. The bent members of the local planning committee enjoy holidays they couldn't possibly afford if they had to live on their legal earnings. And the poor sods whose excellent Victorian homes are compulsorily purchased and razed find themselves rehoused in prefabricated properties which seem to be made out of cardboard and parcel tape and which have such paper thin walls that the occupants have to spend a fortune on keeping themselves warm.

Every six months I pick up a new town map from one of the local estate agents and every time I realise that I no longer recognise the town I'm living in. What really annoys me is that these perfectly decent houses are knocked down on orders from our lords and masters in Brussels. I hate the bastards from Brussels. In the old days we were allowed to do what we wanted to do as long we didn't break the law. These days, thanks to the venomous gnomes from Brussels, everything is forbidden and we are allowed to do what they decide to allow us to do. I feel as though they are changing the rules every hour, on the hour, including nights and weekends, and I can't keep up. They don't even tell you what the new rules are. How are you supposed to know that it's illegal to give a jar of your homemade chutney to a bring and buy sale at your local church?

When William the Conqueror splashed ashore and took charge of our island he banned the English from having fires or lights in their homes after eight o'clock at night. Offenders faced the death penalty. (I strongly suspect that the birth rate must have rocketed.) Today, we've been conquered again. Today, the barking mad rules and regulations originate in Brussels for we have been conquered by an army of administrators and abject, corrupt politicians. The eurocrats call their directives rules and regulations but they can fine us or send us to prison for breaking them and in my book if they can fine you or send you to prison for doing something, or not doing something, then the rule is a law in principle if not in name. I suspect that I now break at least one law a day and I suspect most other people do too. All this law breaking can't possibly be good for our traditional, law-abiding nature.

When I'd worked out my route I wrote out a new list, combining my six visits with Molly's five. I chewed two peppermints, drank another black coffee and set off to do the home visits. I couldn't stop thinking about Molly's article. I was sure she had some arguments and accusations which needed answering. But I was also sure that she'd stuck a stick into a very large wasps' nest full of some wasps who were not likely to ignore the attack.

Chapter 9

The visits, when I dragged myself back into the car and started work again, were exhausting and seemed interminable.

The first visit set the tone for the afternoon.

I got out of the lift on the 16th floor of a block of council flats (it was my treat of the week to find that, although it creaked and wheezed alarmingly, the damned lift worked) and found myself face to face with one of those hideously ugly dogs which have become so fashionable with the unemployed these days (largely because ownership of one of the beasts entitles the lead holder to an additional chunk of money every week in benefits).

I had been holding my breath all the way up (the stench of ammonia was strong enough to strip paint) and when the lift doors opened I must have made quite a noise as I suddenly exhaled in order to make room for a couple of lungfuls of the sort of polluted air they have hanging around on 16th floor landings in blocks of council flats. The noise I made startled the dog which started barking and growling and generally giving the impression that it was auditioning for the lead role in *Hound of the Baskervilles.*

When I started out as a GP I was frightened of dogs, particularly big noisy ones with teeth and a taste for human blood, but over the years I have slowly learned to conquer my fear. I began by becoming less frightened of the little ones (the ones so small that it would make more sense to squeeze them out over the sink rather than to bother taking them for a walk) and have gradually worked my way up to not being frightened by the big ones. The conquering of my fear was helped by the anger I felt when a two year old girl who was a patient of mine was mauled and bitten to death by an Alsatian dog. I was so cross that I told a reporter from the local paper that instead of shooting the dog the police should shoot the rancid owner. At the time this caused some trouble among our many dog-owning patients.

As the dog on the 16th floor landing growled still more I growled back, barked and generally made as much noise as I could. I also held my arms out wide to make myself look as big and as threatening as possible. Experts in these matters recommend keeping still, slinking away quietly or climbing up the nearest drainpipe. Bugger all that nonsense. When the confused dog made its move I simply gave it a hefty clout on the side of the head with my heavy, black drug bag.

`What the hell's going on?' demanded an angry looking man in a dirty vest, crimson jogging trousers and a pair of grubby looking slippers that had holes in the toes to let his feet breathe. Something told me that the slippers were more his style than the jogging trousers. He had an unshaven face and a shaven head and the effect made him look as though he had his head fixed on upside down. He looked at me and then at the whimpering dog, now cowering in a corner.

`What have you done to my dog?' he demanded.

`You called for the doctor?'

`It's the kids,' said the man. `Two of them have got spots.'

`Why do you leave the dog on the landing?' I asked him, genuinely curious.

`If we keep it in the flat the damned thing pisses and shits all over the carpets,' explained the man, who had the arrogant strut of a trades union official combined with the sly look of a child molester. `You're lucky,' he added. `Normally his bite is worse than his bark.'

I looked around and could see that the dog had indeed used the landing as an alternative to the local pavements. Surprisingly, the stench wasn't quite as bad as the smell in the lift.

`You could take it for walks outside,' I suggested. `Let it shit in a nice clean park where other people's children play.'

He looked at me as if I were mad.

When I managed to drag them away from the television set long enough to examine them, I found that the two children advertised as having spots were actually covered in flea bites. I hate fleas which always seem attracted to my person. I wrote out a prescription for something to stop the itching, offered some well-meant but bound-to-be-ignored advice and left quickly. The other five children were doubtless in line to be bitten within hours. Jock has long argued that men and women on benefits should be sterilised or stitched up (whichever seems most appropriate) to halt their indiscriminate breeding and there are days (and this was one of them) when I agree with him. These days it is only investment bankers and those on benefits who can afford to have big families.

On my journey back down to earth the lift groaned and complained for every foot of the way. It seemed as though the whole mechanism was about to jam solid. It occurred to me that maybe someone had thrown an unwanted body down the lift shaft and an arm or a leg had caught up in the cables. High rise, council-managed buildings engender thoughts like this. Down at street level I noticed for the first time that half the cars parked in the vicinity of the building were resting on red bricks rather than black tyres. I was relieved to notice that my car still appeared to be equipped with the required number of wheels.

Eleven visits might not sound much but when you have to find each home, examine every patient, make a diagnosis and decide on treatment it isn't easy to complete a visit in less than fifteen or twenty minutes.

It was going to be a long afternoon. Fortunately, however, the next few visits were fairly straightforward.

A lively pensioner wanted a repeat prescription for her digoxin, a mother had a child with earache which needed an antibiotic and a genial, rather eccentric old man called Walter Kennedy wanted something for an itchy rash on his leg. Mr Kennedy is well known locally for having married a 27-year-old waitress on his 80th birthday. When the vicar asked him if he would take Sharon for his lawful wedded Walter replied impatiently: `That's what I'm here for aint it?' This was generally regarded as one of the least romantic remarks ever heard in the town. Sadly, the waitress left him after a month, complaining that there was a substantial age difference between the two parties. This was clearly something which she had not noticed before the nuptials.

Other septuagenarians and octogenarians dress in beige and favour knitted cardigans and trousers with elasticated waists but Mr Kennedy, may he be blessed eternally, prefers to wear red corduroy trousers, a black frock coat and, whenever he ventures out of doors, a black top hat.

I told him that I had no idea what had caused his rash but assured him that the cream I gave him would clear it up in a day or two. I always carry a small selection of medicines in my drug bag so that I can give patients something to use straight away. I do this because I know that patients who live alone might otherwise have to wait a day or more to find a neighbour to take a prescription to a chemist for them. Some of the medicines I use arc samples but quite a few I purchase from a pharmacy near the surgery. Every now and then Jock has a go at me about this. Most doctors obtain whatever drugs they need in return for favours of one sort or another. (Jock and Deidre both add the drugs they need to prescriptions the pharmacist is already holding. The doctor gets the drugs at no cost and the pharmacist gets the profit on the drugs.) I prefer to spend a few quid buying drugs honestly and Jock objects strongly to this added practice expense.

It had taken the old man an age to open his front door and when I eventually entered the flat I could see why there had been such a lengthy delay. He had no less than four locks on the door. Once I was safely inside he fiddled with two of the locks while I waited. `Aren't you going to lock the other two?' I asked. He shook his head. `I only ever lock two, doctor,' he explained. `If a burglar tries picking my locks he'll always be locking two of them.'

Next, I visited an aggressive, bad-tempered lorry driver (the word `truculent' seemed particularly appropriate) who complained of indigestion. He seemed to find it extraordinary that I should attempt to link his internal travails to his daily consumption of greasy sausages, bacon and eggs. He confessed to eating three breakfasts a day while on the road, insisting that breakfast was always available in the sort of eateries he visited and that it always offered the best value for money. He said he had no intention of changing his diet because it was my responsibility, not his, to deal with his pains. I gave him a prescription and told him to come and see me when he was ready for the operation he would inevitably need.

The fifth visit was to a patient I knew.

Roger Hubbard is a detective sergeant and had been a patient of mine for as long as I'd been a GP. His father is a butcher who still has a small shop in the town and I once delighted Roger by reminding him that William Shakespeare's father was a butcher too.

Roger was very apologetic about calling me out. He suffers from asthma and is terrified that his employers will find out about his condition and that, if they do, he will, as a result, be transferred to duties inside the police station. He is so nervous that someone will find out about his problem that he likes me to visit him at home whenever his wheezing is bad. He's worried that someone might see him sitting in the waiting room.

When I arrived he was in quite a state and his wheezing was so bad that he was on the edge of status asthmaticus. I gave him a steroid injection, which is, from past experience, the only thing that really helps and I stayed with him for half an hour or so while the wheezing lessened. At the end of that time he was breathing pretty normally and could talk and move about.

'If this happens again you must tell the receptionist that you need an urgent visit,' I told him. There had been no indication on the call list that the call was anything other than routine. He told me, nervously, that he always felt intimidated when he rang the surgery. I closed my eyes and counted to ten when he told me this.

I hate the fact that we have one of those damned 'press one if you wish to request a repeat prescription, press two if you would like a non-urgent appointment, press three if you are dying…' telephone systems. (It was only recently that I persuaded Jock to get rid of the premium rate numbers we'd been using. I found out about the damned things when Jock boasted that we had made nearly £10,000 the previous year simply from the telephone calls patients made to us. He was charging up to £3 a minute for patients to telephone for help.)

In fact, there's a lot I hate about the way our surgery is run but there isn't a damned thing I can do about it because most of the rules and regulations we follow are forced upon us by the eurocrats, and are apparently designed to protect the physical and mental interests of our employees, rather than the physical and mental interests of our patients.

Everywhere I go I see signs warning members of the public of the rights of the people who are about to humiliate them. They have these signs at customs posts, where a careless or mistimed remark to one of the arrogant layabouts in uniform can put you in handcuffs in seconds. They even have them in Post Offices where the staff always seem to me to have been hired specifically for their absence of any human qualities. If anyone deserves to be treated with contempt it is the men and women who scowl at our passports and who serve us our stamps and motor car licences. Even at the surgery we have huge signs on the walls telling patients that 'Our Staff Have The Right To Work Without Fear' and 'Aggressive Or Abusive Patients Will Be

Ejected And Reported To The Police'. I sometimes think that we've got all this the wrong way round and that what we really need are signs inside the reception area warning members of staff that patients have rights too. Maybe we need signs saying: `Our Patients Are Frightened And Must Be Treated Sensitively' or `Aggressive Or Abusive Members Of Staff Will Be Fired And Boiled In Oil'. Like most businesses offering what the bureaucrats call an `interface' with the public we seem to do far more to protect ourselves and our own rights than we do to defend the rights of the poor sods we're paid to serve.

I gave Roger my personal mobile number and told him to ring me direct if he had any more problems and to ring the official surgery number only if he could not get hold of me direct. By the time I'd finished with him I was running very late and had only an hour and a half to complete the rest of the day's calls. Visiting patients at home is extraordinarily time consuming and many younger doctors will do anything they can to get out of home visits. I think they're wrong and they're missing out on one of the most important and rewarding aspects of medicine. Some patients are genuinely ill and can't make it to the surgery. They aren't sick enough to be in hospital but they aren't well enough to climb into a car and sit in the waiting room. But the doctor benefits too: I learn a good deal about my patients by seeing their homes. I see how they live, what they read and, often, what television programmes they choose to watch. Hospital doctors see patients as livers, kidneys and hearts. A good GP has an opportunity to see his patients as real people.

Fortunately, none of the visits I had left were particularly difficult to deal with and none of them took me out of the town. (When patients live in outlying villages a home visit can take an hour or more.) Only one of the patients I saw mentioned Molly's appearance on television. The others either hadn't seen it or didn't think it worth mentioning.

The one patient who did want to talk about Molly was a retired Colonel in his fifties who always demanded home visits because he considered himself far too important to make an appointment and visit the surgery like ordinary folk. Deidre and I have both spoken to him about it, and have pointed out to Jock that he is abusing our practice of making home visits without question. But Colonel

Douglas Mortimer, who describes himself as proud to be a blunt Yorkshireman, takes no notice. He inherited his money and lives in a smart area of town where the trees aren't allowed to drop their leaves outside a fixed October fortnight. He met me on the doorstep of his small, modern, faux manor house dressed in his usual tweed suit, waistcoat and old regiment tie and, as I followed him indoors, announced that the practice should get rid of Dr Turner immediately, forthwith and without delay. `I'm a Yorkshireman,' he told me, as he does every time I see him, `and I speak my mind. I don't believe in hiding my views. Straight talking sort of fellow. Get things out, that's my motto. That young woman doctor of yours is a disgrace. Her performance on that programme last night was shocking. How dare she question older medical people who clearly know what they're doing? I've had vaccinations all my life and they've never done me any harm. I don't want that girl treating me. And I doubt if anyone else will. Get rid of her straight away is my advice. If she comes out here I shall send her away with a flea in her ear.' By the time he'd finished this tirade, this absurd rant, he had led me into the drawing room. I'm always surprised by the amount of chintz and the number of plump cushions with which the Colonel has filled his home. Every pair of curtains has a fancy pelmet above and is controlled by complicated looking cords equipped with large tassels.

When the Colonel had finished I asked him if his belief in speaking his mind worked both way. As I spoke I looked out of the window and noticed, for the first time, that there was a fountain on the terrace. It was switched off and I suspected that he only switched it on when expecting visitors he wanted to impress. The Colonel seemed a little surprised by my question but, of course, had little choice but to lie and say that it did. The Colonel had really annoyed me. He seemed to have been brainwashed into believing whatever the establishment told him.

`Is that why you called me out?' I demanded. I noticed for the first time that he had a pair of bushy eyebrows which looked like two small untrimmed hedges. I wondered if he had ever been tempted to try a little topiary work. Turn them into cockerels perhaps. The Colonel said that he had indeed called for a home visit so that he could tell me to fire Molly. `But while you're here you can give me a repeat prescription for his sleeping tablets.'

'You're pompous and rude,' I told him. 'Your comments about Dr Tranter are outrageous and ill-informed. Moreover, you have consistently ignored our request that you ask for home visits only when you are too ill to attend the surgery. And to be honest with you I've known ex-corporals who had more common sense and greater intelligence. You're a disgrace to your regiment and to Yorkshire and you bear about as much resemblance to an English gentleman as I do to a Zulu warrior. Since you have stated that you will refuse to accept treatment from a member of our practice I will write to the relevant bit of the NHS and tell the administrators to find you another doctor. You are a self-important prat and you are no longer a patient of this practice. Good day to you.' And with that I turned and walked back to my car. As I reversed back down his driveway I accidentally on purpose succeeded in driving over a corner of his immaculately trimmed lawn. As I drove away I looked back and noticed with delight that my wheels had cut huge divots out of the grass. However, the Colonel didn't seem to have noticed the damage I'd done to his lawn. He was still standing in his doorway. His mouth was open but I have no idea whether or not he was talking.

I got to the Jock Cohen Health Centre just ten minutes after I should have started the evening surgery and sat down at my desk feeling shattered. I hoped that Molly wouldn't be doing too many more interviews. One of the receptionists (the one with varicose veins) brought me a large mug of black coffee together with the list of patients who'd booked appointments. I groaned when I looked at the length of the list and the height of the pile of medical records which she also brought with her. Most of the nation's medical practices now keep all their medical records on computer. We prefer to continue to keep our records in little cardboard envelopes. Boring men and women from various NHS departments come round from time to time to tell us that we have to adopt the computerised system. But Jock and I always explain that we haven't yet got the hang of computers and our exaggerated ignorance sends them away in despair.

'Dr Tranter's boyfriend called in to say that Dr Tranter couldn't get in for tonight's surgery,' said the receptionist. 'We were going to share out Dr Tranter's patients between you and Dr Cohen but Dr Cohen told us to give them all to you. He said he had to get home because he has a meeting with the builder at the new house he's buying. But to be honest I think he wants to get home because he had a very unpleasant experience at the hairdresser's this afternoon.'

`What sort of unpleasant experience?' I asked. `The barber didn't snip off an ear did he?'

`I'm not supposed to know,' said the receptionist, looking around to make sure that no one, particularly Dr Cohen, was likely to overhear. `But apparently Dr Cohen goes to a unisex salon in Bartholomew Street and suddenly the girl who was cutting his hair screamed and ran across the salon and whispered something to the receptionist who immediately picked up the phone and rang the police.' There was a pause and the receptionist looked around once more before resuming. `Less than two minutes later a squad car screeched to a halt and two burly policemen raced across the salon and pulled back the sheet that the hairdresser had tied round his neck to keep the bits of hair off Dr Cohen's suit. I can't imagine what they were expecting to see but what they found was Dr Cohen quietly and absent-mindedly polishing his spectacles with his handkerchief.'

I grinned and thanked the receptionist for this merry tale. I looked at the list of patients and then at the clock. `This is going to take some time,' I warned her. `Bring me a fresh mug of coffee every half an hour.' As she started to leave I called her back. `Have we got anything to eat?'

`We've got a packet of cream biscuits, half a packet of ginger biscuits and some home-made scones a patient brought in.'

`What are the scones like?'

`Tamarin says they're a bit stodgy but I quite like them. Would you like one?'

`Bring me a scone and as many biscuits as you can cram onto a plate,' I told her. `Have we really got someone working here called Tamarin?'

`She's been here for nine months now.'

`OK. Which one is she?'

`She's the tall, slim brunette. She's married to our postman.'

`Right. Don't tell her I didn't know her name.'

`No, Dr Cassidy.' She paused for a moment, started to leave and then turned back and smiled. `My name is Felicity, by the way. I've been here for two years.'

`I know your face,' I told her. `I'm never very good with names.'

'I know,' she said, nodding. She was still smiling when she left so she can't have been too upset.

The evening surgery was a blur notable only for a visit from a pompous, stout man who called himself Captain Edward Low and said that he was new to the area and was interviewing doctors to find one who suited him. I didn't like to tell him that these days patients are allocated to doctors according to the whims of local bureaucrats and so I greeted him with fake politeness. 'I believe the best way to find a good GP is to ask a doctor who he is registered with,' he told me, taking out a pocket diary and a cheap fountain pen and preparing to take notes. 'I'm registered as a patient of Dr Cohen,' I said. I wouldn't trust Jock to trim my toe nails but if we register as patients with one another it keeps the fees in the practice. 'Ah,' said the Captain. 'Then he's the doctor for me.' 'Splendid,' I said. 'When you see him don't forget ask the name of his doctor.' Captain Low frowned. 'Who is his doctor?' he asked. 'Me,' I replied.

It was after eight when I finished the evening surgery. Just before I left, Tamarin or Felicity or possibly someone else entirely told me that Dr Turner had left a message asking me if I would do her night's duty again. 'She said that she's got a radio interview to do,' explained the receptionist who had, I noticed, a strange way of staring into space when she spoke to me, as though something more interesting was going on somewhere behind me. I thought that perhaps she had been formerly employed in a post office. I groaned silently but managed to find the patience not to scowl at the bearer of these disappointing tidings.

'That's nice,' I said. 'All I was planning to do was sleep anyway.'

On my way home, listening to a jazz clarinet CD in the car, I started itching. The first flea had already started work.

The minute I got through the door I stuffed all my clothes into the washing machine and then climbed into a hot bath. I found the flea in the water and crushed him between two thumb nails. Sometimes you have to be cruel to be kind to yourself.

When I dragged myself out of the bath I caught sight of a decrepit, tired of life old man in his mid-sixties. My skin was grey, my eyes puffy and I looked like a quality control reject. I was still only in my fifth decade but life seemed to have beaten me to a pulp before the contest was half over. If I'd seen myself standing on a bus

I'd have gladly offered me my seat. I tried to work out just where my life had gone and decided that I'd spent too much of it sitting in traffic jams, filling in forms and trying to get back to sleep. A large whisky and a plum jam sandwich woke me up a little and I slumped down in an easy chair to watch the television, although I find that this is a dangerous thing to do when I'm on call. If I find a half-way decent programme to watch the telephone will go, I will inevitably find myself called out to deal with an emergency and I'll miss the end of whatever it was I was watching. Most of the time the call could have waited until after the end of the programme but I can never sit there and wait. When a call comes in I have to go out and deal with it. Usually, when I'm on call I usually dig out a DVD to watch on the basis that if I'm called out I can stop it and restart it when I return. There was nothing I wanted to watch on television and I was feeling too tired to look through the DVDs so I found a Wodehouse I hadn't read for some time and immersed myself in the wonderful world inhabited by the members of the Drones club. I read for half an hour and then the telephone rang.

A man called Gibbs reported that his wife, Catherine, a schizophrenic patient of Jock's, had made a cake and was preparing to take slices round to all the neighbours. `I can see that they might be a bit upset since it's so late at night,' I said, `but why did you ring me?' He told me that his wife had emptied eight bottles of pills, including some pretty potent psychotropic drugs, into the cake mixture.

`Do you think one slice of the cake would do people any harm?' he asked.

I told him to lock the door and not to let the cake out of his sight. I then set off, driving at speeds varying between two and three times the legal limit, and slowing down only when I found myself unable to overtake a cyclist meandering along in the middle of the road. I hate cyclists. They all claim they're saving the planet but every time a motorist comes up behind one he has to slow down and then waste petrol accelerating. I reckon the average cyclist must, as a result, have an even bigger carbon footprint than a standard sized rock star who travels everywhere by private plane.

When I eventually arrived, with smoke coming both from my ears and the brakes, the toxic cake was still intact. I talked Catherine Gibbs into letting me take it away so that I could distribute slices on her behalf. She smiled contentedly, thanked me and went to bed. I put the cake, in its tin, into the car boot and drove home at a rather more sedate pace.

Chapter 10

The Molly Tranter roadshow continued to gather pace.

I confess that I had expected media interest to fade away after a day or so. But a couple of things kept the subject of vaccination in the public eye.

First, Molly wrote an article for *The Daily Telegraph* pointing out the dangers of the influenza vaccine. The publication of her article, provocatively entitled `Licensed to Kill', coincided with the launch of a new Government campaign designed to encourage the elderly to rush along to their doctor and get jabbed. But Molly, who had become a revolutionary army of one, questioned the wisdom of this advice.

`The viruses which cause influenza are forever changing and so anti-flu vaccines are useless,' wrote Molly. `The companies making the vaccines simply guess which might be the strain most likely to produce an epidemic in the coming year. That's about as predictable as forecasting the weather. And we all know how good scientists are at that!'

`How many people know just what is in the flu jab they allow the doctor or nurse to give them? How many know that these vaccines contain mercury – a substance banned from barometers by the European Union?

`Do flu vaccines increase or lower the human body's general immunity? No one knows. Does the widespread use of the flu vaccine spread the flu and cause more illness than it prevents? No one knows the answer to that either, but the list of side effects suggests that it might.'

`The one certainty about the flu vaccine is that the people producing it and giving it are making a lot of money. GPs make thousands of pounds a year out of the flu vaccine. And most don't do anything for that money. The practice nurse gives the jabs and the GP cashes the cheques. Drug companies make billions out of these drugs. But they don't know whether or not they work. They don't even know if they're doing more harm than good.'

`The best way to avoid the flu is to keep away from the aisles in chemist's shops where the cold and flu remedies are sold. The flu victims who hang around in those aisles, coughing and sneezing without ever covering their faces, are deadly dangerous. And the best way to avoid nasty antibiotic-resistant bugs is to keep out of hospitals and away from people who work in them.'

And so the article continued. Molly's arguments were powerful and suddenly people started asking questions. Radio phone in hosts realised that here was a perfect subject for a morning's heated discussion. Leader writers sharpened their quills and took positions. Members of Parliament, scenting a bandwagon about to start accelerating, leapt aboard and started asking questions.

Then a group of doctors wrote a letter to The Times suggesting that the Government should introduce a compulsory vaccination programme. It would be an understatement of colossal proportions to say that their timing was not good. They pointed out that compulsory vaccination had been introduced in the mid-19th century and that it was time to bring it back. The letter was greeted with enthusiasm by a powerful and outspoken group of social workers who claimed that parents who did not allow their children to be vaccinated should be arrested, and that their children should be taken from them. The group's self-appointed leader, a stout, shapeless, bristling feminist with angry eyebrows and a penchant for boiler suits and wooden clogs accused Molly of tilting at non-existent windmills and sneeringly called her 'Donna Quixote'. In a letter of reply, written more to defend her point of view than herself, Molly pointed out that most of the individuals promoting the idea of compulsory vaccination were in the pay of the companies making the vaccines.

This caused an uproar because it was true and nothing upsets the establishment more than the deliberate or accidental spilling of the truth. Molly included a reference to Thomas Jefferson in her letter. 'If people let government decide what medicines they take, their bodies will soon be as sorry a state as are the souls of those who live under tyranny.' And she added that those individuals who allow the State to make medical decisions for them are accepting that the State owns their bodies.

Libertarians everywhere became excited by this and Molly was voted woman of the year by a magazine neither she nor I nor anyone we knew had ever heard of. Still, it was definitely an accolade and not a criticism.

The militant social worker, who was known as Red Ruth as a tribute to her political affiliations rather than because she came from Cornwall, called for Molly to be arrested for creating uncertainty among the proletariat though she didn't call them that, of course. The world is full of bullies these days.

One of the red top tabloids printed pictures of a group of leading doctors who were known supporters of vaccination and underneath the photographs it listed their relationships with a variety of vaccine producing drug companies. It did not look good. It made the doctors look like criminals. The picture editor had done a good job in selecting photographs which made the physicians look shifty and disreputable.

All this activity meant, of course, that Molly was spending as much time on her campaign as she was spending with the practice.

`I'm so sorry,' Molly said, ten days or so after her original television appearance.

She had come into my consulting room at the end of my surgery to apologise for not doing her fair share of calls or emergency duty. I had done most of her home visits and it seemed as though I had been on call for a lifetime. Even when there are few calls to attend to being on duty is exhausting. I can never relax properly when I am waiting for the telephone to ring.

But Molly looked even more tired than I felt and her eyes were dull with exhaustion. She had started wearing smart suits to work, presumably because she never knew when a photographer or television crew were likely to turn up, and she had started wearing make-up. But she looked worn out. It was curious: in some ways she looked younger and less confident than she had looked before but in another way she looked much older, much more self-assured and infinitely more world weary.

`Larry says we have to keep going with this while people are still interested and I know he's right but at the same time I feel bad about letting you down.'

Looking at her I couldn't help wondering if the drug industry and the medical establishment knew that the tough, fearless doctor who was giving them such a hard time weighed less than eight stone and wore shoes made for children because they were the only ones which would fit her.

`Can you do your own calls today?' I asked her. `Jock won't help. And he thinks you're neglecting the practice.'

I was getting worried about her but I knew damned well that I too was working far too hard and needed to slow down a little. I was so tired that I would soon be making mistakes and when you make mistakes in medicine the results tend to be catastrophic. I was worried about Molly not only because she looked so tired out but also because I suspected that she was beginning to believe the old saying that the pen is mightier than the sword. The truth, I suspect, is that the pen is only mightier than the sword when the other person doesn't have a sword. And some of the people with whom she was battling had very sharp swords.

She promised that she would do her own calls. `And I'll take the emergency calls tonight,' she added. She fiddled nervously with the neck of her jumper. `Do you think it would help if I told Jock that any money I earn from articles and broadcasts will be paid into the practice?'

I thought for a while.

`Are you sure about that?'

`Yes.'

`What does Larry say?'

`We haven't talked about it. But it is my money.'

`It would make Jock very, very happy,' I told her. `Money is his second love.'

She looked at me for a moment. `What's his first love?'

`Himself.'

She laughed. `Then I'll do it.' She looked at me for a long, long moment. `Do you think I'm doing the right thing?' she asked. `With all this stuff about vaccination. Or do you think am I being stupid?'

I thought for a while before answering her. `I certainly don't think you're being stupid,' I told her. `But I don't know yet whether you're right and I don't know whether or not I agree with you.'

The truth was that I wanted more time to look at the evidence and to think carefully about the arguments Molly had made. And I hadn't had the time because I had been kept busy racing around the town doing Molly's visits and emergency calls as well as my own.

`You've raised a lot of questions which need answering. And I admire and respect you for it.' I paused. `Someone had to do it. But in a way I'm sorry that it had to be you.'

Molly blushed slightly. `Thank you. '

`But…' I began.

`Ah,' she said with a slight smile `Here it comes…'

`But you're also a member of this practice, albeit a junior one, and regardless of how you consider the importance of your own career you also have a responsibility to the patients.' I felt old and pompous saying this but I also felt it had to be said.

`I know,' she said so softly I could hardly hear her. `I've let you down haven't I?'

`You've perhaps got your priorities mixed up a little,' I told her. `The patients are confused. And Jock is gunning for you. He's fed up of the fact that you're not doing what you're paid for. He even went to the expense of ringing Deidre in Austria. And I bet it didn't take him long to recruit her to the `stomp on Molly campaign'. He's fed up of journalists ringing up and hanging around in the waiting room. He and Deidre aren't campaigning people. They aren't media people. Their world is the Health Centre and to them you seem to be intent on tearing it apart. You've become a threat and to be honest I think they're rather frightened of you.'

She frowned, thought about what I'd said and then nodded.

`And you need to be careful,' I told her. `You've annoyed a lot of rich and powerful people.'

She looked puzzled. `What are you saying?'

`The medical establishment has a habit of crushing people who cause too much trouble. If you make too much noise there's a danger that you might have difficulty getting a job as a partner – particularly if you attract the attention of the General Medical Council.' I took my pipe out of my pocket and stuck it between my teeth. `Now bugger off and let me get on with all this crap.' I waved a hand across the paperwork on my desk and then looked up at her and smiled. `And I'm sorry if I sounded too much like your Dad.'

`Oh, you sound much more like an old fart than my Dad ever did,' said Molly, grinning. `He never even told me off when I dyed my hair green.' She looked down for a moment and her voice dropped. `Actually he wasn't there much at all,' she said. She moved away and then looked back. `You're better than the rest of them,' she said softly. `You pretend to be tough and indifferent, like Jock, but really you're just soft and squishy inside.'

I threw a pen at her.

When she'd gone I wished I'd told her that I was proud of her. I promised myself that I'd tell her next time. The truth was that I was beginning to think of her as the daughter I'd never had and always rather wanted. And I was proud of her. She had much bigger balls than Jock had. Damnit, she had much bigger balls than I had too. Compared to her we were a pair of bloody eunuchs.

No one else mentioned Molly or vaccination for the remaining hours of the working day and I was beginning to think that the fuss was perhaps dying down when Terry Biddles, a patient who'd come to see me for his monthly check up, brought everything to a head again.

`I've been looking at the Internet,' he said, as I checked his blood pressure. `And it looks as if your young doctor is wrong.'

`Wrong about what?' I asked. It is thanks to the Internet that a growing number of people pretend to know everything and fear nothing but, in truth, in private, know little and fear everything.

`About vaccines and vaccination.'

`Ah. In what way is she wrong?'

`Oh, every way possible. I've been onto several sites and it's clear that your Dr Tranter is talking rubbish. I'm surprised you haven't had a word with her, doctor. She's not doing your practice any good.'

I told him to be quiet a moment as I listened to the blood pumping through his brachial artery. `Pretty good,' I told him. `140 over 90.' It had been 165 over 120 when I'd first taken it just a few months earlier.

`Not bad, eh? These drug companies know their stuff don't they?'

`It's not bad at all,' I agreed. It had not escaped my notice that he had given all the credit for the reduction in his blood pressure to the drug company which made the pills he took and absolutely none of it to the changes in his diet which I had persuaded him to adopt or to his belief in the power of what he was taking. The pills he was taking were very mild. Most patients overestimate the value of drugs and underestimate their body's own power of healing itself. The simple fact is that the placebo power of anything that looks like a medicine is enormous. Nearly half of the therapeutic effect of any medicine lies in the patient's belief in the power of the treatment, rather than in the medicine itself. I could cure around 40% of all my patients by giving them a one week course of orange Smarties, though if I tried I would, I have no doubt, have the drug company inspired wrath of the General Medical Council to deal with.

`I wrote down the details of several of the websites,' said Mr Biddles, taking a crumpled piece of paper out of his trouser pocket and putting it on my desk. `I thought you might like to check them out.'

Like many other doctors I have grown to loathe the Internet, which is, as far as I'm concerned, a foreign country where opinions and prejudices survive and breed without the support of, or need for, evidence of any kind or quality. The Internet is an alien land where the words `rumour' and `fact' are synonyms.

I have, over the years, learned that patients can be divided into four simple groups: the ones who imagine they are ill but are not ill at all; the ones who are ill but who will get well whatever is done to or for them; the ones who will deteriorate and die whatever is done to or for them and the surprisingly small group who can be helped by modern medicine. Every day I see patients from all these categories who have consulted websites in order to diagnose themselves or to find new treatments which they can try. The trouble is that before you can use the Internet safely you need to have a considerable amount of background knowledge. Most websites are full of dangerous gibberish. And most of the gibberish has been put there by people with an axe to grind or a product to sell. The Internet may have given a voice to everyone but it's given the loudest voices to those who make the most noise: the ignorant, the self-centred, the self-important, the prejudiced, the bigoted and the snide. Vicious fishwives and mean fascists rule the Internet in a way that they have never quite managed to control the television or the radio. The Internet spreads misinformation, prejudice, anxiety, confusion and bewilderment as efficiently as the modern hospital spreads gastroenteritis. Wikipedia (which can't even spell its own name properly) and Google are less reliable as sources of information than the old woman who used to run the manually operated telephone exchange.

`I'll see you in a month,' I told him, handing over a prescription.

`Thanks, doc. And don't forget to have a word with that young girl doctor of yours. She alarms people and makes them feel uncomfortable.'

I managed to bite my tongue and didn't say a word. I really didn't like Biddles giving me advice about anything. He has twice been found guilty of exposing himself to mature ladies patronising a local public car park. He had been fined on both occasions. When Enid had shown me the story in the local newspaper I'd commented that it was a case of display and pay in a pay and display. She'd said that it wasn't anything to joke about but that he had at least made a clean breast of things and promised to turn over a new leaf. Enid has always had a masterly touch with a cliché. His advice about Molly was absurd and irritating.

And I hate people who call me `Doc'. It always reminds me of that damned cartoon character.

When I'd finished the surgery I switched on my computer, fired up the Internet and looked up the sites that Biddles had listed. It was no great surprise to find that every single one was paid for, sponsored or supported by one or other of the big drug companies. All the sites looked independent but none of them was. The existence of these sites did not surprise me but the fact that the drug companies were concerned enough to create them or support them did concern me. And the fact that Terry Biddles, normally a fairly quiet sort of fellow, had taken such an interest in the subject, and had taken such a firm position on it, also surprised and worried me. It looked as though Molly might be losing the argument. It really didn't matter whether or not she was right. In medicine, as in all areas of modern life, perception is everything.

I looked at some more websites and found, to my astonishment, that organisations which claimed to represent the interests of patients were also accepting drug company money so that they could maintain their websites and publish `advice' for patients and relatives. And, no doubt, so that the people who ran them could pay their Sky television subscriptions and the payments on their wide screen television sets and second cars. The Internet was, it seemed, even more corrupt than I had imagined.

But Terry Biddles, and people like him, believe what they hear and what they read – as long as it comes, or seems to come, with an establishment endorsement.

`Vaccines are safe and effective,' preach the exhortionists. `They save lives. Those who question their value are dangerous Luddites who must be silenced.'

And too many people believe what they are told; accepting, with enthusiasm, the fictions, the spin, the deceits, the distortions and the blatant manipulations. Every senior politician since (and including) Edward Heath has deliberately lied to us. Broken by fear, oppression and self-preservation we accept what we are told; too frightened of the truth to see the lies.

I remembered something that aristocratic rebel Bertrand Russell once said: `In all affairs it's a healthy thing, now and then, to hang a question mark on the things you have long taken for granted.'

Jock sometimes says that I am against too many things and not for enough. I know exactly what he means. I loathe the European Union (the source of almost all the really stupid laws and regulations which curse our lives), the Internet, unlimited immigration, bureaucracy and the unthinking political bigotry which gave us the National Health Service. But sometimes you don't have to be *for* anything to want to change the world for the better. It is enough to be *against* the bad things.

Chapter 11

I had not been looking forward to my weekend off and in the event I was not disappointed.

The film that Enid insisted we see turned out to be one of the dullest productions ever devised for the silver screen. A documentary about Welsh miners would have been more watchable. There was no plot and the script seemed to have been written by the famous team of monkeys who would, if given enough time, produce the plays of Shakespeare but who had, in this instance, not been given enough time to produce even one coherent sentence. If the director had skills they were not associated with the making of films and the actors seemed to have wandered onto the set believing that they had been hired as furniture. The film was so bad that it wasn't difficult to see why *The Guardian's* critic liked it so much. If they gave out prizes to sanctimonious, self-satisfied, complacent, boring, hypocritical nerds the journalists at *The Guardian* would win them all.

The evening with the Stokes was no more of a disappointment (expectations had been too low for there to be any sense of disappointment) but if it ever finds a place in a list of my top 1,000 Saturday evenings it will be towards the very bottom of the list, and it will not be there for any of the usual reasons but because of the curious conversations I had.

`I must say I was very surprised to see that you allowed that young girl to be so outspoken,' said Ms Stoke, as we set about our dishes of prawn cocktail with varying degrees of enthusiasm.

`Which young girl is that?' I asked, disingenuously.

`The one who keeps telling young mothers not to have their children vaccinated,' said the hostess with careless inaccuracy.

`Disgraceful business,' said her husband, stuffing a prawn into his mouth and shaking his head at the same time. Knowing him as well as I did I was impressed at his versatility. He would be walking and talking at the same time soon. `Aren't there rules about doctors criticising their betters? Of course we weren't taken in by it but a good many people must have been terribly confused.'

'People who saw her on that awful television programme wouldn't know what to believe,' said Ms Stoke.

'I was surprised too,' said Enid, eagerly supporting her friends.

I could feel the dagger in my back and wasn't well pleased at this mild act of social treachery. Et tu Brute.

'There are a lot of very gullible people out there,' said Mr Stoke. 'There are probably people who will now believe that vaccination is dangerous.'

'I hope there are,' I said.

The other three stared at me as if I'd suddenly made complimentary comments about Adolf Hitler's road building accomplishments. 'There are too many self-righteous people around who are too blind to consider the awful possibility that their truth might not be the real truth but just a thin veneer of commercially convenient flim flam. Personally, I have a curious feeling that the interfering busy bodies who ban Punch and Judy shows and demand that horse chestnut trees be chopped down are the same folk who insist that everyone   be vaccinated against everything. I'm beginning to think the vaccination of children is just a legally authorised form of child abuse.'

'She's just a publicity seeking girl,' said Enid. She turned to me. 'You want to watch her very carefully. I suspect she wants a media career. She'll be off as soon as she can get her own television programme organised.'

'I don't think she's a publicity seeker, I began. 'On the other hand if she just turns up at one or two more television studios someone is bound to offer her a cookery programme or a spot on an antiques show.'

'Oh, she is definitely a publicity seeker,' said Mr Stoke.

'Definitely,' said Enid.

Ms Stoke nodded her enthusiastic support. The verdict had been reached. I pushed some limp lettuce on top of the prawns in my dish and put down my spoon. As far as I knew neither of the Stokes had ever met Molly. Enid had met her only briefly on a couple of occasions. I was appalled, though not particularly surprised, at the way the three of them happily attacked Molly's reputation and equally horrified at the fact that all three assumed, apparently without reservation, that what she said was wrong and that the medical establishment had to be right simply because it was the medical establishment. It seemed odd to hear three people who regarded themselves as free-thinking intellectuals paying homage to an establishment which had neither earned, nor even tried to earn, their respect.

The conversation continued in much the same manner throughout the main course (rubber chicken that had allegedly been allowed to roam free before being strangled to death, new potatoes that were the size and consistency of cricket balls, fibrous carrots which could have been used as dibbers and another vegetable which I could not identify and which was, I suspect, beyond identification by anyone not equipped with an electron microscope and a couple of armfuls of large textbooks) and well into the pudding course (which was, as a variation on Ms Stokes' well-established theme, a small piece of four-flavour ice cream gateau served straight from the manufacturer's cardboard box).

On several occasions I tried to intervene but each attempt was dismissed as though the three of them were the experts and I the ignorant buffoon wandering out of his depth into uncharted waters wherein they sailed with confidence and equanimity. Every time Enid added her voice to this growing clamour I felt increasingly betrayed and irritated.

At the end of the meal we moved from the dining room to the living room where Ms Stoke served dainty cups of weak coffee. A second bottle of the awful Greek wine had been opened towards the end of the chicken course and the remains of this was brought in from the dining room.

`Are you sure you won't have a glass?' asked Ms Stoke.

`Oh he's being a bit of a spoilsport as usual!' said Enid.

`Whoops, I forgot,' said Ms Stoke suddenly. `You're AA aren't you?'

`AA?' said Mr Stoke, puzzled. `What's that got to do with anything?'

Ms Stoke mouthed the explanation, obviously assuming that the excesses of alcohol I had enjoyed in the past had permanently damaged my ability to lip read.

`You need to let your hair down a bit,' said Mr Stoke. `I'm sure a drop of this stuff won't hurt you. Hardly any alcohol in it at all!' He laughed uproariously at this, as though he thought it funny and winked at his wife who had never seemed to me to be a woman likely to cherish being winked at.

`You tell him!' cried Enid. `I wish he would listen to someone.' She turned to me. `You're becoming a bit of a stick in the mud,' she told me in a not entirely unkindly tone. She patted me on the back of the hand.

I resisted their entreaties and said I'd stick with the coffee. It was hardly drinkable but at least it probably wasn't going to burn a hole in my stomach. As a gesture of defiance I took out my pipe and my smoker's friend and fiddled with the bowl. Enid looked on in horror and mouthed `Don't you dare light that thing in here' at me. I couldn't read her lips but it wasn't difficult to tell what she was saying.

Ms Stoke, who had been moving dirty dishes from the dining room table to the dishwasher (and who had steadfastly refused Enid's help with a series of self-sacrificing facial and body gestures) suddenly appeared in the doorway and beckoned to me with a finger. `Can I borrow you for a moment?' she whispered.

Dutifully, I put down my coffee cup, stood up and followed her into the kitchen. I assumed at first that she wanted my help with the dirty dishes. But that wasn't it at all.

`Since you're here I just want to pick your brains,' she whispered. `As a doctor.'

I thought that this was a bit rich since she'd spent the last hour or two ignoring all my medical opinions but I just nodded.

`Smoke if you want to, by the way,' she said. She pointed to the pipe I was holding.

`Oh no I wouldn't dream of it,' I explained. `I just fiddle with it and give it a suck every now and then.'

Ms Stoke blushed deep red. The blush covered her face and quickly spread down her neck. `That's sort of in a way what I wanted to talk to you about.'

It was obvious what she meant and so I instantly adopted my most serious expression, the one I use when women tell me that they have discovered that their husband has taken to wearing their underwear, and nodded encouragingly.

`I think it's just his age,' she said. `But Rodney is having a bit of a problem in the bedroom department.' The way she said it made it sound as though he ran a department store and was having trouble with an errant salesman.

`Ah,' I said. I nodded understandingly and put my pipe into my mouth. I feel that the pipe, like half-moon spectacles, always gives me a sense of gravitas. I am probably quite wrong about this.

`Can you give me a prescription for some Viagra?' she asked. `Just a few to try.'

`Ah,' I said again. `I'm afraid it's not quite that easy. I'd have to prescribe them for Rodney and he isn't my patient. You aren't either, of course.'

`Oh,' said Ms Stoke. She looked very disappointed. `I wouldn't tell anyone,' she said. `I wouldn't get you into trouble.' She thought for a moment. `I could pay you,' she offered.

I explained that there are rules about these things and that I couldn't wander around prescribing pills for the husbands of friends.

`What a pity,' she said. `You won't say anything, will you? Nothing to Rodney.'

`Say anything about what?'

`Pardon? Oh yes, I see.' She laughed. `Nor to Enid.'

`How are we going to explain this?'

`What?'

`You asking me to come out here.'

`Oh. I hadn't thought. Perhaps I could say I needed you to help move the table.'

`That doesn't sound very plausible,' I said. `Why don't we just say you wanted my advice about a rash.'

`I haven't got a rash.'

`You could pretend.'

`Oh yes, I could couldn't I?' She screwed up both eyes in a bizarre double wink and gave me what I think was supposed to be a smile.

We went back into the living room.

`What have you been up to with my wife?' asked Rodney with forced joviality.

`And what have you been up to with my partner?' Enid asked Ms Stoke.

I really hated it when she called me her partner because it gave our relationship a formality which I didn't think it truly merited. The truth was that when she called me her partner I always felt nervous.

We sat for ten or fifteen minutes and talked about the weather, the council taxes, bad neighbours (one, Ms Stokes insisted, had deliberately strimmed his lawn on the day that Rodney had painted their garden shed) and one or two television programmes I hadn't seen (and wouldn't have watched if I'd been tied to a chair) and then Rodney suddenly reached across, tapped me on the knee and stood up. `I almost forgot,' he said. `I've got something I want to show you.'

We left Enid and Ms Stoke discussing a book they'd both seen reviewed in *The Guardian.* They both regarded the damned paper as the final arbiter on all things requiring any sense of taste or artistic understanding and followed its rulings with the sort of blind obedience with which the children of Hamelin followed the pied piper. When I had a cat for a while I always use to buy *The Guardian* specifically to use as a liner for its litter tray. I never used to read the damned thing; I just put it straight into the bottom of the litter tray every Monday, Wednesday and Friday. I found that if I bought a copy of Monday's paper, the one with the supplement containing advertisements for BBC jobs, it would last me for a month. Twelve litter tray changes out of one newspaper. I wrote to the editor once and suggested that they might like to use a recommendation from me in one of their advertisements. He never had the courtesy to reply.

`I wondered if you could help me with our bedroom life,' said Rodney, when he'd got me safely pinned against the fridge-freezer.

`What can I do?' I asked him. I assumed that he wasn't about to ask my advice on bed linen or curtains.

`The thing is,' he said, `that I love my wife very much indeed but our bedroom life needs a bit of a boost.' He was obviously going to persevere with this silly euphemism.

`Ah,' I said, knowingly. And waited.

`It would help give my wife more confidence in the bedroom if she had, er, more…' he paused, either searching for the word or the confidence to say the word.

I waited partly because I didn't know what the hell he was going to say next and partly because I didn't want to make things easy for him.

`A bigger bosom,' he said at last. He held out his hands in front of his chest in case I didn't know what he meant.

'I thought it would make a nice birthday present for her,' he said.

'Has she asked for plastic surgery?'

'Oh no, she would never ask. She's not like that.'

'So how do you know…?'

'Well, it would give a boost to our relationship. In the bedroom.'

'Have you talked to her about it?'

'Oh no. No. Not at all.'

'Well you'll have to talk to her.'

'I thought perhaps it could be a surprise. A birthday surprise.'

I looked at him, slightly incredulously. 'You mean, she wakes up on her birthday and suddenly finds that she's got bigger breasts?'

'Oh, that would be marvellous! Wonderful.'

'How would we do that?'

'Couldn't you arrange for her to go into hospital for a check-up or something and then while she's anaesthetised the surgeon could do the business.'

'And when she wakes up she needs to buy bigger bras?'

'That's it! Perfect.' He rubbed his hands together.

'I don't think we could do that,' I said. I am always being amazed at just how stupid some people can be.

'Oh.' He looked terribly disappointed. It had never been difficult to guess whose present this would really be.

'I think we'd have to tell her beforehand. The surgeon would need her permission. I don't think we could just anaesthetise her and give her bigger breasts.'

'Oh.' He seemed crestfallen, as though he'd won the lottery but lost the ticket.

'Shall we go back and join the ladies?'

'Yes. I suppose so. There isn't any way?'

'No, I'm afraid not. It's something she'd have to want and ask for herself.'

He shook his head. 'I can't see that happening,' he said, sadly.

'What shall we tell them?' I asked.

'What do you mean? I'd rather we didn't tell them anything.' He looked worried.

'We have to say something. We have to explain why we came out here. What did you want to show me?'

He looked very confused.

'When we came out here you said it was because you wanted to show me something.'

'Oh yes, I did didn't I?'

'Well what have you got that you didn't have? What's new?'

He thought for a while.

'We've got a new kettle.'

'I don't think they're going to believe that we came out here and spent all this time looking at a kettle.'

'No, no, I suppose not.'

'New golf clubs? Fishing rod? Cricket bat? Train set?'

'I bought a new pair of shoes.'

I shook my head.

'A screwdriver set. I bought a new set of screwdrivers. There are both sorts. The ones for the old-fashioned screws and the ones for the new cross head screws.'

And so we went back into the living room and I told them that I'd been looking at screwdrivers. It was very clear that neither of them believed me. But the screwdriver story was probably more plausible than the truth.

'Are you going to fire that young girl?' asked Enid, as we drove back to her house in her car. (She doesn't like to sit in my car, although it is bigger and more comfortable than her own, because the outside needs washing. When we go anywhere together I have to drive to her house and leave my car in her driveway.)

'Good heavens no,' I said. 'I had a word with her about it. It'll be OK. And besides I think she's right. She's a brave girl. And she's done her research.'

'Hmm,' said Enid, disbelievingly.

I drove on for a few more minutes.

'What did Rodney really want you for?' Enid asked.

'You wouldn't believe me if I told you,' I said.

'I know what April wanted,' said Enid.

'Do you?'

'She wanted you to give her some Viagra for Rodney. He can't get it up very well. Actually, he's pretty well impotent. April says that even when he does get it up his erection is very weak; his thingy is too limp to do anything with.'

I looked across at her. 'How do you know all that?'

`She told me, of course.'

`She said she didn't want me to tell you.'

`Well of course she did. But you wouldn't give her any pills. I thought that was a bit mean of you to be honest.'

I ignored this and drove on.

`At least you don't have that particular problem,' she said.

I didn't say anything.

`Did you go to the chemist?' she asked suddenly.

I looked at her.

`For some of those thingies.'

`Oh damn,' I said. `I've been so busy I didn't have time.'

`Oh,' she said. She sounded almost disappointed. Her conversation with Ms Stoke must have enlivened her imagination. `Well if you couldn't be bothered...'

`I've been terribly busy. And I forgot.'

`Don't pubs sell those things? In the lavatories?'

`I suppose they do. But probably not at this time of night. They'll be shut now.' It was after midnight.

`Well, you might as well just pick up your car and get off home then,' she said. `I've got the drama society committee coming round tomorrow morning to choose our next play.'

And so I dropped her off and then went home alone. We didn't even kiss goodnight. It was not a disappointment. In fact as I poured myself a large whisky I realised that I was really rather relieved. And as I sipped the Laphroaig and smoked my pipe I promised myself that there would be no more evenings with the Stokes. I decided that life is too short, and I am too old, for evenings with the Stokes.

Moreover, I realised that any extremely modest affection I might have felt for Enid had disappeared entirely.

I realised I didn't even like the damned woman.

Chapter 12

I was heading home after a dreary day's work when Jock caught me in the corridor. `Do you have anything planned for dinner this evening?'

`Nothing in particular,' I said, surprised by the question.

I couldn't believe that Jock was inviting me to one of his dinner parties. Only members of Local Society (with initial capital letters) received invitations to sup with Jock and his wife.

He wasn't.

`I know it's a bit last minute,' he said, without the slightest hint of an apology in his voice. `But something's come up and I think it might be a good idea if we had a sort of emergency practice meeting.'

`What's the emergency?' I asked. My whole life has been dominated by emergencies. I hate emergencies. Actually, I hate anything new. I hate change. No one seems to realise that change for change's sake (by far the most popular variety these days) isn't progress. `Have you told Deidre?'

`I just caught her in her consulting room,' he said. It was a lie. He's a terrible liar. My guess was that the two of them had fixed this up hours ago. We usually have practice meetings every month. The three of us sit down, usually in Jock's consulting room, and we are supposed to discuss, and make decisions about, all the management issues that come up in the running of what is, in effect, a medium sized business. We have an annual turnover of something close to a million pounds sterling which makes us a damned sight bigger than most of the independently owned shops and offices in the town. The three of us, as partners, are supposed to make all the financial decisions because although Jock owns the building the three of us own the practice and are legally responsible for all the financial matters. In practice Jock, who has taken to describing himself as `Managing Partner', runs everything and Deidre and I rubber stamp his decisions. He does the hiring (and, very occasionally, the firing) of the staff we employ; he has weekly meetings with the accountant; and he discusses with himself whether to do improvements and repairs to the building. He makes sure that we are paid the money we are owed and to be perfectly honest Deidre and I leave him to it because he's bloody efficient at all this sort of stuff and neither of us can find the enthusiasm to deal with paperwork, decisions and problems.

Deidre says she doesn't have time to deal with practice issues because she is too busy being a wonderful mother. In reality, Deidre's children are truly awful creatures with very little chance of growing up into human beings; they show no sign of ever having been given any motherly love. I have no idea what their proper names are but I call them Nadir and Zenith. The boy, who is old enough to have acne spots, is a dedicated fan of Wikipedia and spends his evenings and weekends writing biographies of people about whom he knows absolutely nothing. The girl, who is a little younger, spends her time having body parts pierced and desperately waiting to be old enough to have the breast enlargement surgery which will, she firmly believes, bring her an array of book and television contracts and enduring fame and wealth.

Deidre's experience as a mother, allied to her position as a community pillar, means, naturally, that she is a Governor of both the schools they attend. Apart from her responsibilities as a parent and Governor she does not care terribly much about anything other than the amount of money that pours into her account every month. She and her husband, who is an unemployed opera singer whose highpoint was a single week spent understudying part of the chorus in a performance of Manon Lescault at Covent Garden, also make a small fortune out of a website for non-smokers called 'Noifsnobutts'. They sell a wide variety of products designed to help smokers kick their habit.

I leave things to Jock because I'm just too damned weary to take an interest in the management of the practice. The truth is that I've never been terribly interested in money or in managing things. My out of hours duties have worn me out.

'If you're free I thought we'd have dinner at The Grange,' said Jock. 'I've managed to get us a table.'

The Grange is the most expensive local eatery. It's the place all the nobs go to when they're celebrating something and the place is usually packed with hooray Henrys and Henriettas. It's usually impossible to get a table there unless you book six months ahead. Or unless, like Jock, you know people who know people. The chef is one of those half-wits who regularly appears on television, chopping vegetables at the speed of light and patronising other chefs, celebrities and members of the general public without fear or favour. The entrance hall to the wretched place is lined with plaques and framed certificates showing just what a wonderful and successful person he is. (He is so wonderful and successful that he has been married five times and has enough children to create his own football league.) Naturally, the food he serves is inedible rubbish, served in fancy sauces and offered in minute portions that wouldn't fill a fairy, but it's extortionately expensive and served on fancy plates and so the people who dine there fall on his feet whenever they have the opportunity. At regular intervals during the evening he comes out of his kitchen and wanders about among the diners, accepting compliments and bestowing benedictions on his adoring congregation. He always wears one of those bloody silly tall white hats and a starched and spotless buttoned up white smock that doesn't look as if it has ever been within a mile of a gravy bowl or a spluttering saucepan. I hate the food there and I can't stand him or his band of unctuous sous chefs. I'd much rather have fish and chips from a takeaway chippie.

`Can we afford a table at The Grange?' I asked. A fairly ordinary meal there costs £150 a head before you allow for the wine or the extras. It's the sort of place where they charge £5 for a glass of water and £10 for a bread roll (without butter) and where the waiters are snootier than the clients.

Jock leant towards me and whispered. `We're not paying,' he said. `We've been invited by Jim Zabrinski.' He said this in a way that made it clear that I ought to be as impressed as if we had been invited to dinner by someone really famous and important; someone of the calibre of Alan Sugar or Peter Andre, or the girl who reads the weather on the local television news programme. I looked at him, frowned and waited for him to tell me just who Jim Zabrinski was, and why he was prepared to spend a big chunk of someone else's money taking us all to dinner.

`Jim is national sales manager for ACR Drogue et Cie, the makers of Angipax,' explained Jock, breathlessly. He seemed about to swoon. `He used to play professional cricket. Terrific batter. Really useful bowler. Should have played for England. Everyone says so. Really nice guy. He's got a proposal he wants to put to us.

It's something very much to our advantage. And it's quite an honour, really.'

I was neither surprised nor intrigued.

Jock has close personal relationships with a small but select group of international pharmaceutical companies, and the relationships are generally built on a mutual backscratching basis. If Jock had any best friends they would doubtless agree that he is a grasping, selfish and ruthless bastard who regards altruism as a sin, but he is always eager to help drug companies increase their profits, and it constantly amazes me that he has not yet been awarded a knighthood in the honours list in recognition of his services to medicine and industry. It is something which puzzles him too. He frequently complains that in order to acquire a knighthood these days it is essential to be adept at rowing a boat or riding a bicycle, or to be so rich that a £500,000 donation to one of the major political parties is a worthwhile investment. Still, it's just a matter of time. He came into my surgery the other day brandishing a copy of *The Times* and complaining that a bloke who ran a hedge fund had been given a knighthood after giving the Tory party an armful of money. I told him he should have been heartened by this since it seemed to me to confirm that the system was still as corrupt as it had always been. He thought for a moment before agreeing.

`Yes, but it's become a damned sight more expensive,' he complained. `In Blair's day you could buy a decent honour for the price of a car. These days you have to hand over the price of a good house for a gong. How can that possibly be fair? How is the ordinary, honest bloke expected to buy himself a decent gong when the costs are rising so quickly?'

I suggested that he consider getting himself a job as a lollipop man, and settling for an MBE.

Within moments of Jock asking if I was free for dinner, Deidre appeared, lipstick freshly applied and hair newly flounced, and announced that she was ready and what were we waiting for.

It was the first time I'd seen my female partner since she had returned from holiday. All the bits I could see (or wanted to see) looked tanned but I couldn't help noticing that she hadn't lost the mean, greedy look in her eyes. We set off, in a small line of three cars, to The Grange with Jim (who'd been parked outside doing something important on a laptop computer) leading the way in his super-salesman's steel grey Audi. He had a woman with him in his car. When our small but expensive convoy arrived at the restaurant the doorman opened the passenger doors of Jim's Audi and Jock's Mercedes, took off one of his white gloves, stuck two fingers into his mouth and whistled for a couple of youths to come up and park the cars. I've always been deeply envious of people who can do the two finger whistle. It's a trick I've never mastered, though, in my defence, I can make quite a good whistling sound by blowing across a blade of grass. Having the vehicles valet parked seemed rather pointless since there were plenty of car parking spaces within fifty yards of the front door. But Jim and Jock both tipped the whistling doorman and the drivers so everyone except Jock was happy. Much to the annoyance of the doorman I parked my car myself. But the staff weren't going to let me get away without tipping. I hadn't got two paces through the door before the girl manning the cloakroom grabbed me and asked for my hat. I started to roll it up and stuff it into my already bulging jacket pocket but she took it from me and gave me a small, black plastic token. `Just give the token to your waiter when you've finished your meal and I'll have your hat waiting for you as you leave.'

Chapter 13

The first two hours of the dinner were tedious almost beyond belief. It was as bad as an evening with Rodney and April Stokes. Jim Zabrinski looked like a young Gordon Brown but did not have the Scotsman's legendary natural charm, charisma and general twinkle. He had the dead, staring eyes of a short-sighted television presenter straining to read the autocue and, as a result, looked rather like the third assistant rapist in Deathwish 6.

Jim had brought with him a colleague called Lavinia Something-Hyphenated whom I think he introduced as the regional sales manager, but she could well have been just a bird he'd picked up in the bar while waiting for us to arrive. She looked about 35, dressed as though she were 25 and acted as though she were 15 or thereabouts. She giggled at anything and everything anyone said that could possibly be described as witty, close to witty or even supposed to be witty and she fluttered her outrageously long eyelashes at her boss with such aggressive enthusiasm that I was constantly expecting her to take off and fly around the room. Taking her cue from Jim, who was wearing a dinner jacket, complete with black tie, she was wearing a strapless, backless, almost frontless evening gown which revealed a good deal of a very impressive cleavage while at the same time defying the natural pull of gravity. If I'd been told she was an escort girl I'd have accepted the assertion without any doubt.

`Jim's got a unique proposition for us,' said Jock, as our allocated waiter cleared away the plates, which had contained the remnants of our duck, lobster and something done with salmon and a pungent garlic sauce. The waiter had clearly studied superciliousness at waiting-on-at-tables-college and would have won first prize for plain, unadulterated haughtiness anywhere on the planet. I prefer my waiters to display a little old-fashioned servility.

It had taken two mind-numbingly dull hours for us to get this far and after the first twenty minutes I had been willing my telephone to ring. I'd have happily rushed off to deal with an emergency bruise or a mild headache. I enjoy decent food but I can't bear restaurants which print menus in French and insist on spreading things out for hours. I think some modern chefs must have got their timing from Wagner. But, inevitably perhaps, the patients had let me down and my telephone had remained uncharacteristically silent.

`Jim's company has selected our practice, out of all the practices in the country, to be the first recipient of their new sponsorship programme,' announced Jock. He grinned inanely and looked first at Deidre and then at me as though expecting us to explode with excitement. He waved a hand. `But this is Jim's baby and I'll leave him to tell you about it.'

I was mildly surprised but not shocked by this revelation. The drug companies will do anything to flog drugs. One sales rep once told me that his company hired doctors to speak at medical conferences and meetings not because they expected them to convert their listeners (most of whom would either be emailing their stockbrokers or doing the crossword puzzle) but because they believed they would convince themselves of the wonders of the drug they were talking about and prescribe it by the ton to their own patients.

Nothing drug companies do surprises me. Most doctors, whether they're working in hospital or general practice, make judgements based on what they boldly regard as experience, but too often their conclusions are flawed and baseless because what they regard as knowledge gained through experience is, in reality, no more than a potent and deadly mixture of prejudice and drug company propaganda. Drug companies claim to be ethical but they're all run by the sort of crafty bastards who flog duff watches on street markets. The Colombian drug lords could learn a thing or two about market manipulation from the so called ethical drug industry. The only real difference is that the profit margins are considerably higher in the so-called `ethical' pharmaceutical business than they are in the heroin and cocaine business. Molly had told me that the global vaccine market is now worth £15 billion a year and is growing at nearly 20% a year. That's a lot of money. And the profit margins are obscene. Pills that cost a fraction of a penny each to make can be sold for hundreds of pounds to patients who think the pills will save their lives. The mark up on vaccines would make a jeweller blush. And in Britain, of course, the administrators who work for the NHS are either stupid or corrupt and will merrily hand over lorry loads of taxpayers' money if there's a free pen or a dirty weekend in Skegness in it for them.

The waiter returned with a small clockwork crumb hoover which he ran over the tablecloth. He then skilfully whisked away the newly cleaned cloth, exposing another clean but freshly starched cloth underneath it. When he had made sure that all the creases were nicely flattened, and had asked us all if we had enjoyed our first two courses, he gave us our pudding menus. These were made out of thick cardboard and so huge that when studying them none of us could see anything else. The minute our waiter had presented us with these the sommelier arrived to offer us a choice of dessert wines. The other four ordered an exotic specialité de la maison which, according to Deidre's attempted translation of the French menu, involved cheesecake, brandy, meringue, ice cream, five different types of nut and cubes of braised beetroot. I have no objection to beetroot, a solid enough salad vegetable, but I think it should be kept well clear of ice cream and so I ordered a slice of treacle tart, the only item on the menu which hadn't been given a fancy French name, and which was clearly there to cater for the whims of any poor people who had wandered into the restaurant by mistake. Jim ordered two bottles of something I'd never heard of that cost over £250 per bottle.

`My company has for some time been looking to find a way to show its enthusiasm for the old-fashioned principles of general practice,' he began. `And, after an outstandingly enthusiastic report from Lavinia, your practice was short listed for appraisal by a special and confidential committee appointed by our main board. There was some pretty sharp competition I can tell you but our board members were breathless with admiration for your practice's genuine and heartfelt commitment to good practice and patient care. We were impressed by the fact that, in an era when many practices are turning away from a total commitment to pastoral care, you three medical warriors still continue to provide 24-hour patient care. The board felt this was thoroughly refreshing; particularly so at a time when many practices are turning away from traditional full-time responsibility.`

Jim looked at the three of us, one at a time, and beamed. It was clearly a speech he had written, edited and memorised. Lavinia put her hands together and clapped daintily. Jock smiled modestly and tried to look embarrassed but ended up looking smug. Deidre looked as if she'd just won the lottery, an Olympic gold medal and the BBC's Sports Personality of the Year award. I tried not to look as embarrassed as I felt. I just knew something terrible was about to happen but I couldn't work out what it was going to be. For some inexplicable reason I thought of William Burroughs. `A paranoid schizophrenic is a guy who just found out what is going on.'

`I think I speak for us all when I saw how pleased and proud we are that your company has chosen to recognise our practice,' said Jock. He made it clear that he was speaking on our behalf.

`The board would like to make you our first sponsored practice,' said Jim. He beamed at each of us in turn. `We want to be associated with your practice and, in particular, to your commitment to serving patients with high ethical values.'

`What exactly does this mean?' I asked. `We're not going to have your company's name on our shirts are we?'

It was, I think, Adam Smith who once wrote that people of the same trade seldom meet together even for `merriment or diversion' without the conversation ending in a conspiracy against the public. The old Scot was bang on the button with that one; when greed meets amorality head on there is bound to be considerable collateral damage, with the laity inevitably being the major sufferers.

Jim laughed nervously at my suggestion that we might be wearing logo emblazoned shirts and Lavinia followed suit a split second later. Jock glowered at me.

`Good heavens no!' said Jim. `We'd like to be identified with your practice and so we would like your practice to carry our name. Or, more likely, the name of one of our most successful drugs. Dr Cohen, after whom your practice is currently named, has very kindly agreed to our suggestion and we're grateful to him for that.'

Jock didn't mention that the health centre was supposed to be named after his father and not him, and neither did Deidre. So I didn't say anything either.

`So you want to have naming rights for the health centre?' asked Deidre.

`In the same sort of way that breweries and insurance companies sponsor cricket and football grounds?' I asked. I'd never heard anything quite so tacky in all my life. I assumed we were going to be renamed `The Angipax Centre'.

`Exactly! That's the sort of thing,' said Jim. `We'll just have a nice discreet sign up outside your building and when your receptionists answer the telephone they'll use the new name. And we've suggested one or two other little connections too.'

'What sort of connections?' I asked. I looked at Jock, who appeared very uncomfortable. Even he, a doctor who had long ago abandoned all dignity and self-respect, seemed to recognise that he was exploring new lows in professional degradation.

'We'd like to sponsor your practice vehicles,' said Jim. 'Nothing vulgar. Just something discreet on the doors and perhaps at the back of the car.'

'Just something very tasteful,' said Lavinia. She giggled and jiggled about a lot and emptied her wine glass in a single gulp. 'And we'd like you to agree to use some pens and surgical equipment with our logos on them. That sort of thing. Very discreet and very tasteful.'

'Is this what you dreamt of when you were a medical student?' I asked Jock. 'Is this really what you set out to achieve? A stethoscope with a drug company logo stamped on it? Sell your soul for an endless supply of cheap pens?'

'I don't think so,' Jock replied with a laugh. 'I would never have dared to set my sights so high.' He laughed merrily at his own quip. I looked at him. He looked across at Jim and received a smile of approval.

The waiter turned up with preparations for our puddings, followed by the sommelier with the dessert wine. There was a delay while dishes were put in place and glasses were filled with what turned out to be an utterly hideous (though very expensive) fluid. It looked like engine oil but I think engine oil would have probably tasted more pleasant.

'There will, of course, be a generous honorarium involved,' said Jock.

'Indeed,' said Jim. 'We want, that is to say our board wants, our company to be a part of your practice. And we cannot be a part of your practice without making a financial contribution. We want to help you improve the services you offer.'

'How much?' asked Deidre, who always likes to get straight to the point.

'One hundred and fifty thousand a year, for a rolling one year contract with an initial five year commitment on our side and a 7.5% escalator clause built in,' said Jim.

'That's sterling, of course,' said Jock, now a man of global interests and limitless ambitions; a man whose yearnings had no horizons.

'Of course,' agreed Jim. 'Oh sterling, of course.'

The puddings came at last. I think they must have imported the raw ingredients from South America while we'd waited. There was much murmuring of approval from Lavinia and Deidre. But before we could start eating the culinary wonders set before us the chef himself appeared. His white coat was spotless, his hat as erect as ever. I noticed that he was tanned and his teeth had been whitened.

'Enjoying everything?' he demanded, in a tone that allowed no room for dissent. Everyone nodded and murmured approval and appreciation. Even I, coward that I am, nodded and murmured approval and appreciation.

'Marvellous, marvellous,' oozed the chef.

He squeezed Lavinia's shoulder and she squealed with delight. I'd never before heard a woman squeal.

'Excuse me for asking,' said Deidre, pointing a fork at the pile of small, red cubes on her plate. 'Can you tell me what these are, please?'

'Beetroot,' said the chef with a smile. 'An unusual and impertinent combination I expect you'll agree. None of my competitors would dare put beetroot with a cheesecake. But you try it and you'll be hooked.' He gave Deidre one of his killer smiles, the one he uses in the gravy advertisements. 'We must be thankful to the Americans for the cheesecake but I am responsible for the beetroot.'

'It's a myth that cheesecake was invented by the Americans,' I said. 'The cheesecake photos might have been invented in America. But the cheesecake you eat is English.'

He looked at me as if I'd stood up and pissed on the table. 'Oh no, no, no,' he said.

'Oh yes, yes, yes,' I replied quickly. 'Cheesecake appeared in a cookery book written by King John's chef back in the 14th century. Unless you're suggesting that the Red Indians were making cheesecake before that, of course?' I had read this somewhere and was pretty sure it was correct. I didn't really care whether it was or wasn't.

The chef, who was clearly torn between standing his ground and annoying a customer with two expensive bottles of wine on the able, went as red as his beetroot and stormed off to the next table. ock and Deidre both glowered at me when he'd gone. `You can't irgue with Chef!' said Jock. `He doesn't like it.'

`Good for him,' I said. `There was too much salt in his gravy oo.'

`There's just one little thing we'd ask from you in return,' said im, continuing his interrupted dissertation.

`Quite a fair and reasonable condition, I'm sure you'll both igree,' said Jock.

`The fact is that we wouldn't feel able to associate ourselves vith your practice if you still had Tranter working with you,' said im. `Her reputation and public image really wouldn't sit :omfortably with our board's vision for the company's status and uture development. We would, of course, settle any necessary edundancy payments that were necessary. And cover you against iny potential legal liabilities, though to be honest our legal people lon't think you'd have any difficulties. Tranter has placed herself vell outside the acknowledged ethical boundaries for the profession.'

`We do have to make sure that our corporate partners maintain he very highest standards,' said Lavinia. `And the problem is, of :ourse, that Tranter is doing enormous damage to the reputation of he profession at large. Public trust is being eroded and that is in no me's interests. Members of the public need so much, so very, very nuch, to have faith in their doctors.'

`What do you two think?' asked Jock, looking first at Deidre ind then at me.

`I think it's a very generous offer,' said Deidre. `Flattering and ;enerous.' She paused. `If your company is going to want to put ogos on our cars will you be providing the vehicles?' She didn't eem in the slightest bit concerned at the fact that we were being told o sack Molly if we wanted to get our sticky hands on the extra loot.

`Oh I think that would be quite fair and very reasonable,' said im. `You could, of course, each choose the vehicle of your preference. With a limit of say £50,000 per vehicle? Replacements :very 12 months?'

`That's fine,' said Deidre, who seemed almost orgasmic, and vas clearly sold on the whole damned idea. Jim hadn't blinked vhen she'd negotiated the car deal into the equation. I couldn't help wondering how far he had been authorised to go to persuade us to agree.

`What about you, Dr Cassidy?' asked Lavinia.

`It's a `no' from me,' I said. `Thanks for the offer but I couldn't let you decide who works with us and who doesn't.' I stood up. `And since our practice policy is that major decisions are made only when the three of us are agreed I'm afraid that means that the discussions are over.'

I pulled the linen napkin out of the waistband of my trousers, folded it and put on top of the treacle tart which I hadn't touched. `Thanks for the meal,' I said to Jim. I then turned to Lavinia. `And I don't much like receiving advice on morality from a drug company hack.'

Jim looked as though he had turned into stone. Lavinia, who probably thought she'd been complimented, blushed and giggled.

`You can't just say `no' to an offer like this!' said Jock.

I shrugged. `I think I just did,' I said.

`Can I take it that you aren't objecting to the principle of the naming or the sponsorship?' asked Jim.

`I'm not wild about the idea,' I said. `I suppose I could live with working in the Angipax Building and driving a car with Angipax painted on the sides. But I don't want your company to tell me who I can and cannot work with.'

I'd have probably agreed to accept the bribe if they hadn't included sacking Molly as part of the deal. I would not have had the energy to stand up to Jock and Deidre just to defend my right to work in the Jock Cohen Medical Centre. But then, I was pretty sure that without the sacking of Molly there wouldn't have been a deal.

Deidre, who had probably already spent her first year's £50,000 bonus, and picked out the make and colour of car she'd select, was white with anger. She opened and closed her mouth a few times but didn't manage to say anything.

`Goodnight!' I said, and left.

I had absolutely no doubt that the whole damned proposal was nothing but a plan and a simple old-fashioned bribe to persuade us to dump Molly.

And, of course, to silence her.

If Molly's campaign continued to attract attention, the cost to the drug industry would be measured in billions of pounds. Giving us a few hundred thousand (in tax deductible money) would be a worthwhile expense. The media wouldn't be much interested in a young doctor who'd been fired and who had no job. At that moment I loathed Jock and Deidre and the whole damned medical profession which had, it seemed to me, allowed itself to be bought by the drug industry. Even if Molly had been wrong I felt that she had a right to air her views. Isn't that what people do in a democracy? Moreover, it seemed to me that doctors who allow themselves to be ruled by a trade can hardly call themselves professionals. The Angipax offer had one other result. I was now absolutely certain that Molly's argument was right. If the drug companies had to resort to bribery in order to defeat her then her arguments had to be pretty solid.

As I drove away from the restaurant I felt quite depressed and couldn't help thinking of that single handed practice on the Scottish island. Or maybe I would just retire early and become a bitter and twisted middle aged man. When I got back home, I lit my pipe, poured myself a very large Laphroaig and read a chapter of a Lawrence Block novel about a hit man. It wasn't until I was getting ready for bed, and was emptying my jacket pockets, that I discovered the small black plastic token the hat check girl had given me and realised that I'd forgotten to collect my hat from the restaurant cloakroom.

Chapter 14

Suddenly and unexpectedly, Molly managed to make a new batch of enemies and, at the same time, became the poster girl for all those who believe that modern medicine does more harm than good.

She had agreed to be interviewed for a Channel 4 programme about doctors and hospitals and after answering what had for her become fairly routine questions about vaccines and vaccination she was asked if vaccination was the only area of modern medicine which worried her.

She said it wasn't. And in a couple of minutes she produced a critical onslaught which surprised many with its ferocity and its savagery. Most of all, however, it surprised people because of its obvious accuracy.

`It's difficult to know where to start,' she said. She was filmed in her consulting room at the Jock Cohen Medical Clinic. `Our hospitals are now almost as dangerous as hospitals were in the Middle Ages. Thousands of patients die because doctors make mistakes and because deadly, untreatable infections are endemic. Only cancer and heart disease kill more people than doctors. Most hospital staff admit that they would not be happy to be treated in the institution where they work. Patients who are admitted to hospital at the weekend are likely to die untreated and uncared for because the chances are they won't see anyone with more medical knowledge than a porter until Monday morning. Patients who have had surgery on a Thursday or a Friday are far more likely to die than patients who have surgery earlier in the week, simply because the care at weekends is so appalling. There are millions in this now Third World country of ours who are terrified of falling ill outside office hours. Bank holiday weekends mean that patients are deprived of medical care for three or four days at a time. Patients in hospital are dying of starvation and thirst and doctors and nurses seem to think that this is acceptable. Some hospitals, encouraged by the Government, deliberately starve their patients so that they will die. Did you know that? One third of all elderly patients who die in hospital, die because they have been deliberately starved to death. Doctors and nurses deliberately withhold food and water so that they will die.' The idea is to get rid of old people who are frail and need nursing and who are blocking hospital beds. And the cheapest way to get rid of them is to deprive them of food and water. Don't doctors or nurses give a damn anymore? Actually, they don't. Believe it or not hospital employees are rewarded with financial bonuses if they kill off enough elderly patients. Am I the only person to have noticed that medical staff are quick enough to threaten to go on strike if they want shorter hours or more money but never threaten to go on strike for better conditions for patients? It's no wonder that patients now die because they refuse to see a doctor or go into hospital. It happened in the Middle Ages and it's happening again now. People are turning away from general practitioners – sometimes because they don't trust them and sometimes because they simply can't get to see them – and putting their faith in quack remedies which are promoted and sold by charming hucksters.'

The interviewer, a softly spoken woman who didn't appear on camera, asked Molly what she felt about doctors who accept money for advertising specific products.

'I'm appalled,' replied Molly. 'There seems to be a growing number of doctors who are prepared to climb up on the buckboard and promote the latest miracle medicine. A few years ago doctors got into terrible trouble if they put their names on books they'd written. Today doctors do advertisements on television and in magazines. I've seen real, live, practising doctors advertising chair lifts, hearing aids and vitamin tablets. Whatever happened to dignity and respect? How can anyone take doctors seriously, or trust what they say, when they appear in advertisements? Nurses are no better. I've even seen nurses advertising branded sanitary towels! And hospital nursing is a disgrace – mainly because today's nurses have been encouraged to think of themselves as mini-doctors, far too important to comfort patients, mop their brows or even feed them. Nurses who want to go up the ladder quickly end up working as administrators; they never see any patients at all. I've met senior nurses who work in cardigans. You can't change a catheter in a cardigan for heaven's sake. Florence Nightingale would have had twenty fits. I know nurses who describe themselves as `caring technology specialists' as though the words alone make them good at what they do. The truth is that patients don't give a damn whether or not their nurse has a diploma or a degree; they just want a nurse who genuinely cares and isn't afraid to show a little old-fashioned compassion.'

`What do you think about the situation in hospitals where patients have to wait several hours to be seen by a doctor?'

Molly leant forwards and waved her hands in the air, as though in despair. `I can't believe what's happening,' she said, clearly genuinely angry. `It is now considered acceptable and routine for patients to wait over nine hours in casualty departments before they are seen by a doctor. Nine hours in a city accident and emergency department! The wait is the same whether you're suffering from a heart attack, a stroke, meningitis or a broken arm. There would, quite rightly, be an outcry if Ministers or members of the Royal Family had to wait that long for treatment. It would be quicker to fly to Paris and take a taxi to a hospital there. It's not surprising that when illegal immigrants feel ill they make their way back home for treatment. What a terrible indictment that is. But the medical establishment seems to see absolutely nothing wrong in any of this. The medical profession and the nursing profession have accepted terribly low standards as normal.'

`Reckless doctors have overprescribed antibiotics with the result that many bugs are now immune to them and thousands of patients are dying of bug resistant infections. The fact that our hospitals are filthy doesn't help. Medical education is controlled by the drugs industry – and so doctors merrily prescribe whatever they're told to prescribe, not because it's effective or safe but because it's profitable. Does no one care that drugs tested and classified as `safe' are known to kill tens of thousands a year? Prescribed drugs are responsible for 600,000 hospital admissions a year in Britain alone! Does no one in the medical establishment give a damn that whenever doctors go on strike the death rate goes down? Does it not seem odd to anyone that the patients who are most likely to survive in hospitals are the ones who are tough enough and brave enough, and, sometimes, rude enough to stand up for themselves, while the polite, self-effacing patients are far more likely to die?'

I don't think Molly had planned what she said. In fact I'm damned sure she hadn't. It was all a bit mixed up but it obviously came straight from her heart. As I listened to her I knew that she was right about too many things; right more often than I wanted to admit, even to myself. And she was right to include nurses in her attack.

Student nurses seem to be taught that they are above such duties as lifting patients (bad for their backs) or wiping bottoms (unseemly); they are taught that it is shameful to be `handmaidens' to physicians; they are taught that they are too important to bathe the sick, feed the weak, put flowers into a vase, hold a hand, wipe a sweaty brow and comfort patients who vomit, dribble, leak or behave irrationally or rudely. Modern nurses may have degrees in management but they know bugger all about people or the sick.

I'd heard some of Molly's complaints before, of course. For months, almost since she'd joined the practice, she had regaled me with new and horrifying titbits; new tales of bad doctoring and bad nursing. I think she may have felt that she had me on the ropes; that I was the easiest in the practice to convert to her way of thinking.

The truth is that she didn't have far to go. I have for years been terrified of hospitals; far more frightened of them than prison or extended family Christmases. A citizen has a decent chance of coming out of prison alive, probably healthier and almost certainly with valuable new skills. But for too many people, hospital is their last address above ground. And for too many it is the hospital, and the doctors in it, who are responsible for their deaths.

Perhaps nothing is new. It was, I believe, Molière who said that most men die of their remedies and not of their illnesses.

But while killing patients is bad enough it seems to me that killing patients without any signs of compassion is even worse. Too many doctors these days are simply damned cruel and thoughtless. They have no empathy at all. I saw a television programme recently in which a woman who was taken into a hospital casualty department said to the doctor treating her: `I'm not going to die, am I?' The doctor, a woman old enough to know better, looked at the patient and replied: `I hope not.' Several other doctors and nurses standing nearby did not even blink at this callous and potentially deadly remark. That bloody doctor should have been horse whipped. In the dark days when I was a medical student a nursing sister would have leapt upon any doctor who said anything as crass as that.

The tragedy is that no one noticed. No one blinked. It is nurses who traditionally provide patients with warm hands and soft shoulders. Today, all the patients get are hard faced, ruthless, clock-watching harridans. Patients are treated like supplicants.

Condescending nurses treat all patients as though they've done something wrong.

`Why the hell did you become a doctor?' I had asked Molly once. She had looked at me incredulously. `It's not me that's wrong,' she'd said, with that bullet proof brand of confidence born of youth, courage and passion.

Now, millions of viewers had listened to her and some of them must have known that she was right.

How long, I wondered, will it be before hospitals and care homes follow the advice of satirist Jonathan Swift and sell our old people as food? I read in one of the medical journals recently that two thirds of all the people ever to have reached the age of 65 are alive today. It's no wonder that the sale of beige clothing is booming. Just think of the number of pies that could be made from all those old folk.

Would anyone stop it happening? Would anyone in authority care enough to do anything? The medical establishment would remain aloof and complacent. The General Medical Council, a bloated bureaucracy which is supposed to carry the responsibility of ensuring that patients are fairly and decently treated but which has, instead, become a self-serving source of employment and expenses for an army of meddling Uriah Heeps, would do bugger all of any value. Politicians and administrators would wring their hands publicly but in private they would continue to sweep all the problems out of sight – in exactly the same way that hospital cleaners sweep the dust and the dirt and the dried blood and the vomit and the urine and the faeces under the beds.

And, at that moment, as I was infected by her anger and her sense of outrage, I knew in my heart that she was also right about vaccines and vaccination.

For years our practice has made a small fortune out of vaccines. We buy them in bulk from the wholesalers and our practice nurses jab every patient who keeps still. The massive fees which we are paid go straight into our practice bank account. We get huge bonuses if we vaccinate a high enough percentage of our patients. We, like the rest of the medical profession, have been bought lock, stock and syringe barrel. We vaccinate all our patients because that's what we are told to do. And we believe the people who do the telling because the doing is very, very profitable.

And yet never, not once, has any one of us ever sat down and questioned the value of what we do. We vaccinate because the Government and the drug companies tell us to vaccinate. I knew that Molly was right: no one has ever checked to find out whether vaccines do harm and no one has ever checked to find out whether they work.

Medicine is supposed to be based on science but as far as vaccines are concerned we're practising a variety of black magic. Patients are murdered wholesale and millions of pounds of taxpayers money are spent covering up the evidence, and smothering the truth with a thick layer of lies and deceit.

I turned off the television set and I felt physically sick. I felt ashamed and dirty and furious with myself and my partners.

Chapter 15

The following morning, at the end of my surgery, I rang the Department of Health and asked to speak to someone about vaccines. I wanted to give the establishment one last chance.

`Could you give me references for some research showing that vaccines are safe and effective?' I asked a woman whose name I didn't catch.

`We have some leaflets we can send you,' she said. `We have leaflets for most of the common vaccines.'

`Yes, I'm sure you have. But I was looking for something a little meatier. I'm looking for some scientific research showing that vaccines really do work and are safe – or, at least, as safe as any drug can be. I was hoping you could either send me copies of some papers or give me some references.'

There was a pause. `What sort of research do you mean?'

`The sort where doctors compare a group of patients who've had a vaccine with a group of patients who haven't and then keep a record of how many of each group fall ill. That sort of thing.'

The woman asked me to wait a moment while she transferred me to someone else. I signed some prescriptions while I waited.

`Good morning,' said another woman. She spoke with a harsh foreign accent. `You are some leaflets wanting?'

I explained, again, what I wanted.

`Which vaccine?' she asked.

`Any vaccine,' I said desperately.

`You must give me the name of a vaccine.'

`OK. The whooping cough vaccine. Or the influenza vaccine. Both. Either.'

The woman went away. While I waited I signed half a dozen letters, dictated half a dozen more into a little machine I sometimes use, and signed another pile of repeat prescriptions.

Then there was a click and the woman came back.

`Both these vaccines are quite safe,' she said.

`How do you know?'

`What do you mean `How do I know?'?'

`Who told you?'

`It's very well known' she said. Everyone knows.'

`Yes, but do you have details of any research I could look at?'

`Research?'

`Scientific investigations – to show that vaccines work and are safe.'

`Why would anyone want to do research to show that?'

`To show that they are safe?'

`Everyone knows that they are safe and that they work.'

She said she could send me some leaflets to put in the waiting room.

I rang the Royal College of General Practitioners, the British Medical Association and the Royal Society of Medicine. No one I spoke to could help me. No one I spoke to knew of any evidence proving that vaccines are safe and effective. Nothing. Not a bloody thing.

`Of course they work. Of course they're safe!' said one pompous fellow I spoke to. `Everyone knows they work and everyone knows they're safe. Do you imagine for a second that the Government would be promoting their use if we didn't know they were safe? There are committees who decide that they work.'

And that was what everyone said.

Everyone knew they were safe and effective because everyone said they were safe and effective. And because everyone knew they were safe and effective there was absolutely no need to do any research to find out if they were safe and effective.

It was a confidence trick: the biggest, and deadliest, confidence trick in the world.

I felt confused and bewildered.

I felt like a priest who had lost his faith.

Chapter 16

I didn't see Molly at all the following day, though I kept hoping that I would bump into her. I tried to ring her several times but kept missing her. She had made up the night call duty that she'd missed and that evening I was on duty again so I stayed late at the surgery to deal with the damned paperwork.

When I first started as a general practitioner the paperwork was manageable. There were far too many forms but most of them had a fairly sensible function. No one minds filling in a form to request a blood test or an X-ray. But the number of forms has exploded. Today you have to fill in a form if you want to fill in a form and, like all doctors, I spend more time pandering to the whims of the bureaucrats than I do ministering to the sick. The world of medicine has gone mad and it is nowhere madder than in the National Health Service, the home of socialised medicine. The bureaucrats have taken over completely and our new purpose is not to serve the sick but to serve the whims of the administrators. They have, for years, been commoner than cockroaches in hospitals (though not as attractive or as useful) and now they have found their way into the previously unsullied backwaters of general practice.

Florence Nightingale gave all the real power to qualified doctors and nurses, rather than administrators, and insisted that individuals should accept responsibility for what they did. Her methods were so clearly successful that they were exported around the world and for decades every civilised country practised medicine the Nightingale Way. But Florence's methods had the twin disadvantages of working and being Victorian. And so people had to change things.

In the 1970's a half-wit called Salmon wrote a report, which he modestly called *The Salmon Report,* in which he announced that managers should have all the power in hospitals, and that doctors and nurses should simply do what they were told. Salmon, who was a fool, was chairman of a company called J.Lyons which was famous for running tea rooms for the lower middle classes and he succeeded in wrecking this perfectly excellent company by messing around with hedging and foreign currencies. As an idiot he was way ahead of his time. Naturally, politicians and bureaucrats loved Salmon and approved of his idea that they, not doctors or nurses, should be in charge and so they quickly implemented his entirely untested ideas.

Things were then made infinitely worse when the authorities started listening to a mildly insane and very rigid American called Fred Taylor. The immensely stupid Taylor was a failed manager who had become a management consultant so that he could tell other people how to do what he could not do himself, and he was an enthusiastic fan of outsourcing for the simple reason that it was something of which he had absolutely no experience or knowledge and it was, therefore, something at which he had never failed. His big idea was that organisations such as the NHS should employ outside companies to do essential work on the grounds that this would ensure that the work was done more expensively and less efficiently. Taylor also believed that middle management was a waste of time and money and so the NHS got rid of ward sisters, who had virtually run hospitals and who had made sure that most patients benefited from their hospital experience. Without ward sisters no one was responsible for anything at all. Taylor had no reason for believing that middle management was pointless; it was just a whim of his. 'Against stupidity the gods themselves struggle in vain', wrote Schiller. And when stupidity comes up against such feeble opponents as incompetence and indifference the consequences are firmly set in the direction of disaster.

The result of all this is that today the number crunchers have all the power, no one accepts any responsibility and important medical decisions are made by people with no knowledge of anything at all. Medicine has been raped by ignorant buffoons.

Moreover, things have been made considerably worse by the widespread belief, common among politicians and civil servants, that, if left alone, the rest of us will invariably make flawed and irrational decisions and that in order to get round this problem people must be 'helped' to make the 'right' decisions by constantly being nudged in the 'correct' direction. And so doctors and nurses must now run their professional lives in such a way as to meet a series of arbitrary targets. One result of this is that surgeons prefer to do lots of small operations for non-life threatening problems, and to delay operations that are potentially life-saving but time consuming, because this enables them to deal with a higher percentage of the patients on their waiting lists and, therefore, to hit their allocated targets.

I used to have a small wire basket on my desk for incoming mail. Today I have two huge trays. One is labelled `Forms'. The other is labelled `More Forms'. My mail used to consist of real letters in proper envelopes. Today it consists of paperwork which seems to have been designed and built by bureaucratic robots. The forms and instructions and are sent round in huge packets and delivered by health service employees in special vans. I long ago gave up reading any of it because I know from experience that most of it will be incomprehensible and the rest will simply infuriate me.

An acquaintance of mine is a pharmacist. He complains constantly that although he was trained to produce all sorts of potions and lotions, and learned a good deal about drugs, he spends his life counting out pills and putting them into bottles. Occasionally, for added excitement, he gets to nod his approval when a customer wants to buy pile cream or something for a rash. I used to feel sorry for him. No more. Today, I'm living the same nightmare. I trained to be a doctor; to diagnose and to treat; to prescribe and to operate. But my days are now spent pandering to the latest nonsensical, bureaucratic whim.

Eventually, I got close to finishing the paperwork on my desk and decided to leave the rest for another day. I was tired and hungry and wanted to lie down and stare at the inside of my eyelids for a while.

The `accident' happened on my way back home from the surgery.

It wasn't raining and the roads were relatively quiet. It was dusk but the street lamps hadn't yet been turned off. (The council turns the lights off when it gets really dark in order to save money and free up valuable resources. I suspect that they need the money to pay for better quality biscuits to be served at meetings. There were probably complaints when cutbacks threatened a shortage of bourbon creams and chocolate digestives.)

I was driving just within the speed limit (I apologise if this is beginning to sound like an accident claim report) and was no more than half a mile away from home when a small truck shot out of a side turning and smashed into the side of my car. The impact pushed me half way across the road and the front airbags went off with a bang. It was all rather scary. It wasn't until a good few seconds later that I realised that the other vehicle, the one which had hit me, had disappeared completely. Everything had happened so quickly that I had no idea what make the truck had been. I certainly couldn't describe the colour, let alone remember the number.

Once I had extricated myself from the loving caresses of the over-enthusiastic airbags, and had managed to clamber out of the car, I realised how lucky I had been. I had a sore wrist and a bloody nose and I suspected that my neck was going to be pretty painful in a few hours' time but other than that I had escaped, as they say, without serious injury. My car, on the other hand, looked as if it was almost certainly doomed to be written off and converted, at best, into a source of spare parts or, at worst, into a couple of fridges. Modern cars are made of something not quite as strong as cellophane and a bump on one side leads to dents and distortions everywhere. The absence of a chassis, and the extortionate cost of officially sourced spare parts, means that it is usually cheaper to write-off a damaged car than to attempt to repair it. That's what insurance companies say, anyway, and they're the ones with the power. The smell of fuel suggested both that the tank had ruptured and that it might be wise to move as far away from the wrecked vehicle as possible. I grabbed my coat and drug bag from the front seat, waved away a young man whom I assumed was a Good Samaritan and who was approaching from the far pavement, and plodded away from the wreckage. Only as I passed him did I realise that the young man was holding up a mobile telephone and taking pictures of the wreck. His intention, it seemed, had not been to rescue me but to photograph the scene and, presumably, put the pictures on his Facebook page. 'Today, I had my bowels opened three times and saw a bloke wobbling out of this wreck in the middle of the road.' Self before sympathy; the modern mantra. Television and the Internet have created a race of Bad Samaritans.

English folk are, quite rightly, dismissive of the French. We are, after all, superior to them in pretty well every conceivable way. But, thanks entirely to the Iron Duke's sparring partner, Napoleon Bonaparte, the French do have some sensible legal codes and the most humane is the one which holds every citizen responsible, in an emergency, for the welfare of his fellows. A Frenchman who walked by on the other side of the road to avoid an accident, or who preferred to take photos with his phone rather than offer succour would, if spotted by a gendarme, find himself thrown into the Gallic slammer. (It is not widely appreciated, by the way, that Napoleon had his barking moments. When he commissioned the Arc de Triomphe his original plan was for a 250 foot high elephant with water spouting from its trunk. Sadly, the Emperor lost his nerve, changed his mind and built a boring archway instead.)

It was raining by now, of course, so I took shelter in a shop doorway and as I did so I realised that I was lucky to find a space. Most of the doorways had already been bagged by middle aged men wrapped in cardboard and discarded bubble wrap. I reached into my pocket for my pipe and found to my horror that it had smashed. I was more upset about the loss of my pipe than I was about the loss of the car. A good pipe, like a good cricket bat, has to be selected, nurtured and broken in. This one had been a calabash with a meerschaum bowl. Now that any sort of smoking has become close to criminal, finding a decent pipe shop isn't easy and I knew it would take ages to track down a replacement.

Those interfering Nazis who want smoking banned should know that smoking can save your life. A patient of mine who smokes 60 a day and works as a painter and decorator was the only one of four workmen not to fall ill when there was a dangerous carbon monoxide leak. The other blokes nearly died but the smoker didn't suffer because all the crap in his lungs acted as a filter and kept the carbon monoxide out of his bloodstream. I tell people this but they're never quite as impressed as I think they should be.

Someone had rung the police (quite possibly to complain that the noise made by the denting of metal had spoilt their enjoyment of the latest episode of their favourite soap opera) and a squad car arrived within minutes. The police don't do burglaries or murders these days but they're always quick off the mark whenever motor vehicles are involved. Naturally no one had bothered to ring for an ambulance although, to be fair, one of the two rather officious policemen who arrived did eventually think to ask if I needed medical attention. Not wanting to risk another brush with death I said I would be fine without spending nine hours stuck on a hard chair in the local casualty department. Like most of the doctors I know I do everything I can to avoid putting my life in the hands of the staff at our local hospital.

I rang my insurance company, explained briefly what had happened, and promised to fill in the required forms and to provide them with a fuller report when I'd stopped bleeding. A bored sounding woman in some remote part of Scotland wanted me to fill in the forms online but I refused point blank and told her to post them to me. Heaven forbid that anything should ever happen without a report being written, given a number and filed online. I think she also agreed to send a tow truck to recover what was left of the car. Her accent was so thick that she could have been reading out a recipe for something tasty made with neeps and sheeps' intestines.

Talking to the local constabulary wasn't much more fun. After I had been allowed to explain what had happened I was breathalysed and when (to my surprise and delight) the result was negative the two police officers put up warning signs and controlled the passing traffic with more officiousness than efficiency until the tow truck sent by the insurance company eventually turned up to remove the sad remains of my car.

It was only as we stood waiting for the tow truck that I remembered that I was still on call for the practice patients. I had no vehicle and was beginning to stiffen up. I was, to be honest, also beginning to feel the after effects of the shock. I was shivering and felt slightly nauseous. I silently prayed to whichever God was on duty to stem the flow of emergency calls until I could make other arrangements.

'Do you mind if I get a taxi?' I asked one of the policemen. I explained that I was a GP on duty and that I needed either to sort out alternative transport or to arrange for one of my partners to take over the calls for the night. The policeman said they'd have to wait for the truck to arrive because the wreck was a traffic hazard; and then, to my surprise, he radioed for another police patrol car and when it arrived asked them to give me a lift home.

Chapter 17

`I'm afraid it really is most inconvenient,' said Jock, when I rang him and explained what had happened. I'd asked him if he could cover the emergency calls for me.

`I'm having dinner with two chaps from the manufacturers of the new influenza vaccine. Fascinating work they've done. I'll tell you about it in the morning. They're offering us a special deal on bulk purchases. The more we buy the cheaper the price we pay. I've had an awful day. I was in a meeting with the builders all afternoon. We were going through the plans for the conversion of my new house. You can't imagine how many problems we've got to sort out. We want to preserve the back staircase, the one which used to be for the hotel staff, but we want to remove a wall to improve access to the back bedrooms and we've just discovered that the whole place is a listed building. I can't imagine why I wasn't told before. We've now got to call in all sorts of snotty nosed bureaucrats with cheap pens in their jacket pockets to decide what we can and can't do. And that's not the half of it. Some little twat in a cheap Marks and Spencer suit says we can't cover the roof with solar panels. Crazy isn't it? Does the Government want to prevent global warming or doesn't it? Still, the deal we're getting on this new flu vaccine will help pay for quite a lot of it.'

`I haven't got a car,' I interrupted.

`Oh,' said Jock. He didn't seem to have listened to anything I'd said. `I'd lend you one of ours but I don't think the insurance will cover you. Can't you hire a replacement? Doesn't your insurance company offer you a free hire car?'

`It's nearly 8.00 pm,' I told him. `There's only one hire car place in town and it's closed.` I felt awful. My neck was really quite painful and although I'd managed to stop the nosebleed by stuffing most of a paper tissue up the offending nostril, I had discovered that I'd cut my knee. It must have collided with something in the car. It had bled quite badly, though I hadn't noticed it at the time, and my trouser leg was now stiff with dried blood. It was only venous blood. Blood trickles out of a vein like a motorist out for a Sunday afternoon drive in the 1950's. It moves gently and takes its time.

Blood from an artery comes out with all the speed and venom of motorists on the M25. I really just wanted to pour myself a large whisky and run a hot bath.

'Shouldn't you be ringing Molly?' he asked, suddenly. 'The off duty rota is supposed to be shared between the two of you.'

'I'm sorry,' I said, wearily. 'I just thought...'

The miserable bastard hadn't even asked if I was hurt. My various bits and pieces were by now beginning to hurt like hell. Pain, I was discovering, comes quicker and lasts longer as the years go rolling by.

'If you can't get hold of Molly just use taxis if you need to go out,' said Jock. 'You could charge them to the practice, I suppose.' He paused. 'That damned Molly is probably in a television studio somewhere,' he added. 'It really is too bad of her. She's caused us all a good deal of trouble. I think we'll have to reconsider her position when her contract is due for renewal. We'd have been much better off with that young fellow I wanted to hire. I know he was a bit slick for you and Deidre but he wouldn't have given us all these problems.'

'Thanks, Jock,' I said. 'By the way did you get that note from some idiot at the Department of Health telling us of that new ruling about pregnant women?'

'What new ruling?'

'They have to stay indoors for the final six months of their pregnancies. It's some new EU law. Something to do with pregnant women being considered offensive when seen in public.'

'Really? Have they really said that?'

'Oh yes, I think so, Jock. Perhaps you'd better check it out to make sure. Maybe it's just five months. One of the receptionists is bound to know.' I put the telephone down. I had long ago realised that shouting at Jock did not do any good at all. But making him look a fool in front of the receptionists always made me feel better.

There was no point in my telephoning Deidre. Mrs Canterbury was still not speaking to me. I'd seen her several times since the dinner with Jim and Lavinia but she'd pretended to look straight through me. The only other person I could ring was Molly.

I hadn't telephoned Molly straight away because I knew she had a busy evening. Her boyfriend Larry had managed to obtain a spot on a locally broadcast television programme for young comedy talents. A producer or director he'd met while visiting television studios with Molly had fixed it up for him.

I tried ringing her mobile phone but it was switched off so, after a struggle, I managed to send her a text message. It was full of errors but just about legible. I can't type and have never been able to cope at all with the tiny keyboards fitted on telephones. I then filled the kettle and switched it on. A hot whisky would, I decided, be medicinal. And since I wouldn't be driving it could be a large one. While I waited for the kettle to boil I went upstairs and started to run a bath. Just climbing up the stairs exhausted me. I hadn't eaten for hours but I still felt too nauseous to eat anything. I then limped back down the stairs, made my hot whisky in a Russian tea glass, and crawled back up the stairs to the bathroom. I have great faith in the medicinal properties of whisky and consider it a vastly underrated drug. When I was a young hospital doctor I used to prescribe alcohol for all my patients instead of sleeping tablets. They could choose a large sherry or a pint of Guinness. I had the happiest patients on any ward and my patients always recovered more speedily than anyone else's. When people tell me I drink too much I remind them of Utrillo, the French painter. He used to drink nearly two gallons of red wine before starting work and produced many masterpieces. When he married, his wife moved them both to the suburbs and started watering his wine. His confidence and skill disappeared and he produced an endless selection of mediocre daubs.

I was half undressed when my telephone rang.

`What on earth has happened?' asked Molly. `Are you OK?'

I gave her an abbreviated version.

`Are you injured? Do you need me to come and check you over?'

`No, thanks. I'm just a bit sore and bruised. I've got a cut knee but it's not too bad. I'll put on a plaster when I've had a bath because it'll probably start to bleed again when the dried stuff washes off. With any luck the plaster will stay on for long enough for the bleeding to stop. When I was a kid you had to prise sticking plasters off with a chisel. These days they fall off after two minutes.'

`Do you think they'll catch the bastard who drove into you?'

`I doubt it. I couldn't even tell them the colour of the truck. It was all over in a second. He just drove straight into the side of me and then raced off. It was probably some kid who'd borrowed his dad's truck without asking. How's Larry doing?'

'He's doing brilliantly, thank you. He's recorded his piece. The director said he was really pleased with it. They might have to cut a few bits but they loved the gag about the audience only knowing if he really needed the wheelchair if the studio caught fire. Do you remember?'

I said I did and sent him my congratulations.

'I'm not sure I can manage tonight's duty calls,' I said, having apologised. 'And having no car doesn't help...'

'Put the phone calls through to my mobile straight away,' said Molly. 'I took it for granted that you'd do that. No problem. We've been having a few drinks here in the green room but I'll come straight back.'

'Are you OK to drive?'

'I've only drunk orange juice and a glass of something with bits of fruit floating in it. The director said it was definitely non-alcoholic and suitable for vegetarians!' She giggled. I thanked her, asked her to give Larry my congratulations and told her I'd see her in the morning.

'I'll do your morning surgery and calls,' she said.

I told her I'd be fine for the morning surgery but that if I couldn't arrange a hire car I might need her to do my morning calls. She said that was no problem. I thanked her again, repeated my congratulations to Larry and ended the call. I then finished undressing, climbed into the bath and sipped my hot whisky. My knee started bleeding again but the hot water helped ease the pains in my muscles and joints. The bump hadn't done my arthritis any good at all. I very nearly succumbed to my ultimate remedy: three 300 mg soluble aspirin tablets dissolved in a large glass of whisky.

When I clambered out of the bath I didn't bother getting dressed but just pulled on my striped pyjamas and a frayed dressing gown which was once maroon. The nausea had gone and I was feeling a bit brighter (probably because of the whisky as much as anything else) so I went downstairs and dug a Cornish pasty out of the fridge. I ate that with a couple of slices of bread and butter. I found a piece of pork pie but it looked too much like a pathology laboratory specimen for even me to eat. I then found an old crumpet which was rather stale and crisp at the edges but which would clearly be edible when toasted and buttered, and made myself another hot glass of Laphroiag with water. There is no doubt that of all the malt whiskies the best one to drink warm is Laphroiag. The hot water brings out the peaty taste magnificently well. Cooks and dieticians talk a good deal of nonsense about balanced diets but there's nothing to beat a Cornish pasty, a hot crumpet and a glass of hot Laphroaig.

I'd settled down in my favourite easy chair with a copy of an old Graham Greene novel that I'd hadn't read for years when the telephone went. It was the police. I thought at first that they must have caught the driver who'd caused my accident. But they weren't calling about my accident at all.

`Is that Dr Cassidy?' asked a very formal sounding voice.

I said it was.

`We've had to arrest a young lady called Dr Tranter,' said the voice. `She asked us to call you. Apparently she's a general practitioner and supposed to be on call. She said would you mind taking over the duty calls.'

`What have you arrested her for?'

`Driving while under the influence,' replied the policeman.

I went cold and shivered.

`Has there been an accident? Is she OK?'

`No, no accident, sir. She was stopped by one of our patrols. She failed a random breathalyser test. And the police doctor has taken blood samples.'

`Are you letting her go now? I'll come and pick her up. Is her boyfriend with her? He's in a wheelchair.'

`One of our vans is taking the boyfriend to one of the local hospitals,' said the policeman. `But she'll be staying with us for the night.'

`Why can't she go home now that you've taken a blood sample? She normally looks after her boyfriend herself at night. Someone comes in during the daytime but at night she can manage him by herself.'

`There was a bit more to it than just the drunk driving I'm afraid, sir. She hit one of our officers on the arm. She punched him. He said it was quite sore afterwards.'

`She was probably just upset,' I said. `She wasn't supposed to be on duty this evening. It was her evening off. I was on duty but I had to ring her to take over because I had an accident and my car was written off.'

I could almost hear the shrug of indifference. 'None of that's our concern, sir,' said the policeman. 'We have a zero tolerance attitude towards violent attacks on police officers.'

I could not believe any of this was happening.

'Can I see her?' I asked.

'Not tonight,' said the policeman firmly.

'Tell her not worry about the calls or her surgery tomorrow,' I said. 'And tell her I'll ring a solicitor to come down to the police station as soon as I can.'

I wasn't too worried. The breathalyser test must have been an error.

Chapter 18

It wasn't until ten o'clock the following morning that Nick Yardley, the practice solicitor, succeeded in extracting Molly from the local police station. And I was so busy with my surgery, her appointments and our combined emergency calls that it was two o'clock in the afternoon before I managed to take a taxi to the ground floor flat she shared with Larry. I still didn't have a replacement car. One of the receptionists (the one with the undiagnosed thyroid condition which I keep meaning to talk to her about) had spent two hours on the telephone to the insurance company. They had refused to arrange for a replacement car until they had received my report and spoken to me again. The bureaucrats make all the rules and the games we play are theirs. I'd had to keep a taxi and its driver waiting outside the clinic all morning so that I could deal with any emergency calls. Jock would moan when I gave him the bill but if he'd helped out with the calls, or lent me one of his cars, I wouldn't have needed the taxi.

Molly was in tears when I arrived. Not surprisingly, she looked as if she hadn't slept at all. She looked broken and defeated. Journalists and photographers and a television crew had settled on the pavement outside her flat. A reporter I knew told me that someone, presumably a policeman, had released details of Molly's arrest within minutes of it happening. 'The newsdesk got a tip off,' he told me. 'Don't know where it came from.' It annoys me that the police do this. There is, it seems, always someone in a police station eager to earn a few quid by reporting accidents and incidents to the media. When a celebrity is involved the cash payments can, I understand, be quite substantial. No one seems to realise, or care, that unsubstantiated allegations, however baseless, can ruin a career when reported in the media. I wondered if the person who had shared the details of Molly's arrest with the press had known this. The publicity certainly added to the pressure on Molly and well suited the interests of those who opposed her outspoken views. Death by a thousand cuts.

What was happening to Molly reminded me of Machiavelli's advice that in order to win a battle one should inflict many injuries on an opponent in as brief a time as possible. During the 20th century, military tacticians developed this philosophy and turned it into an ever more successful military strategy known as the 'expanding torrent offence'. The victim has no idea where the next attack is coming from and becomes frightened, disorientated and unsettled by a constant stream of attacks. I had heard that the drug companies had become adept at using this technique when dealing with critics. A man called Stanley Adams wrote a book about his own experiences at the hands of a drug company he had crossed.

I asked her what Nick had said to her.

'He tried to get the assault charge dropped but the police won't budge,' she said. 'He said they're being very stubborn.'

'What happened? Did you really hit the policeman?'

'After they stopped me and breathalysed me I tried to check that Larry was all right. There were two policemen. One of them, a huge brute of a fellow, grabbed my upper arm. He had a very strong grip and it hurt. I just punched him on the arm to try to make him let me go. It was just a reflex; it wasn't much of a punch. To be honest I doubt if he felt it.'

I thought she was probably right. A punch from Molly probably wouldn't have caused a butterfly too much inconvenience. I couldn't see how she could have done a big policeman much harm.

'Let me see your arm.'

She removed her jumper and pulled up the sleeve of her blouse. There were clear finger marks on her skin. 'Have you got a camera?'

'There's one on my 'phone.'

'Let me borrow it.'

She dug her iPhone out of her bag and gave it to me. When she'd shown me how to use it I took several pictures of her arm. 'Does this thing put the date on the picture?'

'I don't know.'

'Can you email from this thing?'

'Yes. What do you want to email?'

'Do you have the solicitor's email address?'

'He left me his card.'

'Send him the pictures I just took. And add a note saying that I took the pictures and will testify that I examined your arm today.'

'Why?'

`Because the pictures are evidence that the policeman grabbed you and used excessive force. And your defence has to be that you only punched him because he was hurting you. I don't know whether or not it will help. But maybe they'll back off from the assault charge if you threaten to sue him for assaulting you.'

Molly sent the email and the pictures to Nick. She then scrolled down the list of new emails she'd received. She was already pale but she now went even paler.

`The editor of the *British Clinical Journal* has sent me a curt note. They're withdrawing my article on vaccination from their records and their website and they've issued an official apology for having published it. They're treating the article as `fraudulent research'.'

`Can they do that?'

`He says they have. He says he has been informed that my arguments were flawed and that the article was published in error.'

It seemed as though the walls were closing in on Molly. We sat in silence for a few moments.

`Did you really not drink any alcohol?' I asked her. `Are you sure you didn't drink anything alcoholic at the television studios?'

`Not a drop. You know me. I don't drink alcohol. The blood test will come back fine and it will all blow over. What's the worst that could happen?'

`This is modern Britain. The penalty for not failing a blood test? They could tear out your fingernails, shoot off your knee caps, nail your tongue to the table, stick hot needles in your eyes, make you eat your liver and then arrange for Her Majesty's Revenue and Customs to audit your last tax return.'

She smiled weakly. `How are you? How are you feeling? Tell me again what happened.'

I told her about the crash and assured her that I was feeling fine. `Just bruised and battered!' I looked around and suddenly realised that there was no sign of Larry. She explained that he was still at the hospital. `He's sitting in a corridor,' she told me. `They said I have to fetch him. But my car is at the police station. I rang two taxi companies but neither of them had cars which can take a wheelchair.'

I rang the hospital, spoke to the sister in charge of the Accident and Emergency Department and asked her to send Larry back home in an ambulance. She moaned a bit but I told her that if she didn't help us out I would send every patient I saw to hospital with a letter demanding an urgent X-ray. I was really pissed off with the world and not in a mood to do anything by the book. '

`Are you trying to blackmail me?'

`I suppose I am. Would bribery be more effective?'

`Try me.'

`I'll send you a large box of biscuits covered in chocolate.' It is my experience that nurses will do just about anything for chocolate biscuits.

She laughed and said that under the circumstances she would send Larry home straight away. While I was on a roll I rang my insurance company, dictated a lengthy report to a sullen teenager working somewhere in Asia, and demanded to speak to a supervisor. I asked for her name and then told the haughty woman that I was a doctor and that I needed a car. `If you don't have a car delivered to my surgery within thirty minutes I will blame you personally for any deaths which occur as a result of my not being able to visit my patients. I will write your name on the death certificate as the cause of death. The police will have to arrest you. You will be summoned to appear in the coroner's court. Your company will receive terrible publicity and you could well end up being charged with manslaughter.'

The supervisor, now considerably less haughty, her voice trembling noticeably, promised that a car would be delivered to the surgery as soon as humanly possible. I believed her. The death certificate ploy has served me well over the years. She then had the last laugh by telling me that since I did not have the registration number of the truck which had hit me my insurance company would not be able to trace the other driver's insurer and so I would either be liable for the damage myself or I would lose my no claims bonus. This reminded me, as if I needed reminding, that insurance companies always win in the end.

Finally, I rang the Jock Cohen Health Centre and told one of the receptionists (since we were on the telephone I had no idea which one) to call a taxi to take her to the local Accident and Emergency department. `Take some money from the petty cash tin. On your way to the hospital stop at a grocery store and buy the largest and most expensive box of chocolate biscuits you can find.

When you get to the hospital tell the taxi driver to wait. Go inside and give the biscuits to the sister in charge with my compliments. And then take the taxi back to the surgery.'

When I put the telephone down Molly was laughing. She was still crying, but now she was laughing as well. `That's the most impressive five minutes of telephone work I've ever seen.'

I grinned at her. `Sometimes you have to play the system the way it's been designed to be played. And occasionally it works.' I felt quite proud of myself; as though I'd achieved something. Sometimes we all delude ourselves.

Less than ten minutes later there was a knock on the door and when Molly answered it two ambulance-men wheeled Larry into the front hall. They were cheerful and kindly and it occurred to me for the millionth time that we pay the wrong people the big money. Ambulance men and women should get the high salaries but society gives the big salaries to models whose only discernible skill is being able to walk while wearing clothes and to television presenters whose sole talent is to be able to read while sitting down.

Larry was spitting nails at having been left in a hospital corridor for hours. I told him and Molly that I'd speak to them later but that I'd better get back to the surgery to take delivery of my replacement vehicle.

Chapter 19

I suppose it is just about possible that the insurance company might have been able to find a smaller, dirtier, less powerful car if they'd had more time, but in the few minutes I'd given them they had done pretty well.

I don't know what make it was because most modern cars look the same to me and the little badge at the back, which might have given me a clue, was covered in mud, but it was filthy on the outside and filthy on the inside. It looked as if it had been used by a sales representative who'd done 2,000 miles a week in it, slept in it and used it as a dining room. Judging by the refuse which had been left in the car he'd probably died of a hard-earned heart attack. Burger wrappers, coke cans and crisp packets suggested that he or she hadn't been a health freak. The stench of congealed, cold animal fat was so bad that I had to open the two windows which worked.

When I turned on the ignition and pressed the accelerator the car made a noise like a faulty washing machine. Still, it moved forwards, it was a car and it was what that I needed.

I visited a widow called Mrs Brustwarze who'd suffered a deep vein thrombosis and had run out of her warfarin tablets. She had taken rat poison pellets instead. 'They're the same thing, aren't they?' she asked. I agreed that they both contained the same basic ingredient, but told her that I would rather she took my nice little tablets because I could control the dose more easily. She promised me that she would take my tablets in the future because the rat poison pellets had turned out to be rather expensive and in view of her age she got her prescriptions free. In the meantime I called an ambulance and when it came I persuaded her to get into it so that the hospital could check her blood and keep an eye on her for a day or so. When the ambulance had gone I had to take her two cats to the local cattery. They were fat, lazy house cats which probably explained why a woman who lived with two cats also had a box of rat poison pellets under her kitchen sink.

'You doing animals now, are you doctor?' said a neighbour when he saw me climbing into my grotty little hire car with one of those huge plastic carriers which people use for transporting cats. I told him to shut up and weed his front garden.

When I'd dropped off the cats I visited a man who told me he wanted a sex change operation because he'd heard that women lived longer than men and then called on an old woman who took 25 minutes to undress to a point where I could poke the end of my stethoscope through a small gap in the armour plating and manage to listen to her chest. `Do you always wear so many layers?' I asked her. `Oh no,' she replied. `I dressed up because I knew you were coming.'

I then had a phone call from Jock. He was in a filthy mood.

`Why did you tell me all that rubbish about pregnant women?'

`What rubbish about pregnant women?'

`You said they have to stay indoors for the last six months of their pregnancies! I've spent half the morning telephoning people to check it out. I've made myself look a complete idiot.'

`Is it not true then?'

`You know damned well it's not true,' said Jock.

`Well maybe the people you spoke to just hadn't heard about it,' I told him. `It's always safer to check these things out thoroughly.' I ended the call. Jock really is an idiot but if he didn't exist someone would have to invent him.

The complications of the day meant that I got back to the surgery half an hour late for the evening surgery. I wanted to go home, climb into bed, pull up the covers and shut out the world. There was a small revolution brewing in the waiting room. Jock had already seen five patients and mine were getting restless. I stuck my head round the door, apologised and explained that I'd been busy with an emergency. It wasn't quite the truth but it was near enough and took up less time than explaining about the cats and the impenetrable corsetry.

`Is there any food back there?' I asked one of the duty receptionists before I hurried upstairs to my consulting room. It was one I hadn't seen before. She was fat and had red hair. She didn't seem to have any health problems but she was sitting down and I couldn't see all that much of her. Knowing our luck she probably had rabies, leprosy or distemper. She'd either bite a patient or leave fingers stuck in the filing cabinet drawers.

She looked at me as if I were barking mad. 'Just biscuits and chocolates,' she said, rather sternly I thought.

'Put some on a plate, please. And make me a mug of tea.'

'We don't serve food to clients,' she said, going red all over. I wondered if she were maybe menopausal and having a flush.

'Are you new?'

'Yes.'

'I'm Dr Cassidy, one of the partners,' I told her, silently wishing that Jock would introduce us to the new members of staff he hires. 'And I'm starving. Bring me up something to eat, there's a sweetheart. And a drink. If you haven't got whisky a tea will do. And for the record this isn't a hairdressing salon so the folk who come in here are patients not clients.'

I'd just dealt with my third patient when the flushed receptionist finally turned up with the refreshments. She had put two chocolates and two digestive biscuits onto a plate. It wasn't exactly a feast. The chocolates looked like the sort filled with toffee. I can't eat toffees when I'm seeing patients.

'I don't appreciate being called 'sweetheart',' she said, slamming the plate down on my desk. 'It's sexist and demeaning. And since we're all supposed to be professionals here I don't think it's my job to make cups of tea for co-workers.'

I looked at her. 'Sorry, love. I didn't mean to offend you.'

She stared at me, went red again, and stormed out. I'm pretty sure that if my door didn't have one of those springs on it she would have slammed it. I decided she was almost certainly menopausal and that an exhausting rush of hormones must be flooding through her body.

My first patient was a youth of 19 who had injured his leg taking part in the annual cheese rolling event which seems to be a vital part of social life in Gloucestershire. Before he left he asked me to sign a petition to have the event included in the next Olympics. I did so happily. As far as I'm concerned chasing a rolling cheese down a grassy knoll is far more worthy of a place in the sporting pantheon than synchronised swimming. Next, I saw a poor sod who'd managed to escape from the local hospital after a botched operation to remove a misbehaving gall bladder. The scar they'd left was horrendous and if it had been created by a make-up artist working on a horror movie I'd have told them they'd overegged the pudding. The wretched fellow looked as though he'd been operated on by a team of workmen moonlighting from their jobs digging holes for the council. He wanted a sick note.

`What's your job?' I asked him.

`I'm a Gravestone Testing Consultant.'

`What does that entail?'

`I go round the cemeteries pushing gravestones to see if they fall over.'

`And if they do fall over?'

He shrugged. `I leave them where they land. It's less grass to cut.'

`Are there enough gravestones to keep you busy?'

`Oh yes. When I've finished I just start again at the beginning.'

`You'll need at least three months off work,' I told him. I signed a certificate and handed it to him. He seemed pleased. `Come back and see me in three months and I'll perhaps give you another three months.' It seemed to me that both he and the rest of the world would be better off if he stayed at home.   There then came a woman of eighty three who wanted her varicose veins attended to so because she said they didn't look very nice. I tried to persuade her to wear thicker stockings in lieu of surgery but she wasn't about to be cheated of her right to smooth legs. Before she left she asked me if I'd like to follow her on Twitter and become her friend on her Facebook page. I told her, quite honestly, that I'd never visited either of the sites and had no intention of doing so. Only the other day I read somewhere that Coca Cola had 65 million friends on Facebook and around a million Twitter followers. I simply don't understand any of this. Why would so many people want to be `friends' with a tooth rotting, gut burbling fizzy drink? How can any sane person possibly `follow' the literary meanderings of a cola? There are, apparently, thousands of apparently sane citizens who voluntarily `follow' the twitterings of British Gas. These are surely sad manifestations of the existence of lonely generations. She seemed to take my refusal to become a `friend' and a `follower' as a personal affront and sniffily told me that if I felt like that about her she would be looking for another doctor.

My next patient was a boy of eight. He told me his name was Doug. His mother had brought him in because he had a nose bleed that wouldn't stop. The poor little devil had been sitting in the waiting room for the best part of an hour with his mother constantly stuffing bits of tissue up his nostril. She had a handful of blood stained tissues and her blouse and skirt were both blood stained. She looked quite a sight. Apart from the absence of mud she looked as if she'd been nursing in the trenches on the Somme. Still, if the little chap had gone to casualty he'd have been lucky to have seen a doctor in less than half a day. Nosebleeds don't appear high on the list when the nurses are deciding which patients should be seen first.

I had to pop out of my consulting room for a moment to fetch some packing gauze from the room the nurse uses for doing dressings (when she isn't in a meeting with our ever present horde of social workers) but the whole exercise, including the stuffing of the exsanguinating nose, didn't take more than five minutes.

'Go back down to the waiting room and I'll see you again in twenty minutes,' I told them. 'It should have stopped by then.'

'Thank you very much,' said the mother who politely held her hand over her mouth which seemed to be full of something. The boy, whose nose was full of clotted blood and who also seemed to be eating, just mumbled inaudibly. He sounded like one of those Romanian refugees imported into Britain to sell the *Big Issue* magazine. 'And thank you for the nibbles,' she added. 'We were both starving.'

I didn't know what she meant at first but when they'd gone I inspected my desk and saw that the plate of goodies the receptionist had brought me was now empty. The toffees and the digestive biscuits had all disappeared. I stuck a pencil in my mouth and chewed on that, hoping that the rumbling of my empty gastro-intestinal tract would, if heard by a patient, be mistaken for a fault in the central heating. Not that our central heating is ever efficient enough to be that noisy.

When I'd finished the surgery and had tottered back downstairs, the flushed receptionist handed me a plastic bag which contained a pair of heliotrope pyjamas and a blue toothbrush in a plastic case. For a moment I couldn't understand why I was the beneficiary of such a generous gesture and then I recognised the pyjamas and realised that they were the pair I'd kept at Enid's. I didn't recognise the toothbrush but it was a fair guess that it was the one which had recently been domiciled in her bathroom.

`Looks like you've been given the heave-ho,' said the receptionist who had clearly peeped into the bag.

I was too embarrassed to think of a witty reply. The pyjamas were not in the first flush of youth and the toothbrush bristles were flattened beyond reasonable use. As I left the surgery I tossed the bag and contents into the plastic wheelie bin outside the surgery.

It wasn't until five minutes later that I realised that Enid had surgically removed me from her life. I was so delighted that I stopped off at the chippie on the way home and bought myself a large portion of cod and a bag of chips. I asked for extra vinegar and extra, extra salt, put the chips on my lap and ate them in the car as I drove home. The chip shop staff had put my chips into a plastic dish and wrapped them in drawer lining paper (the interfering do-gooders will not let them recycle old newspapers) but the warmth still came through. If there's a better way to celebrate the ending of a painlessly deceased relationship I cannot think of it. The health fascists who want to ban salt from chip shops should be boiled in brine.

Without Enid in my life there would be no more dull dinner parties, no more tedious evenings watching amateur dramatics and no more nights with that damned ankle length nightie. I idly wondered why I had stayed with her so long. Lethargy? Loneliness? Had it been simply by default? For the sake of a desultory once a month tumble in her doughy bed? I really couldn't think of a reason. As I scrambled around in the little plastic dish for the crunchy bits of batter which always hide away I realised that I had achieved my freedom while remaining the innocent and injured party. My joy was not in the slightest bit diminished by the discovery that the grease from the fish and the chips had seeped through both dish and the paper and had left a permanent mark, in a difficult to explain position, on my trousers. What's the value of a pair of grey flannel trousers when compared with a man's emancipation?

Chapter 20

Despite the court case hanging over her, Molly was back at work the next day. She seemed subdued (which was hardly surprising) but it was clear that she didn't realise that there was another shoe waiting to drop.

Whenever a registered and licensed medical practitioner is arrested the police automatically file a report with the General Medical Council. A court might take away her licence to drive (thereby making her life as a general practitioner difficult and expensive) but the General Medical Council had the power to take away Molly's licence to practise medicine (making the loss of her driving licence of rather less significance). And all this was assuming that the assault charges didn't stick. Molly's defence union solicitors, who had taken over her case, were still fighting the assault charges but did not seem particularly optimistic that they would be able to prevent the police trying to get Molly convicted of some variety of assault. 'The police are always keen to prosecute when anyone punches a copper,' said one of her lawyers. 'And the courts always tend to be sympathetic. The copper who got punched will turn up in court with his arm in a sling and will say that he hasn't been able to work since the incident. He'll probably claim that he gets nightmares and may never be able to work again.'

The publicity she had received in recent weeks meant that Molly's arrest made the front pages of the local evening papers and she was quite high on the agenda for the local television and radio stations. A part-time snapper with a mobile telephone had, inevitably, managed to capture Molly's 'moments of shame' (as they were described by one reporter) and the photograph of her struggling with a huge policeman appeared in numerous publications. She wasn't quite so prominent in the national press or on national broadcast media but they certainly didn't ignore the story. 'Anti-Vaccination Doctor In Boozy Night Brawl', was one of the least offensive headlines I saw.

And, again inevitably, some of her newly found opponents displayed their enthusiasm for giving a good kicking to anyone who had dared to express an anti-establishment point of view. Doctors who regarded themselves as important figures within the British Medical Association almost fell over themselves in their excitement and their determination to take full advantage of Molly's misfortune.

'I sincerely hope that the General Medical Council takes firm action against this young woman,' said one professional committee member. 'Her drunken escapades and her alcohol fuelled ramblings have done irreparable harm to the profession and caused enormous concern among anxious parents. Thousands of young children could die as a result of her wild accusations.'

Another self-appointed defender of the profession took pains to point out that Molly was living ('shacked up' was the phrase he chose) with a would-be comedian. 'There is no doubt that this wretched couple have chosen to risk the health of the nation's weakest and most vulnerable citizens in order to promote their own careers,' he told a reporter from *The Times* newspaper.

'I think we have to fire her immediately,' said Jock. 'We can find a locum to help with the night and weekend calls.'

Deidre agreed with him. 'She's a disgrace to the profession and to her sex,' she said. 'I hope she's struck off for life. We can't have her working here any longer. What will the patients think?'

'We can't fire her just because a few doctors are being rude about her!' I protested. 'She hasn't been found guilty of anything yet.'

'I don't think we can afford to wait until she is found guilty of something,' said Jock. 'My father established this practice and I've spent my life continuing his work. This young woman has destroyed our reputation in days. Patients are leaving the practice in droves.'

'Are they?' I asked. It was the first I'd heard of it.

'Well not yet,' admitted Jock. 'But they will do. I know damned well I wouldn't want to entrust my health to a doctor who's been branded a drunk and a thug.'

'Maybe we should just hang on a bit longer,' I suggested. 'Wait and see exactly what happens. She's due to appear in court in two days and we'll know then where we stand. The General Medical Council will soon let her know if they're going to do anything.'

'They're bound to strike her off,' said Deidre. 'Damned good thing too.'

'I think we might be wise to have a word with the lawyers before we sack her,' I said. 'If we fire her before she's found guilty of anything she could sue us.'

'Sue us?' said Jock, shocked. 'Could she sue us?'

'I've no idea. But I would have thought so.'

A telephone call confirmed that she could, indeed, take legal action against the practice if we fired her because of comments that had appeared in the press, rather than because she had been found guilty of doing anything wrong. Both Jock and Deidre seemed to think that this was outrageously unfair but, with great reluctance, they agreed to wait a day or two.

However, despite this temporary respite, there was little doubt that the writing was on the wall for Molly. It seemed extremely unlikely that she would be a trainee with the practice for very much longer. I was devastated by what was happening. She was, I realised, a girl I would have been proud to have had as a daughter.

'We'd better have another meeting in a couple of days,' said Jock. Deidre and I agreed.

'Can we assume that you'll be happy about the sponsorship arrangement with the Angipax people when Molly has gone?' asked Jock.

I was reminded of something Confucius once said: 'The superior man understands what is right; the inferior man understands what will sell.'

'I wouldn't have any objection,' I said wearily. 'If they still want to go ahead with it.'

'Why on earth wouldn't they?' demanded Deidre. 'The stumbling block would have disappeared.'

'It wouldn't surprise me if they withdrew the offer,' I said.

Jock and Deidre looked at me and then at each other.

'That's crazy,' said Deidre. 'Molly was the only reason the deal didn't go ahead the other evening. Jim had the contract papers with him in his car. We could have signed up for the sponsorship there and then!'

'They wanted you to fire Molly because she dared to speak out about vaccines!'

'She's a maverick!' said Deidre, spitting out the word as though she could not think of anything more contemptible.

`Being a maverick just means she hasn't been branded,' I snapped. `What's wrong with not being owned by anyone?'

`It's not our place to question these things,' said Jock pompously.

`What is our `place'?' I demanded angrily. `Are we supposed to just do as we're told, like squaddies marching over a cliff because that's what the sergeant tells us to do? Is it our `place' to do as we're told even if we know that what we're doing is wrong? Is it our `place' to stick needles into people without ever asking whether what we're doing is going to help them? Or is it our place to just bank the cheques, spend the money and keep our mouths and our minds firmly shut?' I sighed. I could tell that they both thought I'd gone barking mad. `When is our locum arriving?' I asked.

`Locum?' said Deidre. `What do we want a locum for?'

`Because at the moment I'm on call every night and every weekend,' I said. `And if we don't hire a locum quickly you and Jock are going to have to start doing some emergency calls.'

`If you hadn't put a stop to that sponsorship deal we'd be able to afford a locum,' said Jock.

`Quite,' said Deidre. `You'll just have to soldier on for the time being.' She looked at me over the top of her spectacles and paused. `Until we get the sponsorship deal sorted out.' She paused for a long moment, staring at me as if seeing me for the first time. `You're becoming a bit of a dinosaur, you know,' she said. `I'm beginning to think you spent far too much time with that Tranter woman. You're becoming as bad. And you know what happened to her.'

I looked at her, was about to say something anodyne and realised that I really did not have to be polite to Deidre and, more important, that I really didn't want to.

`Oh, fuck off Deidre,' I said wearily, but with remarkable and searing wit. `There is no way that I can carry on looking after all the emergency calls. Since neither you nor Jock want to get out of bed at night we're going to have to do what 99% of other practices do and turn all our emergency calls over to whatever the damned company is called which provides emergency cover for this area.'

`Oh I don't approve of that,' said Jock. `We have always taken pride in providing patients with 24 hour cover for 365 days a year.'

`You've always taken pride in the extra money we make,' I told him. `I'm now the only doctor providing all the cover. You and Deidre just rake in the extra cash and do nothing.'

`You're paid extra for taking on out of hours calls,' said Deidre. I suddenly realised that when Deidre spoke I always felt like her gardener or odd job man being told to rake the lawn or clean out the drains, and to damned well make sure that I made a good job of it.

`I'm paid a very modest bonus for doing the out of hours calls,' I pointed out. `But neither of you would take on the extra work for the little I'm paid. And when Molly was doing weekend and night calls she didn't get an extra penny. I like the practice providing 24-hour cover because I happen to think that's what GPs should do. But I'm absolutely knackered and without Molly or a locum I simply can't go on providing cover for 168 hours a week.'

`That's very unfair of you,' said Jock.

`Fair or unfair it's ending,' I told him. `I'm buggered and as from today I'm resigning from out of hours cover. Unless you and Deidre want to start clambering out of bed at three in the morning you can make arrangements for our weekend and evening calls to be taken by the agency which provides cover for this area.'

`You've changed!' cried Deidre. `You really don't care a toss about us, do you?

`It's certainly not been a change for the better,' said Jock.

`Perhaps it was about time I did change,' I said.

Jock and Deidre both tried to speak at once but I left. I was half way down the stairs long before they'd manage to sort out who was going to speak first. As I hurried away, free at last from the tyranny of the telephone, I felt ten years younger. I was about to leave one of the receptionists (the fat, red-headed one) told me that the police had brought round a cake tin which they had retrieved from the boot of my wrecked car.

`It looks rather nice,' she said.

For a long, long moment I was tempted to tell her to share it out among the social workers, administrative assistants, community workers and other hangers on who frequent the surgery. But deep inside my soul there lingers a part of me that is forever responsible. To my regret, I couldn't do it. `Leave it in the tin and throw it into the rubbish,' I told her. I couldn't be bothered to explain why.

`Are you sure? It's a lovely looking cake. Smells most unusual too. Is it cinammon?'

`Throw it away,' I told her firmly before I hurried away.

I turned back and saw her lifting the lid and looking in at the cake rather longingly.

`It's got arsenic in it,' I warned her sternly. `If you eat it, you'll die.'

Chapter 21

I telephoned the General Medical Council to try to find out how they were doing to deal with Molly.

'We cannot comment on a specific case,' said a snooty woman who sounded as though she'd had very large plums inserted in both ends of her intestinal tract. She spoke English as though it were her third or fourth language.

'Does the GMC have a general view on doctors who disapprove of vaccination?' I asked.

'Vaccination is being an essential plank in the preventive health programming,' replied the woman, after I'd repeated the question several times.

'Does the GMC have any evidence to show that vaccination is safe and effective?'

'It is not our placing to be doing evidential research.'

'No, I realise that. But since you believe that vaccination is an essential plank in the preventive health programming do you have or know of any evidence to support that belief?'

'Everyone knows that is the case. It is widely known.'

'Yes, I appreciate that. But it is also widely known that you cannot get pregnant if you have sex while standing up.'

There was a pause and then a request that I repeat my last remark. I repeated it.

'Good heavens!' said the woman. 'I was not knowing that. That is very interesting. But what has this to do with vaccination?'

'I was merely using that piece of folklore as an example,' I said. 'To show that people sometimes believe things to be true when they are not.'

'Are you now saying that it is not true that I cannot be pregnant if I do it while I am upstanding?' She sounded disappointed. I hoped that she was not now going to claim that she had already become pregnant as a result of our misunderstanding.

'No, it's not true,' I told her. 'But how do you know that vaccination is a good thing?'

'Oh, yes, it is a very good thing indeed. Everyone knows that.'

It was my turn to pause while I tried to think of a different approach.

`What is the GMC's view of doctors who disapprove of vaccination?' I asked.

`Oh we take a very dim view indeed of that,' said the woman. `There is a young woman doctor who has been saying that very thing.'

`Dr Tranter?' I asked, surprised that the conversation had now turned to the very specific case I wanted to discuss.

`That is the one. Molly Tranter. We take a very dim view of her. Everyone knows that vaccination is a very good thing indeed. Dr Tranter is a bad lady. Very naughty indeed. She has been blowing whistles and scaring the communes. The GMC does not approve of scare mongering.'

`But she merely tried to encourage a debate on the issue of vaccination.'

`There is no need for debating. The issue is cut and dry and quite clear. Vaccination is a very good thing. Anyone who says it is not a good thing must be a bad person and must be stopped from saying these things.'

`Do you know if the GMC is taking any interest in the police case relating to Dr Tranter?' I asked.

`The police have arrested this woman? This we did not knowing. Why have they arrested her?'

I cursed myself quietly, thanked her, reminded her to take all proper precautions if she had sex while standing up, and put the telephone down. The General Medical Council would hear soon enough about Molly's arrest. But it didn't seem as though Molly was going to stand much of a chance with them. The odds on her staying on the medical register would have been much better if she'd simply killed a few dozen patients through ignorance or neglect.

Molly's problem, I realised, was not that she'd acquired dangerous new information, or that she had discovered some previously unpublished facts, but that she was prepared to tell the truth about things the medical establishment desperately wanted to be kept locked in a cupboard.

Chapter 22

I think everyone working at the practice knew that Molly's days with us were numbered. I hadn't said anything to anyone but it seemed pretty clear that either Jock or Deidre, or possibly both, had told a receptionist a nurse or a social worker that Molly was going to be fired when she'd been found guilty of whatever it was that she was being charged with. They probably wanted to distance themselves from her as quickly as possible. And there was certainly no shortage of people with whom they could share their confidences.

I can remember the days when we managed the practice with three doctors, two receptionists and a district nurse. Over the years we had, by some remorseless, unstoppable process, acquired what I believe is called a 'team' and I long ago lost track of how many people are in the team, let alone what their names are or what they are supposed to do. I blame it all on progress. As Ogden Nash said, progress might have been all right once, but it has gone on for too long. We had acquired enough receptionists to staff a large hotel and enough nurses, of various kinds, to empty bed pans and plump up pillows in a decent sized cottage hospital. We had accumulated platoons of health visitors and social workers and our biscuits were regularly munched by hordes of bureaucrats with impressive but incomprehensible titles. Some of the outsiders wore white plastic badges pinned to their chests, the rest had plastic identity tags hanging from coloured tapes around their necks. These were adorned with name, photograph and title. I've never really been able to trust people who label themselves in this way but thanks to these badges and tags I knew that we had a continuity care manager, a continuity nurse who had the most supercilious and insincere smile of anyone I'd ever met, and the almost constant presence of a discharge facilitator from the local hospital who had ill-fitting dentures and a nasty looking mole on the back of his left hand. It's just a pity that the insincere smile wasn't as malignant as the mole undoubtedly is. These were not wallahs, patiently pampering to the needs of sweating doctors hacking away at the coal face of life and death, but self-important stars in their own eyes. They were all soulless do-gooders, earnest box tickers who saw trees but never saw woods and who all had neat hypocrisy running through their veins. Moreover, they were as lazy and as incompetent as any squad of motorway repair workers. They never seemed to do anything other than drink tea, gossip or read a newspaper. They rarely seemed to finish doing whatever they were not doing and if they did finish, and moved on, you could not see what they'd done, or why they'd done it.

And yet, despite the presence of all these people, there was no doubt in my mind that the service to patients had become worse than ever. There was always a queue at the reception desk, patients were always complaining that it had taken them half an hour to get through on the telephone and it had become so impossible to persuade a nurse to call round at a patient's home and change a dressing that I'd taken to managing these small chores myself. It was quicker and less soul destroying to collect a bandage, some gauze stuff and a roll of decent, professional sticky tape and pop round and do the dressing than it was to persuade a nurse to skip one of her endless round of daily meetings, get into her taxpayer provided motor car and attend to a real, live patient.

When you have so many people working together there will, inevitably, be a good deal of gossiping. Our reception area is tiny but always packed with people. I only go in there to pick up the details of each day's calls, which the reception staff enter in a big book as the requests come in, but while I'm there I invariably overhear snippets of some very strange conversations and only rarely does it seem to me that these are of any clinical significance. Patients might be surprised if they knew that phrases which I have never begun to understand such as `she's no better than she ought to be' figure large in the conversations of well-paid, highly trained health care professionals.

`Is it true that Molly is going to be fired?' asked someone I only vaguely recognised. The question wasn't asked out of sympathy. There was nothing more than morbid curiosity in the questioner's voice.

`I doubt it,' said someone else with a snort. `She's like dog shit on your shoe. Very nasty and difficult to get rid of.' A few people tittered.

I looked around the room. I doubt if I recognised more than a quarter of the people there. `Haven't you lot got any work to do?' I shouted, before glaring at the woman who'd asked about Molly. I didn't have the foggiest idea who she was but her hair needed washing so she was probably a social worker of some kind. I remember noticing that when she walked she always looked as though she were wearing wellington boots. 'You're a bunch of gossiping old hags. The ones who work for this practice can get back to work please. And the ones who don't work for us can bugger off back to where they came from.' I then stormed out and would have slammed the door if it hadn't been another one of those self-closing things that is connected to its frame by a powerful spring. Those doors may well be convenient but they're damned irritating when you want to slam them. I was furious. Didn't these lazy bastards realise what Molly had been campaigning for? She was worth more than the whole damned lot of them put together but all they could do was gossip about her downfall. The Germans may have the word for it, schadenfreude, but by heavens the modern English enjoy the feeling just as much as the damned krauts ever did. Frustrated at not being able to slam any of the damned doors, I drove out of the car park too quickly and banged into a couple of small vehicles on my way out. I didn't care and I didn't stop. They probably belonged to the gossiping hags in the reception area and with any luck they'd never stop talking long enough to notice.

Chapter 23

I was sitting in the bar at The Bell when Molly telephoned. I'd finished the day's calls and the evening surgery and was enjoying a pre-prandial glass of Glenmorangie and waiting for the chef to prepare my dinner. There was no one serving at the bar when I'd arrived so I'd found one of the waiters I knew in the restaurant and given him my order. He'd poured me the whisky, left the bottle on the bar and told me to help myself if I needed another. I'd asked for steak and kidney pie, roast potatoes, parsnips, carrots and broccoli with a double helping of spotted dick with custard to follow. I probably wouldn't eat the carrots or the broccoli but their colours would liven up the plate. The chef at The Bell made much better meals than Enid, if he whinged while he cooked I didn't have to listen and I didn't have to wash up afterwards. He probably looked just as good in a nightie too.

Molly sounded bright and upbeat and was clearly trying hard not to cry.

`I've just telephoned Jock and resigned,' she said. `I would have rung you first but you're such a sweetheart that you'd have tried to talk me out of it and probably succeeded and that would have been a mistake.'

`Why the hell did you do that?' It sounded harsher than I meant it to sound. But I was angry and I didn't quite know what to do with the anger. `I'm sorry,' I said immediately. `Why did you do that?'

`I don't have much choice,' she said. `The blood test was positive.'

`How on earth…?'

`I don't know. Maybe my drink was spiked. The punch perhaps?'

I couldn't think of anything to say.

`I spoke to a lawyer at the Medical Defence Union,' she said softly. `He seems to think they can keep me out of prison if I plead guilty and grovel a good deal. But whatever happens I'm going to lose my driving licence and I'm going to be struck off the medical register. The GMC doesn't mind doctors slaughtering their patients wholesale but it takes a firm line with doctors who get into trouble with the law and it takes an even firmer line with doctors who get drunk when they're supposed to be on call. The best I can hope for is that I might be allowed back on the register in a couple of year time.'

I wanted to say something but I suspected that the advice she'd been given was probably correct.

'I keep trying to cheer myself up by thinking of campaigners who've ended up in prison: doctors like Guevera, Semmelweiss and Paracelsus and writers such as Cobbett, Paine and Wilkes. But then I remember that if I go to prison it won't be because I opposed the Government but because I hit a policeman.'

'Let me ring them,' I begged her. 'Maybe I can help,' I said in that hopeful yet hopeless way we do when we want to do something but don't have the foggiest idea what to do. I have never had any important contacts and never acquired any influence whatsoever.

'You're very kind,' said Molly. 'But there isn't anything anyone can do. It's all my own fault anyway.'

'No! It's my fault,' I said. 'If I hadn't had that damned crash. If I hadn't called you…'

'If I had kept my mouth shut about vaccines perhaps Jock and Deidre wouldn't have been so determined to get rid of me.'

'What about the photos I took of the bruising on your arm? Doesn't that prove that the policeman was violent? I know that doesn't help the drunk driving charge but surely it gets rid of the assault charge?'

'The policeman says the bruising on my arm happened after I'd hit him. He says he had to restrain me because I was violent. And the solicitor says that courts always believe policemen.'

'But that's a lie!'

'Yes.'

'You could fight it! Tell the truth.'

'If I fight it and lose then they will almost certainly send me to prison for assaulting a policeman. And then the GMC will never let me back on the medical register. My career will be over before it's started. I'm going to plead guilty to a charge of drunk and disorderly and to driving while under the influence.'

For a few moments neither of us spoke. Everything seemed to have happened very quickly. And nothing that had happened seemed fair.

'When are you leaving?

'I've left I'm afraid. Jock didn't want me to go back to the surgery. He said that he'd put all my stuff into a box and have it brought round to the flat. But he's promised to find a locum to help you with the calls and to do my surgeries.'

I knew Jock wouldn't hire a locum. It costs a small fortune these days to hire a temporary doctor. You have to fly them in from Germany and pay them in diamonds. And Jock had a brand new house to pay for. He wouldn't want any extra expenditure. I also suspected that the mean bastard would probably welcome Molly's resignation because it would save the practice money.

I spoke to Molly for a little longer and promised to ring her the following day. It worried me a little that she seemed so quiet but she said she was just preoccupied; worrying about the future; concerned about getting a job of some kind. She laughed and said that outside doctoring she didn't have any saleable skills. 'I can't even type!' she said. 'If I'm lucky I'll end up stacking shelves in a supermarket.' There was a long pause while we both contemplated this awful possibility. 'Promise me that you'll have me put down if you hear that I've taken a job with an estate agency.'

I said I would. Then I promised her I'd do anything I could to help. 'We could hire you as a medical assistant of some kind. A sort of super-nurse.'

She shook her head. 'Jock and Deidre will never accept that.'

'Then I'll hire you as my driver. I'll pay you myself. Jock and Deidre can't stop me doing that. And you'll be tax deductible.'

She said I was to stop worrying because everything would be fine. Then she said goodbye and we ended the call. I rang Jock and told him to fix up for one of the agencies to take all our emergency calls. He moaned and said it was short notice but when I told him that it was either that or take the calls himself he gave up complaining. Shortly afterwards my dinner arrived. I pulled out my orange Penguin paperback of country stories by H. E. Bates. I was using as a bookmark the advertisement for a doctor to work on a Scottish island and I picked up the cutting and looked at it again. Every time I looked at it the job sounded more and more attractive. I checked the date. They'd probably found someone by now. I was depressed about Molly's position but didn't feel much better about my own. I seemed doomed to spend the rest of my days coping with the mean spirited whims of two doctors who I loathed (probably almost as much as they loathed me) and Molly was doomed to spend her immediate future stacking shelves in the local branch of Tesco.

'Would you like a refill?' someone asked.

I looked up. A woman I vaguely recognised was looking at me and holding the bottle of Glenmorangie. Slim but curvy in the appropriate and recommended places she looked to be in her early thirties. She had dark hair, twinkly eyes and a warm but gentle smile. It was a real smile and not one of those toothy grins that are so popular among celebrities and politicians. It was only when she laughed that I could see that she had a piece chipped off one of her incisors. She was wearing a white blouse with a grey skirt and a grey waistcoat and in that respect only she looked like a female version of Harry. The management at The Bell likes its staff to look smart. I suppose it's cheaper to keep the staff looking well-dressed than to have the place painted and decorated and to buy new furniture.

I nodded.

'A double?'

I nodded again.

She poured a double tot into a measuring cup and tipped the whisky into my glass. They don't use optics for the malt whiskies at The Bell.

'Do you mind the, er…? I held up my pipe.

She shook her head. 'But if someone else comes in…'

'I know,' I said. 'Is Harry off tonight?'

'Just for tonight. He's gone to a Status Quo concert. I'm sorry I wasn't here before. I had to fetch some peanuts from the storeroom.' She pointed to a large cardboard box on the bar.

I looked at her, surprised. 'I can't see Harry as a Status Quo fan,' I admitted.

'He's just a big rocker at heart.'

'Put the whisky on my tab. I'll settle up for everything when I go if that's OK. Can I buy you a drink?'

'Thanks. I'll have a white wine spritzer.' And unlike most bar staff, who accept the invitation but simply pocket the money, she poured herself a white wine spritzer.

We talked for a while about this and that and the time passed more than pleasantly. It had been a long time since I'd enjoyed the luxury of wasting time on inconsequential chit-chat. And then a waiter brought my meal from the kitchen and the barmaid tactfully moved away while I ate. She put some of the peanuts into a display box and stashed the rest in a cupboard, polished glasses and generally tidied up the bar. I knocked the ash out of my pipe, ate and read my paperback. They lie flat if you break the spine. I called her over when I was ready for my coffee.

`Black, please. No sugar.'

`Would you like another whisky with your coffee?'

`I would like one very much but I'd better not have one. I'm driving.' I nearly told her that I was also on call but then I realised that I'd told Jock to fix up for an agency to take our calls. I looked at my phone. I was about to turn it off but didn't. I didn't trust Jock to fix up alternative cover. I decided that I'd keep my phone switched on just in case he hadn't fixed up the agency. Anyway, I didn't want to tell the barmaid that I was a doctor. I learned, many years ago, never to tell people I've just met that I'm medically qualified. Pleasant conversations have a nasty habit of turning into free, private consultations. One minute you're talking about a film you've both seen and enjoyed and the next moment you're peering down their throat or listening to a detailed analysis of their bowel movements. In pubs, cafes and hotel bars I've had complete strangers pull up their jumpers, trouser legs and skirts to show me rashes, scars and funny little bumpy bits. It's difficult to recover the mood of the conversation when that's happened. I was thankful that I had, as always, left my tell-tale drug bag locked in the boot of my car.

The bar was still empty so I asked her if she wanted another drink. She said she'd have a coffee too but that there was no need to put it on my tab because she was allowed to help herself to coffee. When she brought my coffee she brought her own and we talked again. We talked about music and films and books and I enjoyed the conversation. Talking to Enid and her friends had always been a competition to see who could score points by being sharper, or snappier or nastier than anyone else. This conversation wasn't like that at all.

Suddenly it was half past ten. I realised that unless Jock had put through our phones I had been on call for several hours without my phone ringing once. I took it out of my pocket and checked that it was switched on. It was, and that the battery was still good. I then realised that I could check that Jock had hired the agency by ringing our surgery number to see what happened. Two minutes later an agency doctor answered the phone. She had a foreign accent and was probably sitting somewhere on another continent. I told her I was just checking that the phone was working and ended the call. I then turned my phone off and put it away.

`What do you do when you're not working here?' I heard myself asking.

She smiled and titled her head to one side. `I look after my boy, I do a lot of shopping, cleaning and washing, I watch too much bad television and to keep the wolf from the door I do occasional shifts at a couple of other pubs. It's mostly just standing in when the regular bar staff are away or sick.'

`You're married?'

`Divorced. My son's father left. I haven't seen him for months but he turns up occasionally when he wants money. I believe he's living with a stripper. I think he's probably her pimp. He never liked work very much so pimping would be his style. He once spent three months working at a car wash with some Romanians but they sacked him because he seemed curiously reluctant to do any actual car washing. If he'd been an animal he'd have been a sloth.' She said all this with a smile which suggested that the original bitterness had been replaced by a mixture of bewilderment and contempt.

I asked her for the bill. She gave it to me. I paid it, took some of my change and left her a decent tip. She thanked me.

`May I buy you dinner one evening? And the cinema perhaps? Something pointless and frivolous?'

The questions clearly surprised her. They surprised me even more. I hadn't known I was going to ask them until I heard them.

`Are you asking me out on a date?'

`I think that's the idea,' I agreed. I suddenly realised that I desperately needed a little fun in my life.

For a moment she seemed uncertain how to reply. But then she made up her mind. `I'd like that. I'd like that very much.' She paused. `You're not married?'

I shook my head. `Not married, not engaged, not going steady. No ties. Not even a cat.' I paused. Full disclosure. `I was married but it ended about fifteen years ago. We never had any kids. She's a consultant anaesthetist, married to a consultant surgeon. I don't know whether or not they've got kids. The good thing is that they both earn more in a month than I earn in a year so any alimony cheque I could send would be petty cash and an embarrassment. And I did have a sort of arrangement with a bookshop owner until recently. But that's over now.'

`Is it OK for you to ask me out?'

`Why shouldn't it be? Does The Bell have a rule about the staff not dating the customers?'

She laughed. `No, I don't think so. I just wondered...' She left the rest of the sentence unspoken.

`What's a good night for you?'

`I'm not working on Friday. I can get the girl next door to babysit. Actually, I shouldn't say `babysit'. My son is eight. He wouldn't like being referred to as a baby. He likes to think of himself as the man of the house.'

I climbed off the bar stool and stretched my legs. `Friday then?'

`Friday.'

I started to move away and then stepped back. `It would help if I knew your name.'

She smiled. `Clarice, Clarice Dempster.'

`That's a lovely name.'

`No it isn't. It's horrid. I've never forgiven my parents.'

`I meant the Dempster.'

She laughed. `That's the only thing my ex-husband ever gave me. I used to be a Bottomley so I did well out of the name change thing.'

`My name's Harry. Like the barman Harry Cassidy.'

`Yes,' she said, as though she knew.

Shall I pick you up or meet you somewhere?'

`Is it convenient to pick me up at home?'

`Yes, of course. But you'll need to give me your address.'

She told me where she lived. And then wrote it down for me on the back of a bar menu. I took the bar menu, folded it and put it into my pocket without looking at it.

I said goodnight and left, thinking it hadn't been such a bad day after all.

But then, on the way, home I remembered Molly and wondered what the hell she was going to do and how she was going to cope with the sky falling in on her world. Thinking of her reminded me of Jock. When I got back home I rang him.

`Did you fix up a locum to do Molly's surgeries?'

'Do you know what time it is?' he demanded.

I looked at my watch. 'It's seven minutes past eleven. Don't you have a clock in your house?'

'I know its seven minutes past eleven!' said Jock. 'I didn't ask you because I wanted to know the time. I asked you because I wanted to know if you knew the time.'

'Of course I know the time. I've just told you the time. It's seven minutes past eleven. Well, actually, it's nearly eight minutes past now...'

Jock sighed wearily. 'What the hell do you want?'

'Did you fix up a locum to do Molly's surgeries?'

'I'll fix something up in the morning. We have to find someone qualified and suitable. There are formalities. Forms to fill in and so on. Running a practice isn't just a matter of scribbling out prescriptions, you know.' The line went dead and I realised that he had turned off his phone.

That's the trouble with mobile phones.

You can't slam them down on the receiver any more than you can slam a door with a spring on it.

Technology has taken so much of the fun out of life.

Chapter 24

Early the next morning a distraught Larry telephoned to tell me that Molly had killed herself.

He told me he'd found her lying in what looked like a bathful of red water. He said he had found a note by the side of the bed telling him not to go into the bathroom but to ring me. But he'd struggled out of bed, crawled to the bathroom, opened the door and been sick. I asked him if he was sure she was dead and between sobs he said he was. I told him I'd be there within fifteen minutes and not to do or touch anything.

She had dissected out her left radial artery and then cut into it; she hadn't taken long to bleed to death. If you cut a vein, death comes slowly. But cut into a major artery and you don't have long to change your mind. As I would have expected she'd done it very neatly. Unlike many GPs she really was very good with her hands. She would have made an excellent surgeon. The scalpel she'd used was lying neatly in the soap dish. Next to it was the small alcohol soaked swab she'd used to clean her skin. I knew without looking that the neatly torn wrapper from which she had taken the swab would be in the waste paper basket. Even at the end she'd done everything properly. It's strange how doctors do that. I've read that the American doctors who give lethal injections to prisoners on death row always use a neat, little piece of gauze soaked in alcohol to clean the skin of inmates who will be dead in seconds. And although she was lying in a bath full of bloody water she was wearing a bra and a pair of knickers and I immediately understood why. She knew that Larry would call me and she wanted to retain a little dignity. She didn't want to be seen naked. We had never said anything but she knew I looked upon her as a daughter. And in my heart I felt that she looked upon me as a sort of father. No father should have to see his daughter lying naked in a bath of her own blood. I looked down at her and I could feel the tears running down my cheeks. I felt sadder than I could ever remember feeling before. The voice of conscience is delicate and unmistakeable; but so easy to stifle. Deep inside me, hidden just underneath the sadness, I could feel the beginnings of a huge, stark earthquake of a fury. She'd been the doctor all of us should have been; brave and honest and caring.

Her only mistake had been to think that being right was enough. And, perhaps, not to realise that thinking ahead of your time can be a dangerous thing to do if the world doesn't keep up with you. Her own hand may have held the scalpel, but the system had killed her. Someone once said that there is no tragedy in dying, only in never having lived. Well, that was bollocks. If there was ever tragedy in anything there was tragedy in Molly dying.

I was angry because we live in a world of thieves and liars. And the thieves and liars control what we do, how we do it and when we do it. I was angry because I realised that it is now impossible to underestimate the intelligence of the people who are destroying our society; or, more importantly, to overestimate their dishonesty. I realised that for the establishment, reality no longer matters. All that matters is whether or not people believe what you say.

Every successful politician knows that reality is of no bloody significance at all and any doubt about that disappeared in the bombing years of Bush and Blair. The self-righteous and self-serving majority close their eyes so that they do not need to care. I knew at last why I had felt so damned tired for so long. I realised that for too long I had nurtured an undirected and unrecognised rage against an establishment which had been built on betrayal: betrayal of obligations; betrayal of responsibilities; betrayal of history and betrayal of purpose, self-respect and commitments.

For the first time in my sheltered life I realised just how right Voltaire was, and how dangerous it can be to be right when the people with the power are wrong – especially when the people in power within the medical establishment are owned lock, stock and syringe by an utterly ruthless and unethical pharmaceutical industry.

And I thought of another writer too. Turgenev. 'What aim do you wish to achieve, where are you going, what is in your soul? In a word, who are you? What are you?'

Whatever the hell has happened to my profession? What has happened to integrity?

During the first Crusade a French nobleman called Baron d'Anglure was taken prisoner by Saladin and held to ransom. 'If I may visit my chateau on the Aube,' the Baron told the Sultan, 'I will return with the money you have demanded.' Saladin agreed to let the Baron go. But when the Baron reached home he found, to his dismay, that his wife had spent all his money. Every last sou had gone. All had been frittered away on frocks, minstrels and wine. Empty handed the Baron returned to the Sultan. `I have no money,' he confessed. `I have only my word.' Saladin, who was nowhere near as bad a stick as we now like to think, gave the Frenchman his freedom on condition that his children would always bear the name Saladin, that the Baron's coat of arms would incorporate the crest of Islam and that he would build two mosques when he got back home and had managed to save some money. The Baron agreed. And, as promised, the crescent was put into the family crest, two mosques were built, and all the Baron's male descendants have born the name Saladin. Now, that's integrity.

I rang some people and arranged for Larry to be taken to a nearby Cheshire Home where he could be looked after indefinitely. He certainly couldn't stay in the flat by himself. I contacted the police and spoke to the coroner's officer, arranged for the undertaker to call and somehow managed to find time to ring the surgery and tell one of the receptionists that I would be late, and that patients who did not need to see me urgently should make a fresh appointment and go home. And I spoke to Jock who was furious because he'd had to go out on an emergency call during his morning surgery. He didn't give a damn that Molly was dead. I knew without asking that the first call he would have made when he heard the news would have been to his good friend Jim of ACR Drogue et Cie. I knew that to Jock, Molly's death would mean that a problem had been solved and a sponsorship reopened. He was far too stupid to understand that Jim and Lavinia, and their board of eminent directors, would regard Molly's death as a small financial windfall of their own. There would no doubt be bonuses and champagne all round. Another problem solved. And a problem solved without making a dent in the marketing budget.

`Can I have a word with you, please?' asked Jock, when I'd finally struggled to the end of my morning surgery. I'd started nearly two hours late but most of the patients had insisted on waiting. Neither Jock nor Deidre had offered to help by adding some of my patients onto their morning surgery lists.

Innocently and naively I'd thought he wanted to speak to me about Molly. Maybe he felt guilty about what had happened. Perhaps he wanted to talk about the funeral arrangements. Or maybe he wanted to tell me about the locum he had arranged to take her surgeries.

But Jock didn't want to talk about Molly at all.

'I'm afraid I've had a number of complaints,' he said adopting the rather pompous tone he usually reserved for dealing with tradesmen who'd come to fix the guttering.

'What about?'

'About you, I regret to say. And I'm sorry to have to say that they are all serious complaints.

'Crumbs. What have I done?'

I felt more concerned than I sounded. Complaints are as much a part of the modern doctor's life as parking tickets and form filling but the problem is that as the number of complaints has grown so too has the bureaucratic machinery for dealing with them. It is terribly easy for people to make complaints and terribly difficult for doctors to defend themselves. Moreover, and in my view rather paradoxically, it is easier to complain about a doctor's manner than it is to complain about his lack of skill. Doctors who are tired and short tempered with patients are likely to be disciplined whereas doctors who kill patients through ignorance or arrogance are likely to get off scot free.

No one ever complained about Dr Harold Shipman because the wise old bird was always polite to everyone – right up to the moment when his chosen victims were slumped and cooling off in their favourite armchair. Even when they put the sod in prison he remained charming and reputedly had an excellent bedside manner with the other residents who used to queue up for medical advice. Apart from the fact that he was the world's most toxic serial killer, my only real complaint about old Shipman was that the genial bugger was woefully unimaginative. When bored I often spend my time thinking up ways to knock people off without getting caught. There are many far more subtle ways to bump someone off than merely jabbing a needle into a nice, plump vein in the antecubital fossa, and squirting in an over enthusiastic dose of morphine. For example, stuffing a needle connected to a syringe full of insulin into the external haemorrhoidal plexus would produce a corpse in no time at all without any real risk of discovery. No pathologist would ever notice. No coroner would ever know.

'Tracey has complained that you called her 'love', Colonel Mortimer has complained that you called him a Zulu, threw him out of the practice and drove over his lawn and Stella Saxon and someone else whose name I've temporarily forgotten have complained that you raised your voice and used intemperate language when speaking to them.'

'I don't know any of these people!' I protested. 'Who the hell are they?'

It occurred to me, as I spoke, that Jock is a patient of mine and that, with any luck, he will one day come to me complaining of symptoms of prostate enlargement. It would be oh so easy to tell him that I had noticed a little venous swelling in that delicate region around the anus, to offer to deal with the problem with a quick blast of some sclerosing substance such as sodium alkyl sulphate, and, instead, to give him a lethal blast of entirely undetectable insulin.

'Tracey is one of our receptionists!' said Jock. 'She's been with us for seventeen weeks. She has complained that you ordered her to make you tea and that you spoke to her in an over familiar way. Colonel Mortimer is a very long established private patient of mine. And Ms Saxon and the one whose name I can't remember are attached to the Social Integration Unit in the Community Care Office of what used to be known as our local Primary Care Trust and which is, this month, known as the, er, ah, something else.'

'I didn't know we had any private patients,' I said.

Jock blushed. He went quite red and looked embarrassed 'I do see a few private patients,' he admitted. He sounded rather defensive about it.

'They pay you money?'

'Of course.'

'Does that money go into the practice coffers?'

Jock went an even deeper shade of red. 'These are patients who see me outside normal surgery hours.' He seemed extremely uncomfortable.

'And they pay you cash? Discrete little wads of folding money?'

'It makes life easier for them. People prefer to deal in cash. It saves the bother of having to deal with invoices and cheques and so on.'

'You naughty boy!' I said, pointing a finger at him. 'You're been diddling us and diddling the taxman haven't you!'

Jock went so red that I thought for one glorious moment that he might spontaneously combust and become a front page story in one of those American supermarket tabloids which specialise in that sort of thing. *Angry British Doctor Catches Fire And Burns To Crisp. Distraught Widow Identifies Husband By Remaining Shoe.*

But the good things don't usually happen when you hope they might. Not to me they don't.

'Don't think you can turn this around and put me in the dock!' Jock said angrily. 'These are serious complaints.'

And with that he stalked out.

When he'd gone it occurred to me that our professional relationship, which had been going through something of a bad patch for the last twenty years or so, had probably reached rock bottom.

Chapter 25

When I'd finished my morning visits the next day I went round to the local Cheshire home to see Larry. I wanted to see how he was coping, and to talk about the plans for Molly's funeral. He was being well looked after. He told me that her parents had arranged for her body to be taken back to their home town.

`They're both in a pretty bad way,' Larry told me. I immediately felt guilty. I knew I should have rung them, although I had no idea what I would have said.

`They don't want me or what they call outsiders at the funeral. Just close family,' he said.

I'd never spent any time with Larry without Molly being present and I realised that I didn't really know him very well. I certainly didn't really like him. For one thing he appeared to me to be surprisingly sanguine about being told that he couldn't attend his girlfriend's funeral. I got the impression that he was far more upset about the fact that the television company was no longer planning to use his recorded contribution. It was all he wanted to talk about.

`They couldn't do enough for me before the day of the recording,' he told me. `The director himself spoke to me several times.'

`That sounds encouraging.'

`Exactly what I thought,' said Larry. `To be honest I half suspected that they wanted me on the programme to make some sort of political statement. You know, bloke in wheelchair on TV sort of thing. But he did seem really keen. Television directors and producers and editors have researchers and assistants and gofers to make telephone calls for them. But he was desperately enthusiastic. He really wanted me on the programme. He was producing the programme as well as directing it and it seemed to be a big opportunity for him. He was terribly keen for us to be there.'

`You said `us'. He was keen on Molly being there?'

`Absolutely. He was terribly keen Molly went with me. He said he very much wanted to meet her. To be honest at one point I was convinced that it was really Molly he wanted to see, rather than me. I wondered if perhaps he wanted her for some other programme he was making.'

`And now you don't think they'll use the piece you recorded?'

Larry shook his head. `I've rung the studios stacks of times. No one wants to speak to me. Alfred Lunt, he's the director, is always busy. They say he'll ring me back but he never does. I spoke to one of the researchers and asked her if they had a date for the screening but she just said it was all very fluid, whatever that means. They'd heard about Molly and I very much got the impression that now that she's dead they didn't want to know about me.' He looked really miserable. `Do you know what really pisses me off? It's when people say that hard work always pays off. Or when they say that you get what you deserve. No one could have worked harder than I have. Am I going to get what I deserve?' I saw tears forming in his eyes. And then, embarrassed, he looked away. `I made the mistake of succumbing to hope,' he whispered.

I stayed about three quarters of an hour and when I left I felt distinctly depressed. I knew that Molly had cared desperately for Larry. She had looked after him, and cared for him, in every possible sense of the word. Working in general practice and caring for a paraplegic couldn't have been easy. But it seemed to me that Larry missed her only because she had been useful to him. He certainly didn't seem heartbroken. It had been Larry, I remembered, who had pushed Molly into doing the television and radio interviews. It had been Larry who had been excited by the idea of her working regularly in the media. It had been Larry who had fixed up most of the interviews she'd done. It had been Larry who had been building up a network of useful contacts on newspapers and in radio and television.

I drove back to the surgery feeling very sad. And I wondered if Molly had noticed that Larry was using her. Was she, perhaps, beginning to suspect that Larry was using her, wasn't quite as fond of her as she was of him, and was taking advantage of her unexpected celebrity to boost his own burgeoning career.

Until Molly had suddenly found herself in the limelight Larry had been struggling. He'd had a couple of gigs in pubs but I'd always suspected that the places where he had appeared would have given a gig to anyone who'd asked for one. And I had no doubt that he expected the wheelchair to open doors for him.

Now he was wallowing in self-pity and building up a fairly large reservoir of resentment.

How much had he known? How much had he suspected? Could he have been aware that Molly's drink had been spiked?

I didn't know the answers to any of these questions.

And, I realised, I didn't ever want to know the answers. It's only in books that people get the answers they think they want.

All this was going through my mind when I got back to the surgery. But my mind was soon dragged back into the murky folds of reality.

Chapter 26

'Would you ask Dr Jock and Dr Deidre if they're nearly ready for their evening surgeries?' asked a new receptionist I didn't remember seeing before. She had bad dandruff, a Scottish accent as impenetrable as porridge and varicose veins as thick as pencils. I only understood what she'd asked after she'd repeated it three times. She was as incomprehensible as those BBC presenters who are imported from Scotland to make Scottish nationalists feel 'included'.

'Where are they?' I asked her.

'They're in Dr Jock's surgery,' she explained. 'They've been in a meeting for two hours now.'

'Just the two of them?'

'No, there are two drug company people with them as well.'

'A man and a woman?'

'That's right.' She seemed startled that I'd guessed. 'We were surprised you weren't in there with them.'

I wasn't in the slightest bit surprised. I could imagine what they were discussing. And they would have all found the discussions easier to manage without my presence.

'It's just that the evening surgeries are due to start in a couple of minutes,' said the receptionist. 'We've tried ringing through on the intercom but no one answers. And we've tried tapping on the door.'

'No reply?'

She shook her head.

'They're all still in there? They haven't snuck out without anyone noticing?'

'Oh no. I took them some tea about an hour ago. And we haven't heard a peep out of them since then.'

I climbed the stairs to Jock's consulting room and knocked on the door. There was no reply. So I opened the door.

The tableau inside would have been a credit to Madame Tussaud, the waxworks impresario. At first I thought the four of them were dead. But a closer examination showed that they all were merely unconscious. Jock, sitting behind his desk and slumped in his black leather executive chair, was snoring loudly. He had his head to one side. Deidre, sitting beside him in a dining chair, one of the carver chairs with arms, was dribbling and a large damp stain, clearly produced by saliva, had formed on the front of her blouse. Jim and Lavinia, the two drug company executives, had clearly been sitting in the two chairs reserved for patients. They must have been uncomfortable because three quarters of an inch had been shaved off the front legs of both those chairs. (The idea of shaving the front legs is that patients sitting in them will be forever sliding forwards and, without quite knowing why, constantly feeling a need to get away.) Jim was still sitting in his chair but Lavinia had fallen off hers and was lying slumped on the floor. She was snoring loudly.

It was not a pretty sight.

It didn't take me long to decide what had happened and I didn't need Sherlock Holmes or his medical friend to help me work it out. There were two trays on Jock's desk. The first tray still carried a teapot, a milk jug and a bowl of sugar cubes. And spread around on the desk there were four of our best bone china cups and saucers. The second tray carried the remains of a large fruit cake which I recognised. And four empty plates, strewn only with a few remaining crumbs, were evidence that all four had eaten well.

I picked up the telephone, dialled 999 and called for an ambulance. `Actually, 'I told the operator when I'd given my name and the address, `you'd better send two.' When I'd fixed up the ambulances I telephoned the local Accident and Emergency department and told them to be ready to do stomach wash outs on four unconscious patients.

`Do you know what they've taken?' asked Elvis Rathbone, the casualty doctor.

`Not yet,' I told him. `But one of my receptionists will ring you in a couple of minutes with a full list of the drugs they've swallowed. They're all psychotropics. You can, I think, safely assume that they've all had some of everything.'

`What the hell…'

I explained about the cake and then ran downstairs to the reception desk and told them (rather breathlessly, I'm afraid, for I had forgotten that the first rule of medical emergencies is that one should never run) that two ambulances were on their way.

`Fish out the medical records for Catherine Gibbs,' I told one of the stunned receptionists when I'd got my breath back. `And then ring Dr Rathbone, who is one of the casualty doctors at the hospital, and give him a full list of everything listed on Catherine's notes.' I looked around. 'Where did the cake come from?'

'What cake?' asked the receptionist who was supposed to be fishing out the records for Catherine Gibbs. She'd stopped what she was doing and was staring at me gormlessly.

'Get on with digging out those records,' I snapped at her. 'The hospital will need what's on them.' I looked around once more and repeated the question about the cake.

'We found it in a cupboard,' said a girl with a squint. 'It was in a tin. ' She was wearing a white coat and looked as if she could do sterling duty in a concentration camp so I assumed she was another one of our receptionists. Where the hell Jock finds these women I simply cannot imagine. He certainly doesn't choose them for their personalities or their decorative qualities. And why don't we ever have male receptionists? Are there any male medical receptionists anywhere I wonder?

'Where's the fat, red-headed receptionist?' I asked.

They all looked horrified so I repeated the question.

'Do you mean Hazel? Hazel Thickett?' asked one.

'Is she fat with red hair?'

'Well…'

'Is she fat with red hair?'

'Yes, I suppose so.'

'Where is she?'

'She's not on duty today.'

'Well ring the stupid woman and tell her that she is fired. And if she moans at being fired tell her that if she is very, very, very lucky she might just get away without being charged with attempted mass murder.'

That shut them all up.

'Now tell all the patients waiting for Dr Canterbury and Dr Cohen that they won't be seen tonight. If they've got urgent problems I'll see them. Otherwise they'll have to make new appointments.'

I then marched out and climbed quickly back upstairs to make sure that none of the four victims choked while I waited for the ambulances. It occurred to me that I'd never had to order two ambulances at once before.

Chapter 27

Jack and Deidre weren't terribly happy when, after two days, they were discharged from the local hospital and allowed back home. The two drug company hacks, Jim and Lavinia had been whisked away to a private hospital in London as soon as they'd been deemed safe enough to be moved, but Jock and Deidre were treated locally and were lucky enough to obtain valuable experience of what it's like to be National Health Service patients, starving to death in a typically brutal, uncaring National Health Service environment. They had, naturally, both demanded to be moved to the local private hospital but their demands had been turned down on the grounds that the local private hospital had been designed and staffed to deal with patients requiring minor cosmetic surgery, rather than anything which might require some serious nursing. `We can cope with postoperative mammoplasty patients,' said the Medical Director. `But we're not so hot on the death defying stuff.'

`We were poisoned!' complained Jock, not entirely unreasonably, and certainly not inaccurately.

We were sitting in the large and expensively furnished conservatory at his home. He was sipping plain water. I was drinking a malt whisky which carried the name of a well-known supermarket in two point print on the label. It tasted as if they made it in tankers off the Korean coast. I suspect they also put the same stuff in bottles labelled `Oven Cleaner' and `Mouthwash'. Even when he's well Jock doesn't drink whisky and he doesn't like spending money on stuff he doesn't drink.

`Jim, Lavinia, Deidre and I were all damned near killed! Have you ever tried eating the food in that damned hospital? You could use it for filling in potholes but it isn't fit to eat. I developed food poisoning and they wanted to keep me in on a closed ward. I only got out of the place by threatening to sue everyone in sight. Moreover, Jim and Lavinia will probably never speak to me again. Do you have any idea how important that guy is? He has an unlimited personal expense account! He's got an American Express platinum card and direct e-mail access to the European Marketing Director of one of the world's biggest pharmaceutical companies!'

He paused, trying to decide whether or not to share the next piece of information with me. In the end he couldn't resist it. `He's pretty well made it clear that any chance of my getting a decent gong in the next honours list has gone out of the window. If that deal had gone through I'd have probably been in line for a K.'

`A K?'

Jock sighed. `A knighthood. That's what they call them. Ks. The company has a lot of clout in Whitehall. They have a lot of high ranking civil servants on the payroll. These people fall over backwards to please the big drug companies. I could have probably got something for you too. Not a K, of course. But probably an MBE. Maybe even an OBE.' He took a sip of his water.

Jock has been desperate for a knighthood for years. If he ever gets one he'll have the practice notepaper reprinted before the courtiers have finished polishing the sword.

Jock stared at me. He looked pathetic, like a beagle begging for a biscuit. `Why didn't you destroy the damned cake?' he asked, plaintively.

`I gave it to the receptionist to destroy. She apparently thought it looked too good to throw away so she put it in a cupboard. And someone else found it there, and put it on one of the best plates, when you had Captain Hook and Tinkerbell round to tea.`

`We're going to have to give her an official warning,' said Jock.

`I've already fired her.'

`You can't do that! You can't fire receptionists. There are procedures to follow. You have to give them warnings and allow them representation.'

`I fired her. She's too stupid to expect procedures to be followed. If she wants to sue us then let her. What did it taste like?'

Jock frowned. `What?'

`The damned cake, of course. What did it taste like?' I was genuinely interested. To be honest I was surprised that none of the four had noticed that it didn't taste of the usual ingredients. I would have thought someone would have noticed that the usual mixture of eggs, flour, milk and so on had been supplemented with a few handfuls of powerful pharmaceuticals. But maybe they all noticed but no one liked to say anything. This does happen. A local hotel once served 150 wedding guests with prawns which had decayed and were so far past their best that, when called to help treat the heaving and leaking hordes, I felt nauseous after simply sniffing one of the offending portions. Not one of the guests had complained or refused to eat the damned things. They'd nibbled away delicately and it wasn't until the dancing was in full flow that the consequences of their willingness to stuff rotten shellfish down their throats became only too apparent. The ballroom floor was, I remember, inches deep in the evidence of their misplaced faith.

`It may come as a surprise to you to know that I cannot remember eating it, let alone what it tasted like. How many drugs were in the damned thing?'

`Five anxiolytics, two antidepressants and two sleeping tablets. It's all your fault, of course. Catherine Gibbs was your patient. Why do you give people so many different pills?'

`She has a very complex medical condition. She needed a cocktail of medicines to control her symptoms.'

`Sadly, it rather seems that your cocktail didn't control her very well.'

`That's easy to say now,' snapped Jock. He rubbed his forehead and sighed. `So, how many pills do you think were in the cake?' He still seemed drowsy and confused.

`Her husband said she emptied all her bottles. Looking at her last prescriptions, and assuming that she'd been taking them according to your recommendation, Elvis and I reckoned that she had about 150 pills left and so there were 150 pills in the cake. You all had decent sized slices so, assuming that she gave the mixture a good stir, I reckon you probably had about fifteen pills each. It's not surprising you were all flat out. Oh, there were some antibiotics in there too. Her husband said she had two unused packets of amoxicillin which have disappeared. But he couldn't remember what they'd been prescribed for or how old the packets were.'

`I don't think we'll tell Jim any of this,' said Jock, who had gone even paler. `Better for him not to know.' He frowned. `How did Elvis come to be involved in all this? I thought he was dead.'

Chapter 28

My last patient at that evening's surgery was Roger Hubbard, the local policeman who suffers from asthma. He had come to pick up another prescription for the inhalers he uses. I checked his chest, talked to him about his illness for a while and wrote out a prescription.

'I was very sorry to hear about Dr Tranter,' he said, as he stood up and slipped the prescription I'd written into his breast pocket. 'She came out to see my youngest once. He had earache. She was very good with him.' I realised with a great wave of sadness that Roger was the first person who'd shown any sadness about her death. Roger and I talked about Molly for a few minutes.

'The whole thing was so very odd,' I told him. 'My accident was bizarre, then Molly, who had taken over the on call responsibilities, was stopped and breathalysed for no very good reason. And the press found out and the whole thing spiralled out of control.'

'Do you know why she was stopped and breathalysed?' asked Roger.

'I've no idea,' I admitted. 'She wasn't involved in an accident. She was never charged with speeding or breaking any traffic regulations. She was just stopped and breathalysed. And she doesn't drink alcohol. I suspect that someone at the television studios gave her something with alcohol in it.'

'Or someone had spiked her drink.'

I nodded. 'Are traffic policemen allowed to stop cars for no reason?'

Roger looked uncomfortable. 'The traffic guys are a bit of a law unto themselves,' he said. 'The law doesn't allow them to stop a driver unless they have reason to suspect that a law has been broken. Technically, they can't just wave someone down for no reason and get them to blow into the bag.'

'But they did,' I said. 'They were apparently very aggressive about it too. I knew Molly well. She wouldn't have punched that copper if he hadn't been manhandling her rather roughly. And then, within minutes, someone rang the papers and the whole incident got completely out of control.'

`I know the two blokes involved,' said Roger. He paused and thought. `To be honest they're a pair of tearaways. Always pushing things a bit further than they ought to. I think she was probably a bit unlucky to be stopped by them.'

`Who would have rung the papers?' I asked.

`They might have done it themselves. But they probably passed the tip to a bloke in the station. One of the sergeants is usually the one to pass stories onto the papers. He rings them up every evening. Sometimes, if it's a really good story he'll sell the exclusive to one of the journalists he knows. But usually he just rings round all the papers. They settle up with him at the end of the month and he then pays off the copper who gave him the tip in the first place. I don't know about other stations but on our manor it's usually only the uniformed guys who get involved.'

`Do they make much out of tipping off the papers?'

Roger looked uncomfortable. `It can be quite a bundle if they've had a good story,' he admitted. `I did hear they got a few thousand for that story about a cabinet minister last year. One of the bobbies took some pictures on his mobile phone.'

`Could you find out why they stopped her?' I asked him. `And who tipped off the papers?'

He looked uncomfortable.

`I'm not planning to complain about anyone,' I assured him. `I'm just curious. It all seemed odd at the time and looking back it seems even more bizarre. A lot of coincidences.'

`I'll have a sniff around.'

Chapter 29

When I'd finished the evening surgery I drove out to The Grange to collect my hat. I parked, plucked the plastic token from my pocket, nodded a greeting to the whistling doorman and walked straight over to the girl in the cloakroom who was standing guard over a small collection of expensive overcoats, umbrellas and briefcases. I have no idea whether or not it was the same girl. It didn't matter. I gave her the token, which she exchanged for my hat, and then gave her a quid as a tip. To be honest I doubt if the hat was worth a quid but I've had it a long time and we've become good friends.

As I was about to leave I glanced towards the bar, wondering whether or not to have a whisky before driving back home. To my surprise I saw Jim Zabrinski, sitting on one of the barstools. The man sitting next to him, the only other person at the bar, was a fellow of about thirty. He was balding prematurely and had shaved his head to disguise the fact but it was easy to see that, even without extending his morning shave, he would have had a pretty meagre head of hair. Despite the chilly weather he was wearing a white linen suit and an open necked blue silk shirt. Zabrinski, of course, was wearing his usual immaculate grey silk suit, white cotton shirt and striped tie.

My first inclination was to sneak out before the drug company guy spotted me but on reflection that seemed rather cowardly so I wandered over to ask how he was feeling, and to offer my apologies for the mix-up that had led to his being poisoned. He can't have been particularly pleased to see me; our previous meeting had hardly ended happily and since then our practice had succeeded in putting him in hospital, but he had the skills and superficial charm of all professional salesmen and he immediately got off his stool, gave me the full 100 watt grin, shook hands and told me that he and Lavinia were fully recovered. He then introduced me to the bald guy in the white suit who turned out to be a film director called Alfred Lunt.

When Jim asked me what I wanted to drink it seemed rude to say I had to rush away, though I did explain that I was really only here to pick up my hat. `I'll have a Laphroiag,' I said. `Just a small one.'

While Jim turned to the barman to order my drink I asked Lunt if he'd made any films I might have seen.

'Doubt it, very much!' he said. 'Not yet. I've been working in television for a few years. It's the easiest way to get your director's ticket.'

'What sort of programmes have you been working on?'

'Oh, the usual mix of stuff. A couple of local documentaries. I did one about local crafts and trades that you might have seen. We discovered a chap who thatches roofs. He got his own series on Channel Four on the back of it. '

I confessed, with the appropriate apologies, that I hadn't seen the documentary, or heard of the celebrity thatcher.

'Recently, I've been doing bits and pieces for the local news programme and also working on a comedy talent show that the station is quite keen on.'

'The Laughter Factory?' I said.

'That's the one. Have you seen it?'

'I caught an episode. Very exciting stuff.' Suddenly, I remembered where I'd heard the name Alfred Lunt.

'Oh, it's all a bit parochial. Low budget stuff with a bunch of comics who aren't really ever going anywhere to be honest with you. But with any luck all that's about to change. I'm making a documentary feature for Jim's company. Two full sixty minute programmes. Massive budget. Great opportunity for me to spread my wings as it were.' He looked and sounded extremely pleased with himself.

'What are the programmes about?'

'Vaccination: a very important topic. The first film is about the importance of childhood vaccination programmes and the second film is about vaccinations for the elderly – particularly anti-flu vaccines. The company wants to inform people of the importance of following proper vaccination schedules. Both programmes will be shown on BBC 1 at peak times.'

Jim, who had finished ordering my drink, and refills for himself and Alfred, turned back to us. 'How's Jock?' he asked. 'And Deidre?'

'They're pretty well recovered,' I replied. 'I think the stay in hospital did them more harm than the poisoned cake.'

`I'd invite you to stay and have dinner with us,' said Jim. `But Keith Messenger, our Public Affairs Director, is coming up from London and the three of us are having a rather boring business meeting.' He looked at his watch. `He should be here any minute.'

I finished my drink, picked up my hat, shook hands with Jim and Alfred and left.

`The Laughter Factory' was the name of the programme for which Larry had made a recording on the night that I'd had my accident; the night when Molly had been arrested. My world was beginning to become uncomfortably full of coincidences.

I went home and cooked myself a three course meal (a glass of pineapple juice, a slice of toast with a poached egg sitting on the top and two chocolate biscuits) and then poured myself a large whisky. Now that I no longer had to worry about night calls I could enjoy the luxury of spending a little time relaxing. But something kept nagging at me and I couldn't work out what it was. I felt I had to do something or be somewhere. But I couldn't remember what or where. I was so damned tired that I fell asleep and woke up several hours later with a terrible cramp in my neck.

Chapter 30

I had a huge surgery the next morning.

I long ago gave up trying to work out why some days are busier than others. Mondays are obviously the busiest days of the week (signs and symptoms having been carefully nurtured over the weekend) and it is understandable that in the winter, during a flu epidemic, the waiting room will be crammed with patients coughing and sneezing and exchanging germs with one another, but I have absolutely no idea why, say, one apparently routine Wednesday should be quiet to the point of being boring while another will be hectic to the point of being like a twelve hour constant emergency.

When I'd finally worked my way through the two and a half dozen patients desperately needing advice, information, prescriptions or referrals to someone wiser or more skilful with a knife than myself, I was presented with a long list of patients who had asked to be visited at home. I knew them all, and knew where they lived, so it took me only a moment to sort them into a sensible visiting order that wouldn't have me retracing my steps and driving backwards and forwards across the town.

First came a request to visit Mrs Penelope Devereaux. She is in her seventies and rapidly approaching another of those landmark ages for which the greeting card companies produce special cards, but the casual observer would probably assume that she is in her mid to late fifties. She and her husband, who is a few years older than her but who also looks as if he is yet to celebrate his 60th birthday, live in a small cottage just outside town. They have a thatched roof, roses around the front and back doors, no central heating and a septic tank. Their water comes from a spring about a hundred feet away from their back door and they share the cottage with an army of woodworm whose presence they ignore on the grounds that they will both be dead long before the woodworm bring down the roof. They both suffer from slightly elevated blood pressure. They don't have a car and there is no bus service past their house and so every six months they get a taxi into town to visit the surgery to have their blood pressures checked and do any shopping they can't do at the village shop. It's the only time they ever come into town. I don't think either of them is in danger of having a stroke or a heart attack and so I have yet to prescribe hypotensive drugs. The side effects associated with drugs prescribed for high blood pressure range between mild and deadly and whenever possible I prefer to avoid using them.

Penny (as she insists I call her) was in bed when I arrived. As he led the way up the narrow staircase her husband told me that she had a swollen and painful right calf. He was right. Her calf was very swollen and clearly very painful. The diagnosis wasn't difficult to make.

`You've got a deep vein thrombosis,' I told her. `I'm going to get you into the local hospital for a few days. If we take it seriously and get it treated straight away it won't be anything at all to worry about.'

`Is it dangerous?' asked George, her husband.

`She'll be fine,' I said, putting an arm around his shoulder. `She'll be back home in a day or two.'

While George, acting on Penny's instructions, started to pack a few things in a suitcase I telephoned the hospital, spoke to the duty house physician and arranged for a bed. I then rang the ambulance service and asked them to send an ambulance round. By the time I'd finished these two calls George had completed the packing and had the suitcase standing beside the front door. While all this had been going I had been aware of a good deal of whispering going on between Penny and George.

`What are you two worrying about?' I asked them, as we all waited for the ambulance.

`I want her to take the spectacles,' said George.

`I won't need them,' said Penny. `He'll need them here.'

I told them I didn't quite understand.

`We both need reading spectacles,' said Penny. `But we only have one pair. We share them.'

`I read for half an hour and then she reads for half an hour,' explained George.

`Usually we read to each other,' added Penny.

I asked the obvious question. `Why have you only got one pair of reading spectacles?'

`We can't afford two pairs,' said George. `We get free eye tests. But the lenses and frames are so expensive.'

`You only need glasses for reading?'

They both said they did.

`You can buy reading spectacles for £1 in one of the bargain shops in town,' I told them.

They looked astonished at this.

`Put the spectacles in Penny's case,' I told George. `I'll bring you a pair of reading spectacles later on today.'

After I'd seen Penny off to hospital in the ambulance I visited Wendy Bramble. She too is on the wrong side of 70 but she pretty well lives in her bed. She says that her get up and go has all got up and gone and that, as a result, she suffers from something she calls `the weariness'. Once a year she makes a complete but temporary recovery, gets up from her bed and travels to London for the Wimbledon tennis championships. She stays with her sister, who lives near to the tennis courts, and every day the two women stand in a long queue to buy their tickets. They never manage to see tennis on the main courts, of course, but Wendy says that the atmosphere on the outside courts is exciting enough for her. Since it wasn't Wimbledon season, Miss Bramble was lying in bed. The television was on and a couple of presenters I'd never seen before were interviewing someone I didn't recognise.

`Can I turn this down?' I asked, looking for the volume switch on her remote control. As a doctor I have always believed that I am no more than a guest in my patients' lives. When they see me it is usually because something has gone wrong. No one ever wakes up and says: `Whizzo! I'm off to see the doctor today.' I am, of course, also a guest in their homes but, as an invited guest, I do feel that I am entitled to a certain amount of respect. And I am not prepared to try to examine a patient while the television set continues to blare away in the background.

The television suddenly went off and Miss Bramble triumphantly held up the remote control which she had been holding under the bedclothes. `I've heard about your little tricks!' she told me with a smile. I smiled back at her. It is clearly becoming known that if I visit a house where patients refuse to turn down the sound on their television set I fiddle around with all the knobs, switches and buttons that I can find – occasionally even loosening one or two wires at the back of the set. I'm told that after one of my `attacks' it can take a trained television engineer half a day to retune a television set.

'I've got indigestion,' she told me. 'And heartburn and gastritis.'

'How long have you had it for?'

'Nearly fifteen years.'

'Has it got worse?'

'No. But I'm fed up with it.'

When I examined her I was surprised to see that even though she was in bed and wearing a nightdress she was also wearing an old-fashioned whalebone corset. The corset was pulled so tight that the straps had made deep, red indentations in her shoulders. I was surprised that she could breathe while wearing it.

'Do you always wear that?'

'Always,' she said. 'I wouldn't feel properly dressed without it.'

'But you aren't dressed,' I pointed out.

'No. But I don't want the postman or the paperboy seeing me without my corset,' she said.

It turned out that because she spent so much time in bed she always left her front door open so that callers, including the postman and the paperboy, could walk straight into her house and climb up the stairs to her bedroom.

'I think your symptoms might be a lot easier if you left off the corset,' I told her. 'I'm sure no one will mind. And maybe you'd be a little more comfortable if you replaced the whalebone with something a little more modern and more forgiving.' I told her that it is now widely accepted by scientists and academics who study these things that the greatest invention of the 20th century was not the jet aeroplane or the Internet but the two way stretch foundation garment, a piece of high technology equipment which surpasses even the cross-your-heart bra in importance.

'Can't you just give me some medicine?' she asked. 'I'll have an operation if it's necessary.'

I eventually persuaded her to leave off the whale bone corset and promised that if her symptoms weren't easier in 24 hours I would prescribe some medicine.

Some days I spend more than half of my time making diagnoses and decisions which have absolutely nothing to do with the things I learned at medical school. Doctors who work in hospitals tend to see their patients as malfunctioning kidneys, livers, hearts or lungs rather than as human beings. I see all my patients as real people whose real lives are being disrupted by some, hopefully temporary, disorder.

Third on my call list was Mick Leyton.

Mick describes himself as a businessman and carries a pocketful of visiting cards which are embossed with the words 'Leyton Industries International' and 'Import/Export'. Over the years he has operated a number of schemes; some profitable and some not so much so. He told me once that his most profitable scheme involved persuading the manager of a small transport company he knew to put 'How's My Driving?' stickers on the back of its vans and lorries. But instead of the usual free telephone number he put on the stickers a premium rated number charged at the rate of £5 a minute. Angry motorists who rang the number to complain didn't find out until they received their phone bills just how much their moan had cost them.

Mick works from home, a council house in a particular run down area of town, and as usual his terraced house was packed from floor to ceiling with cardboard boxes. There were boxes full of television sets, mobile telephones, computers, microwave ovens and computer games. I have no idea where he obtains all the stuff he supplies but I strongly suspect that he doesn't do much business with the usual wholesalers. He's the sort of fellow who prefers to beg for forgiveness than ask for permission.

'Where do you get all this stuff?' I asked him.

He touched a finger against the side of his nose and winked. He really did. 'It all comes off the back of lorries. Sometimes it's lifted off and sometimes it falls off.' He laughed, as though this were very funny.

He told me that his wife, who was upstairs in bed, was suffering from sickness. 'I think it's something she ate,' he said. 'But it's been going on for a few days now and the poor old girl is worn out.'

I left him opening boxes and went upstairs. This wasn't easy. Half of every tread was occupied by boxes. On the upstairs landing there were more boxes. And his wife was lying in a bed surrounded by boxes. I asked her questions, listened to her, examined her, congratulated her and went back downstairs.

`Congratulations!' I said.

`Thanks,' said Mick. `She's a good looking girl isn't she?

`I think you'll find that your wife's got something to tell you,' I told him.

He looked puzzled, frowned and then hurried past me and up the stairs. Left alone in the living room I looked around the boxes.

`Hey, doc!' he called down, a few moments later. I could hear him thumping his way down the staircase. He was obviously used to coping with a stairway that was just half the normal width. `Fantastic news. I'm going to be a dad!'

`Yes,' I said. `I know.'

`Golly news travels fast. How did you know?' He laughed, climbed round some boxes, opened a desk and took out a bottle of gin and then two glasses. `Have a drink with me!'

I drank a large, neat gin and shuddered. I don't much like gin but it seemed rude to say `No'.

He reached into the desk again and took out a packet of cigars. He gave me one. I thanked him and put it into an inside pocket.

`What would you like, doc? New TV? Mobile phone? You name it. Present from us. All brand new and state of the art. Some of these phones aren't in the shops yet.'

I thanked him and shook my head and then had an idea. `Do you have any reading glasses?'

`Course I have!' He moved some boxes, clambered over others and finally produced a large white cardboard box. `What sort do you want?'

I scratched my head. `I'm not sure,' I confessed. `They're for a patient who needs reading glasses.'

Mick rummaged around in the box and took out six pairs of spectacles, all contained in neat metal tubes that looked like posh cigar cases. `Here you are, two of each sort.'

`How much do I owe you?' I asked, reaching for my wallet.

Mick waved his hands and shook his head. `No charge,' he said, thrusting the spectacles at me. I thanked him, put them into my black drug bag and headed for the door.

`Do you want any old-fashioned light bulbs?' he asked as I was leaving. `I bet you're a fellow who likes proper light bulbs aren't you?'

I stopped and turned back. `The real, old-fashioned bulbs?'

`The real old-fashioned ones. Bayonet or screw in. I'm getting two dozen boxes in next week. You can have 40 watt, 60 watt or 100 watt.'

I did a deal with him and he agreed to deliver 100 mixed light bulbs to me at the surgery.

I then finished the rest of my visits, took the spectacles to George Devereaux, who was delighted with them, and drove to The Bell for a light, late lunch.

Chapter 31

'Clarice was asking about you,' said Harry, the barman, when he'd served me my usual whisky and a ploughman's lunch that I doubt if any ploughman in history would have been able to afford. Tastefully arranged on a large plate were three bread rolls (one made with olives, one with sesame seeds and one with bits of date), large hunks of Cheddar, Leicester and Cheshire cheeses, a huge mound of Branston pickle, a tomato cut into halves and two crisp lettuce leaves.

'Clarice?'

'Clarice Dempster.'

I thought for a moment and shook my head. The name didn't mean anything to me though to be honest I was feeling so shattered that I probably wouldn't have recognised my own name.

'She stood in for me when I was on holiday. Lovely woman. Nice figure. Thirty something.'

Suddenly I remembered who Clarice was. I felt very cold, very hot and very cold, sequentially and then, impossibly, all at once. She was the woman I'd arranged to meet; the woman I'd promised to take to the cinema and to dinner; the woman who had arranged a babysitter and who had, undoubtedly, got dressed up, sat and waited and waited and fumed and cursed me and then sent the babysitter home and poured herself a large drink as she thought up some more curses. I cursed myself. I was angry with myself because I'd let her down and I was angry with myself because the date with Clarice had been the one thing I'd been looking forward to. How the hell could I have forgotten?

'She just wanted to know if you'd been asking about her,' said Harry. 'She thought perhaps you might need her address or telephone number. Wondered if you might have forgotten them. Said I should give it to you if you asked. But that was last night at about half past eight.' He handed me a small piece of paper, torn from a telephone message pad. Written in blue ink, in Harry's neat, almost childish writing, were printed her name, her telephone number and her address. I waited until Harry had disappeared, prayed that she would be at home, and telephoned her.

She answered the phone on the tenth ring and sounded slightly harassed. I immediately wished I'd thought of something to say before I'd dialled her number.

`Can you hang on a minute, please?' she said, before I'd had to chance to apologise.

`I'm so sorry,' I said, in case she was still there, listening. But she wasn't. In the background I could hear noises but I couldn't work out what they were. I sipped at my whisky and waited. I didn't want to eat anything in case she came back to the phone and I had a mouthful of bread roll.

`Sorry about that,' she said eventually. `The washing machine has flooded the kitchen. One of the pipe things has come away from another one of the pipe things and there's water everywhere. Who did you say it was?'

`It's the plumber, madam,' I said.

I have no idea why I said this. It just came into my head. I wished I hadn't said it the moment the words had emerged. But by then it was already too late and for the duration of the phone call I was stuck with being a plumber.

`The plumber?' she sounded puzzled. `How did you know…'

`We're proactive plumbers,' I said, trying to sound like a plumber, without any idea what a plumber sounds like. `We use information received direct from your mobile phone. Via the infrared camera. That's why we're called Proactive Plumbers. Our motto is: `We mend your leak before you know you've got it.' Not always, of course. I mean, you know you've got your leak this time. But that's our motto.' I didn't have the faintest idea why I'd started this daft plumber stuff but it was too late to stop.

She sounded puzzled and more than slightly disbelieving. `My phone doesn't have a camera.'

`Oh, all mobile phones have cameras nowadays. Some of them are secret cameras but they're all built in. It's to comply with a new rule from the EU. All phones have to be fitted with cameras. Even the ones made in China.' I was gibbering. Surprisingly, horrifyingly even, what I said even seemed to make a bizarre sort of sense.

`Can you see me now?'

`Yes madam. But if you'd rather I'd not look I'll turn my head away.'

There was a cry of anguish. 'This is awful. I'm soaked to the skin. I look as if I've entered a wet T-shirt contest. Look away immediately!' There was a pause. 'I don't believe a word of this. There can't possibly be a hidden camera in my phone. Can there? Are you looking away? This should be illegal.'

'I'm looking away now, madam. You look very nice indeed but I'm looking away. Would you like me to send one of our consultant technicians round to take a look at the washing machine?'

'How much will it cost? Are you sure about phones having cameras fitted? Where is it? Are you definitely not looking? You promise?'

'Definitely not looking, madam. The first hour is free. After that we'll quote you a price. If you don't like it you can just send our consultant technician away.'

'The first hour is absolutely free? No charge at all?'

'No charge at all.'

'If the man you send can put the two pipes back together in less than an hour I don't have to pay a penny?'

'That's right, madam. Our consultant will be with you as soon as possible.'

'Wait! Do you have my address?'

'Yes, we have that thank you, madam. Look out for the large yellow van with the big tap on the top. Unmissable.'

'How did you get my address?' asked Clarice. She sounded nervous. Big Brother was watching too closely.

'Just using the Google geographical software attached to your telephone, madam.'

'Oh.' There was another pause. 'I didn't know you people could do all these things. Well, don't be too quick. I need to change my top and mop up some of the water first.'

'Will about half an hour be all right, madam?'

'That'd be fine, thank you.' She still sounded a trifle uncertain. 'And you sure the first hour is completely free?'

'It's completely free, madam. It's an introductory promotional offer we're running in conjunction with Google.'

I turned off my phone and looked at my watch. I just had time to finish my lunch.

Chapter 32

I was half way to Clarice's house, hoping that I would somehow be able to mend her washing machine and wheedle my way back into her good books, when my telephone rang. It was Roger Hubbard.

`Something odd,' he said. `I asked around and found the guy who'd rang the papers about your doctor friend.'

`Who was it?'

`Rather not name names,' said Roger. `But it doesn't matter anyway. When he rang his usual contacts he found they'd already got the story. He rang three papers and two television news studios. They all had the story.'

`So someone else rang them all?'

`Exactly so.'

I overtook a red Audi which was travelling so slowly that the driver was either looking for somewhere to park or having a heart attack. An oncoming van driver tooted unnecessarily.

`If you're driving I hope you're using a hands-free kit!'

`Of course I am,' I lied. `Could it have been some kid in the street with a mobile phone who called in the story? Kids are getting very media savvy these days.'

`Not very likely is it. How would they know who it was? It was dark and Dr Tranter wasn't immediately recognisable was she? I mean it wasn't as if it were the Duchess of Cambridge being breathalysed. And even if someone did recognise her it's a bit unlikely that they'd ring all the papers and television companies. They might ring one. But all of them?'

I had to agree with him. `So who was it?'

`There's something else,' said Roger. `My mate at the station, the chap who rang up the papers, said that one of the editors told him they'd had the story for an hour.'

I thought about this. `That's not possible,' I said at last.

`Seems strange doesn't it? But my mate was absolutely certain about it because he thought it was a bit funny too. He rang the first newspaper about fifteen minutes after the call came in to the station. Allow another fifteen minutes for the patrol guys to make the call to the station and that editor had the story thirty minutes before it happened.'

`Which editor told your mate that they'd had the story for an hour?'

`Haven't the foggiest I'm afraid, doctor. One of the nationals.'

`No, I mean was it the first, the second, the third…'

`Oh, I see what you mean. I don't know that either. But it doesn't make much difference. He wouldn't have taken more than ten minutes to make all five calls. The guys on the news desks don't hang around making polite conversation about the weather.'

`But how…'

`I really don't have the faintest idea, doctor. But it does seems to suggest that someone, somewhere, knew that Dr Tranter was going to be stopped and breathalysed and arrested before it happened.'

`Before it happened!'

`Exactly.'

`How the hell could that be?'

`I have absolutely no idea. No idea at all.'

I thanked him and switched off my phone.

Who the hell would have known that Molly was going to be breathalysed before she was breathalysed? It had to be someone who had rung the police, given them her car number and told them that the driver had been drinking. But no one could have seen her drinking because she hadn't been drinking. So it had to be someone who had spiked her drink. So it had to be someone at the television studios. And that could be any one of a hundred people.

I pulled up outside Clarice's house; a neat looking semi in a row of neat looking semis. They all looked identical. The doors and window frames were all painted the same shade of light blue. The landlord, whoever he was, had clearly managed to arrange a good deal on the paint. I wondered if he'd bought it all from Mick Leyton.

It was time to stop puzzling about Molly for a few minutes and to start worrying about mending a washing machine and a badly damaged relationship that hadn't even started.

Chapter 33

Clarice opened the door, looked at me and didn't say a word. In fact she put her hand over her mouth in that way that people do when they are surprised and either can't think of anything to say or don't want to say anything until they have thought through what they think they might be planning to say.

'I'm from Proactive Plumbers,' I said, trying to smile.

She still didn't say anything. Her hair was pulled back from her face in a pony-tail and she was wearing very little make-up. She was wearing a plum coloured sweater and close fitting jeans. I thought she was the most beautiful woman I'd ever seen. And she had a terrific figure. I couldn't imagine why she'd agreed to go out with me. It occurred to me that she might not even remember that we'd met before. She might not remember that we'd had a date.

'It's me,' I said. 'Harry Cassidy. We met at The Bell. I was having dinner. You were working there.'

'I know,' she said. 'I haven't forgotten.'

'I am so sorry about forgetting our date.' I suddenly realised that I should have brought flowers. Flowers and chocolates. I was making a real mess of this. 'I really will have a look at your washing machine,' I said.

She looked at me and raised an eyebrow.

I felt myself going red. 'I don't know why I did all that plumber stuff. It was pretty stupid.'

'That was you?'

'Yes. I'm afraid so.'

'You pretended to be a plumber?'

'I was ringing you to apologise and…I don't really know what happened.'

'Has my mobile phone got a camera in it?'

'I don't know. I don't know anything about mobile phones. I don't even know if my mobile phone has got a camera in it.'

'Do you know anything about washing machines?'

'No. But I can look at it.'

'You couldn't really see me when I was soaked?'

'No.'

'You told me a whole load of lies.'

`Yes. And I don't know why I did it. When you answered the phone I sort of panicked. I was really cross with myself and nervous that you'd tell me to go and, well just go, and so I suppose I was frightened to admit it was me. I do feel really bad about forgetting our date. It's been a pretty horrid time to be honest and I just forgot. I just got home, slumped in a chair and sort of fell asleep.' I winced. It didn't seem a good idea to keep pointing out that I had forgotten that we had a date. I should have said that I'd been stuck with an emergency. Racing around up to my knees in blood. Saving lives. Preferably children's lives. Small, cute, blonde children. But I didn't want to lie to her. I couldn't start our relationship with a lie. Apart from it not being the right thing to do I would probably get found out.

Clarice didn't say anything. She looked as if she was trying to decide whether or not to just shut the door.

I sighed. `I'm not very good at this sort of stuff.'

She smiled. `You're not, are you? No one could accuse you of being a smoothie!'

I went down on my knees. `I'm really very sorry,' I said. `Will you please forgive me?'

She laughed out loud. `The woman across the road is peeking. She probably thinks you're proposing to me.'

I looked around, over my shoulder, just in time to see a net curtain twitch.

`You'd better come in,' she said. `Would you like a coffee? You can continue grovelling while I put the kettle on.' She turned and walked along the hall. I shut the front door and followed her. The hallway was narrow. There was a door into a living room on the left and a narrow staircase on the right. Everything was neat and clean. As Clarice disappeared into the kitchen, which was straight ahead, I couldn't help noticing that the view from behind was pretty good.

`It's a lovely house,' I said.

It smelt clean and fresh. Not the sort of clean and fresh that you get out of an aerosol but the sort of clean and fresh you get when a house is kept, well, clean and fresh. GPs go into far more homes than most people. I'm always surprised how many houses look and smell like refuse tips inside. I've been in houses which were so dirty that I wiped my feet when I left.

She was filling the kettle. 'No it's not. It's pretty horrid and it's small but there's only the two of us. And it's all I can afford. I rent it furnished so you don't have to be polite about the furniture. Be careful on the linoleum. I tried to dry it off but it's still a bit damp. Would you like a biscuit?'

'Just the coffee please. Black. No sugar. Where's the washing machine?'

She plugged the kettle in, turned and looked at me. She was smiling broadly. 'Guess.'

Puzzled, I looked at her.

'Guess which one is the washing machine.'

I looked around the kitchen. There were four appliances. None of them was new. They all looked as if it had been a long time since anyone had unwrapped them and made appreciative noises. I pointed at one of them. 'That's the oven.'

'Good start. I'm glad you recognised that one.'

'And that's the fridge.'

'Fridge freezer if you don't mind. The estate agent made it very clear.'

'Sorry. Fridge freezer.

'You're down to two.'

'One will be the washing machine and the other will be the tumble drier.'

'I haven't got a tumble drier. They cost too much to run. And there isn't room for one anyway. '

'One's a dishwasher and one's a washing machine.'

'And the washing machine is which one?'

I peered at the knobs and dials. 'The one with the glass door on the front will be the washing machine. People always like to watch their clothes go round but never seem to want to watch their cups and plates being washed.'

'I'm impressed.'

'Can I have a look at it? Where are the leaky pipes?'

'You have to pull it out. The pipes are at the back. I pushed it back in when I cleaned the floor.'

I pulled out the washing machine. There seemed to be an endless number of pipes and leads behind it. I took out the small pen torch I use for looking down inflamed throats, switched it on and crawled in behind the washing machine. `The thin wiry things carry the electricity don't they?'

She laughed. It was a beautiful laugh. I began to think I might be winning.

`There's a pipe at the back that looks as if it ought to be joined up with another pipe,' I said.

`A red one and a green one,' she agreed. `I think those are the two that came apart. I tried to screw them back together but I couldn't. My fingers aren't strong enough. And I don't have any tools. Well, I have a screwdriver and a hammer but I don't have one of those wrench things.'

I tried to fasten the two pipes together but I couldn't manage it either. I crept out from behind the washing machine. `Just one minute,' I said. I ran out to the car, collected my drug bag and ran back. I opened the bag and took out two pairs of artery forceps. I keep them in case I ever have to stop arterial bleeding in an emergency. Needless to say I haven't used them since I started work as a GP. Holding my torch in my mouth I fastened one pair of forceps around one of the pipes and used the other pair to hold the other pipe tightly. I then managed to screw the two pipes back together.

`I think I've done it!' I announced with considerable pride and some surprise. `Do you want to try the washing machine?'

`You've mended it?' she sounded surprised.

`I think so.'

She turned on the washing machine and I sipped my coffee. It was an excellent cup of coffee; made with Arabica beans and strong. We both watched, listened and waited. There was no sign of water seeping out from underneath the machine.

`You have mended it!' she said eventually.

`Proactive Plumbers always aim to please,' I said proudly.

`Thank you. And the first hour is free?'

`The first hour is definitely free. Am I forgiven?'

She pretended to think for a minute. `I think so,' she said at last. `Just this once.'

`I'm not really a plumber,' I confessed.

`I know. '

`Were you absolutely totally furious with me?'

`Pretty furious,' she admitted.

'Can we try again?'

'OK.'

'Tonight?'

She shook her head. 'I need to fix a babysitter.'

'Oh yes. Tomorrow?'

'That should be OK. '

'I'll pick you up at eight.'

'Fine.'

'I forgot to give you my phone number last time,' I said. 'Do you have a piece of paper?'

She rummaged in a drawer and gave me an envelope from the electricity company. I wrote my mobile number down on the back of it. And, for good measure, I then added the surgery number.

Just then the back door burst open and a small boy entered. He had muddy knees and was carrying a large sports bag. 'We beat them, mum!' he announced, tearing off his shoes and then putting them neatly beside the back door. Then he saw me and looked puzzled and alarmed. He had clearly recognised me. He turned to his mother. 'Are you OK, mum?'

'I'm fine darling,' she said. 'The washing machine broke down.'

'Oh,' said the boy. He sounded slightly surprised by this. He was wearing neither a baseball cap nor expensive trainers and so I liked him straight away. I suddenly realised that I knew him but I couldn't think why.

'Do you remember Doug?' asked Clarice. 'You stopped his nose bleeding.'

'Oh yes,' I said. I paused and went ice cold. 'When was that?'

'Last week. In the surgery.'

'Of course.' I remembered. I remembered it all.

'Say hello to Dr Cassidy, Doug.'

Doug said hello. I said hello.

'I didn't know doctors mended washing machines,' said Doug.

'Oh yes,' I said. 'We do all domestic appliances.'

'You need a bath, ' Clarice told her son. 'Go up and I'll be up n a few minutes with a clean towel.'

Doug disappeared.

'He's a patient of mine?'

`Yes, of course.'

`You're a patient of mine?'

`Yes.'

I didn't speak for what seemed like a year or two but was probably quite a bit longer.

She spoke at last. `You didn't remember?'

`You looked different then.'

`I hope I did. The last time I saw you I was covered in blood.'

`You did look different. Have I seen a good deal of you?'

She laughed out loud.

I blushed. `I'm sorry. I didn't mean…'

`I know…it just seemed funny.'

`Have you been to the surgery much?'

`No. We're fairly new patients. Doug and I joined your practice when we moved into this house.'

`That's good. I mean it would have been embarrassing if you'd been to see me every week and I hadn't remembered you.'

`I assumed you knew I was a patient. That's why I asked you if it was OK for you to ask me out.'

`I thought you meant because you were working at the bar.'

She laughed. `No. I think barmaids are allowed to go out with their customers. I was worried because you're our doctor.'

`Yes.'

`It's not all right is it? I should have realised and said something. Can we just forget tomorrow?'

`No!' I said. `I don't want to forget tomorrow. I want to see you.'

`Are you sure?'

Yes. Very sure.'

`It's not as if we're doing anything we shouldn't.'

`No. Just having dinner. And going to the cinema.' I suddenly caught sight of the clock. `Crumbs. Is that the time? I must fly. I've got a surgery to do.'

`Thanks for mending the washing machine.'

`Pleasure. Always available for all your plumbing needs.'

`Proactive Plumbers!'

`That's me!'

`I look forward to seeing you tomorrow.'

`I look forward to seeing you too.'

`Are you sure it's OK?'

`Definitely, positively, certain.'

I wasn't, of course. I wasn't entirely sure that Jock and the General Medical Council would approve. But I didn't care. We could sort things out later. It wasn't as if we'd kissed or held hands. Not even the GMC could complain about my mending her washing machine.

I walked to my car and looked back. Clarice was still standing on her doorstep.

I waved, she waved and I drove away. About two hundred yards down the road I looked in the rear view mirror. Clarice was still standing on her doorstep. I opened my car window, stuck my hand out and waved. She waved back.

Chapter 34

The evening surgery went slowly. I didn't want to be behind my desk, writing out prescriptions, and I didn't want to be standing beside my examination couch prodding fat bellies and listening to what was going on inside sweaty chests. I wanted to go home, pour myself a large whisky and think. I wanted to think about what Roger Hubbard had told me about Molly. But, even more than that, I wanted to think about Clarice. I liked her a lot. I liked her more than a lot. I thought that life with her could be a good deal of fun. It would certainly be far more fun than life with Enid. But how did I feel about her having a son? I didn't think I minded that at all. He seemed a decent enough boy. But how would he feel about his mother finding a new man? Were his mother's feelings about me as strong as mine about her? And how much of a problem was it that she was a patient of mine? I hadn't treated her so I didn't see how I could be accused of taking advantage of the doctor-patient relationship. It seemed that nothing in my life could be simple. Suddenly, it dawned on me that it was a little early to be thinking of all these potential problems. I'd only met her twice. Three times if you counted the time when she'd brought her son to the surgery – which I most certainly didn't count. We hadn't yet had what could be called a date.

My first patient was a man who looked to be in his fifties. He didn't speak a word of English. He came with two relatives, a woman of the same sort of age and a man in his late twenties or early thirties. I assumed that the older man was my patient because he sat in the chair on the other side of my desk. The other two sat on chairs at the back of the room. The woman was wearing a yashmak and all I could see of her was her eyes. The two men were wearing dark blue suits that hadn't been cleaned or pressed for a generation or two, and grey shirts without ties. The shirts may well have been white when they had been sold. None of these people was registered as patients of ours but the man who sat on the other side of my desk had handed me a form which suggested that he was a `temporary resident'. The receptionist had been no more successful than I was at understanding who they were or what they wanted. In the space headed `name' someone, presumably one of the three, had written something I could not read. Nor could I read what had been put down to explain where they'd come from or where they were staying. I tried speaking to them with a few words of Spanish I'd acquired on a couple of almost forgotten holidays but that proved as ineffective as my attempts to speak to them in English. I didn't know where they came from, what they wanted or what language they spoke.

I hate trying to treat patients to whom I cannot talk. Without being able to communicate with someone it is impossible to take a medical history and one is in a worse position than a vet, who can at least always ask the person accompanying a sick animal for information.

Eventually, after ten minutes of sign language that made me think we were all playing a Christmas parlour game, I realised that the patient was not the older man who was sitting opposite me but the woman who was sitting at the back of the room. And she, I gathered, was the wife, mistress or companion of the younger of the two men. I assumed, probably wrongly, that the older man was the father of the younger man or the woman. I got up from behind the desk and approached her. It quickly became apparent, however, that this wasn't a wise move. The two men stood up quickly and placed themselves in front of her. It seemed that a physical examination was not an option. So, no history taking and no examination. I retreated and sat down again. I then began the tedious business of trying to make a diagnosis by pointing to bits of my own body until eventually the older man confirmed that I was getting warm. A little more mime and some rather poor play acting on my part led me to suspect that the woman was suffering from constipation. I wrote out a prescription for a suitable product and handed it to the older man. I told him firmly that the woman should see her own doctor as soon as possible so that the existence of any underlying pathology might be excluded. The three of them then left. The whole business had taken me over half an hour and put me well behind. The patients sitting in the waiting room would, I suspected, be getting restless.

The next dozen patients were easier to deal with in that they all spoke English and none of them refused to be examined, though a woman who wanted a fresh supply of her contraceptive tablets was quite put out when I wanted to take her blood pressure. 'Dr Cohen never bothers with that,' she moaned. An elderly man, old enough in body to be my father and young enough in spirit to be my son, came into the surgery complaining that he was going deaf and, after I had syringed his ears and removed about two pounds of compacted, accumulated wax, left humming to himself and talking of miracles. I handed out prescriptions for aspirin to five patients suffering from colds or flu (and handed handkerchiefs to the three who sneezed all over me without bothering to use either hand or hanky to deflect their germs) and prescribed a soothing cream for a child who had developed a tiny patch of eczema. A couple who had been trying for a baby and who were under the impression that oral sex was the best way forward were sent away with some basic advice about conception. A man in his forties who was losing his hair left promising to complain about me to the Minister of Health when I told him that I couldn't prescribe a hairpiece for him.

At that point the evening surgery was interrupted. One of the receptionists telephoned to tell me that there was a man downstairs threatening to close down the surgery.

`Can't you ring Dr Cohen?' I asked. Jock is, after all, the senior partner. `Dealing with lunatics from the council is one of his responsibilities.'

`Dr Cohen said he's not to be disturbed,' said the receptionist. `He's got Mrs Oliphant with him.' Mrs Oliphant is a young widow who visits Jock once a fortnight and stays with him for an hour at a time. None of us knows exactly what they get up to but, knowing Jock as I do, I very much doubt if it is anything illegal, immoral or worth gossiping about.

I hurried down the stairs and found a man with a clipboard waiting for me. He was wearing one of those yellow vests that motorway workers wear while they read their papers, make the phone calls and drink their endless mugs of tea. I was slightly surprised to see that he wasn't wearing a hard hat. He was in his early twenties and under the yellow vest he was wearing a cheap grey suit, a blue shirt and a tie that looked as though it had been designed by a regimental quarter master after a night out with the lads.

He told me that he had made a spot check and that he was going to have to close us down because our chairs weren't all fastened together.

'In an emergency exit situation a chair could fall over and impede egress,' he told me.

'Go away,' I said.

He showed me a piece of plastic that was hanging around his neck. 'I'm from health and safety. And that's not all. Your entrance door is two point four centimetres too narrow. If a woman was pushing a double pram she would not have easy access to your building. That needs to be changed before I can allow the building to continue to be used for its present purpose.'

'That's sexist,' I told him.

He stared at me, uncomprehending.

'You said that if a woman was pushing a double pram. That's a sexist remark. You are assuming that only women push prams.'

The man with the clipboard looked worried. These people take these things very seriously.

'If you're going to close us down then you must tell all those people to go home,' I told him, pointing behind me to the waiting room. 'And you must sign to take responsibility for what happens to them.'

He looked at me and frowned, clearly puzzled.

'They're all here because they need drugs or treatment,' I explained. 'If they go home untreated some of them may die. If you're sending them home then you must take responsibility for the ones who die.'

'No one said anything about taking responsibility for people dying,' said the youth.

'It's what we do here,' I explained.

He stared, uncomprehending.

'We take responsibility,' I explained. 'The buck stops here. If people die we're responsible. So if you want to take over then you must take our responsibility.'

'I'm not signing anything like that,' said the youth, edging towards the door.

'Then go away and stop wasting our time,' I told him.

'I'll be back,' he said. 'I'll have to make a report. You haven't heard the last of this.'

'If I see, hear or smell you within a mile of me I'll certify you insane,' I told him. 'And if you annoy me I'll certify you officially dead. It'll take you weeks to unravel the mess that will make of your life.'

He left, clutching his clipboard. I set off back for the stairs. Before I could start climbing, a receptionist popped out. 'Did you see that man who was threatening to close down the surgery?' she asked.

'Mistaken identity,' I told her. 'He thought we were a branch of McDonalds.'

'Oh,' she said, seemingly unconcerned and unsurprised by this. 'So we're not shutting then?' She sounded disappointed.

'No. We're not shutting.'

The rest of the surgery went smoothly and ended with a woman in her thirties reporting that she was having difficulty sleeping and demanding that I give her some of the wonderful capsules I had prescribed for her friend. She had brought one of the capsules with her, carefully wrapped in a paper tissue, so that I could be sure to prescribe the correct medicine. I recognised the capsule immediately. It was huge. It looked like the sort of thing pharmacists use in their window displays. One half of the capsule was green and the other half was yellow. The ingredients were nothing more potent than vitamins and the capsules were my favourite placebo.

As I've mentioned earlier, I am an enthusiastic believer in the power of the placebo. The evidence shows that between a third and a half of all patients will respond to a placebo and will recover from whatever ails them when given an entirely inert and harmless medicament. The trick is that the prescriber must believe in the power of whatever he is prescribing (or must convince the patient that he believes in it).

'Does your friend sleep well with these?' I asked.

'Better than ever,' came the reply. 'She's tried all sorts of things given to her by Dr Cohen. But your capsules work best. They've got rid of her depression too.'

'Are you having difficulty in sleeping?'

'Terrible difficulty,' said the woman. 'I've got two teenage kids. They're going through a bad patch. My daughter has had metal rings put through her nose and her tongue and other places too that I won't mention if you don't mind. My son is waiting to go to court for stealing a car. And my husband is drinking too much.'

'Are you depressed?'

'Wouldn't you be?'

'These capsules are very powerful,' I told her, writing out a prescription for thirty capsules. 'You must only take one and you must take it at 9 o'clock at night. Not a minute earlier and not a minute later. You must swallow the capsule with 100 mls of water. You must keep the bottle locked up somewhere safe so that no one else can find them.'

I have found, over the years, that the capsules work best when given with very precise advice. I once experimented with telling patients that the capsules had to be taken green end first but stopped this after a woman rang me in tears to tell me that she had taken a capsule yellow end first. She was convinced that she would die.

The sleepless patient was very grateful and left clutching the prescription as though it were the Holy Grail. I do believe that doctors should use placebos more often. I have tremendous faith in their power. I suspect that I could help cyclists win the Tour de France by giving them supplies of my green and yellow vitamin capsules.

And so the early evening went.

When I'd seen the last patient I had a telephone call from the only receptionist remaining on duty. I have no idea which one it was. She told me that Jock wanted to see me. She made it sound as if I were a schoolboy and he the headmaster.

'I've had another complaint about you,' said Jock, the moment I walked through his door. 'Someone from the Regional Health Authority rang and bollocked me. Apparently you haven't filled in your XD109s.'

'I haven't filled in my whats?'

'Your XD109s. These new forms we're supposed to fill in every week.'

'What the hell are they for?' I long ago gave up trying to keep up with all the forms we are supposed to complete. There are forms for licensing, revalidation and compliance and a zillion and one other things too. Any doctor who fills in all the forms he's supposed to complete must be failing his patients.

'I don't know,' admitted Jock. He looked a trifle embarrassed. 'Apparently I haven't filled in mine either.'

'I bet Deidre has.'

'Oh yes, Deidre has.'

Deidre is a star at filling in forms. Nothing – and I think I probably mean `nothing' - gives her greater pleasure than sitting down with a cheap pen and a pile of questionnaires. I, on the other hand, find it difficult to take forms seriously. Not a week goes by without some idiot somewhere in the National Health Service thinking up a reason for another questionnaire.

`Tell them Deidre has used up all the forms and we need another supply,' I told him.

`And those social workers from the Social Integration Unit are still carrying on with their complaint about you. I tried to persuade them that you'd had a nervous breakdown but they wanted an apology in writing and I knew you wouldn't do that.'

I took out my pipe and started to scrape out the bowl. Just the sight of my pipe always annoys Jock.

`Just tell them to go away. They'll slink back into their dark cave.'

`I don't think I can do that. They're making a complaint so we have to take them seriously. You're not going to light that thing are you?'

`Or?'

`Or what?'

`Or what will happen if we don't take them seriously?'

`I don't know. They'll probably send someone round to crush your morning biscuits and let the air out of your tyres. I don't know what these people can do.'

`Don't worry about them. Tell them I've left the country. What morning biscuits?'

`The biscuits you get with your coffee at eleven.'

`Do you have coffee at eleven? With biscuits?'

`Yes, of course.'

`Oh.' I made a mental note to tell the receptionists I wanted coffee and biscuits half way through every morning. I stood up, tapped out the contents of my pipe into Jock's waste paper basket and sat down again. `Tell the Social Integration Unit that I'm making a counter complaint because they interfered with the provision of care to a patient. Tell them I feel that their actions threatened the state of mind of a vulnerable individual. Tell them we can't respond to their complaint because to do so would be a breach of privacy regulations. Tell them I've gone insane and been appointed Minister of Defence. Tell them I was battered and abused when I was a child and that I regard their complaint as a continuation of that bullying. Tell them I've become a Muslim and that I regard their complaint as an ethnic slur. Tell them I'm homosexual and regard their claims as specifically directed at my choice of sexuality. Tell them I'm having hormone treatment because I'm a transsexual and that my presence of mind was disturbed by a rush of progesterone.' I paused for a moment. 'Tell them that I've got early onset Alzheimer's disease and that I don't remember who they are, what they want or who I am.' I took out my tobacco pouch and started to refill the pipe.

'One of those might work. Do you really want me to tell them that? The only snag is that the GMC might want to take away your licence.'

I turned and headed back towards the door. 'I'll make a miraculous recovery and write a book giving all the credit to green and yellow capsules.' I sighed. 'To be honest Jock I don't give a fig what you tell them or what they do. I can't even remember what the complaint is about. They can't have me put down and they can't send me to prison. The worst they can do is ask the NHS to sack me. I doubt if they can do that but if they do I will be utterly delighted. I'll live off the State and spend the rest of my days sitting around in my pyjamas watching daytime television.'

'I've been meaning to ask you about those green and yellow capsules,' said Jock. 'What the hell are they? What is in them? I've had five patients begging for them this week. I had to palm them off with Angipax, which I told them were much stronger.'

I started to light my pipe and left.

I really was getting very tired of my job.

Chapter 35

On my way home I called in at The Bell. It had occurred to me that Clarice might be working but, sadly, she wasn't. I ordered the steak and kidney pudding with mashed potatoes, carrots, broad beans and cauliflower. While I waited for the chef to create yet another masterpiece of traditional English cooking I asked Harry to pour me a large Laphroaig. I then sat on my usual bar stool and thought long and hard about Molly; and about why and how someone had managed to ring the newspapers to tell them about an accident that hadn't yet happened.

The `how' was all too easy. Someone had spiked Molly's drink when she and Larry had been at the television studios. And someone, probably the same someone, had made a few telephone calls. The first, as a concerned citizen, had been to the police to tip them off about a driver worth breathalysing. The others had been to various news desks. The chances were that the drink had been spiked and the calls made by Alfred Lunt. And his reward had been a commission to make a couple of documentary films. The other part of the puzzle had doubtless been easy to arrange. A joy rider in a stolen truck had been given £50 to drive into the side of my car to put me out of action for the evening. I could prove none of this. And I suspected that no one else would ever be able to prove it either. But in my heart I knew it was the way it had happened. In real life, sadly, the baddies get away with things more often than they should.

The `why' wasn't difficult either. Molly had annoyed some very powerful people in the drug industry and the medical establishment. She had become a serious threat to the vaccine industry and someone had decided to silence her. Had she found new evidence of some additional, particularly egregious example of corporate malfeasance? Or was she a threat merely because she had dared to speak out? Had men in suits sat around a large walnut boardroom table and made the decision to end her professional life to save their profits? Had some eager underling gone further than even they had ordered – a la Murder in the Cathedral? Initially, it seemed difficult to believe that huge, international pharmaceutical companies would actually destroy a doctor's career in order to shut her up. But why should I find that so difficult to believe? Every doctor worth his salt knows that drug companies have knowingly sacrificed thousands of patients by keeping drugs on the market even though they are aware that the drugs they are selling are killing people. Time and time again evidence of serious side effects has been suppressed by executives eager to extend a deadly drug's profitable lifespan. Doctors who have dared to speak out have been excoriated, ridiculed and eventually destroyed. Whistleblowers who posed much smaller threats than Molly have been metaphorically hung, drawn and quartered in order to protect the bottom line profits and the sanctity of the executive bonus scheme. It seemed clear to me that the drug companies had decided to discredit Molly, and to ensure that the GMC took away her licence. The assault on the policeman had been a small bonus. The suicide had been a big bonus.

I decided I wanted to see what research Molly had accumulated. Larry was in the Leonard Cheshire home and there was no one living in their flat. Her parents had taken nothing of hers. They hadn't even visited the flat to see where she had lived (and died). They had, I knew, instructed Larry to deal with all her belongings. But I was pretty sure that he hadn't.

I finished my whisky, paid Harry and drove to the Leonard Cheshire home. I told Larry I wanted to go through Molly's papers to see if there were any letters or notes relating to patients she had seen. He happily gave me the keys. 'Her desk is in the bedroom,' he told me. 'There's a small, three drawer filing cabinet next to it. It's dark green. We bought it in a junk shop just off the High Street. It weighs a ton but she insisted on carrying it back herself. All her papers are in that. Take whatever you need. None of it's any good to me.'

He didn't seem to care about Molly now that she was gone and of no further use to him.

The flat was cold and smelt empty. It was full of furniture, clothes, books, CDs and DVDs but it still seemed empty. It took me no more than a minute to find the filing cabinet. It had been around for a long time. Over the years the corners had been chipped and bashed by clumsy removal men. The side of the cabinet had been hit hard with something very solid and there was a big dent in it. For a moment, just before I opened it, I wondered if it might have been emptied; if someone had broken in and removed the contents. But the three drawers opened smoothly and easily and all Molly's papers were in there. Someone, presumably Molly, had oiled the runners. I didn't expect to find anything startling. I suddenly got the feeling that the drug companies had been more frightened of Molly and her willingness to tell what she knew than they had of her having unearthed some new and devastating information.

I opened the three drawers of the filing cabinet and flicked through the files they contained. There were dozens and dozens of scientific papers. They were crammed in so tightly that it was difficult to slide the files in or out. Some of the papers had been torn out of medical journals. Most were photocopies which had library stamps on them to prove that the copies had been made legally. Some were reprints of papers which had been sent to Molly by the authors. Medical journals don't usually pay their contributors in cash; instead they pay them in reprints of the articles they've written and these reprints are distributed enthusiastically by the proud authors. There were no letters or private documents, though one cardboard file contained copies of articles Molly had written and a contract from a publisher for a book she had been commissioned to write. The title of the book was to be *Bad Medicine*. I started to read through the papers but quickly realised that there were too many and that I needed to take them home with me. I found a roll of black plastic rubbish bags in a cupboard under the kitchen sink and filled three of them with files from the cabinet. I then carried the sacks out of the flat, dumped them in the boot of my car and drove home.

It took me six hours to skim (not read) through the papers and articles I'd collected. Individually the articles were troubling. En masse they were devastating. Some of the papers dealt with iatrogenesis as a whole, with analyses of the harm doctors do, but most dealt with vaccination. Molly had clearly collected together every medical or scientific article about vaccines and vaccination that she could possibly find. Judging by a few scribbled notes I found, it seemed that a sympathetic librarian in London had helped her. And the evidence she had accumulated showed conclusively that vaccines were simply neither safe nor effective. Every accusation she had made had been entirely accurate; every conclusion she had drawn had been correct and fair. Nothing she had said had been taken out of context; nothing she had written had been an exaggeration.

It was three in the morning when I finally sat back. There were piles of papers on every available surface – including the floor. I realised, for the first time, just how bad things had become and just how complete the corruption of the medical establishment had been.

We all know that bankers and politicians lie and cheat but I had not realised just how much doctors also lie and cheat to protect and defend their true masters – the drug companies. The papers which Molly had collected proved without any shadow of a doubt that the lying and the deceiving is done routinely and dispassionately and that it has spread everywhere throughout the profession. Molly had evidence of drug companies suppressing inconvenient truths and lists of members of the medical establishment who had close, financial links to the drug companies they were charged with regulating. There was even evidence of corruption among scientific journals. All this was printed openly. Available but largely unread. It was clear from what she had discovered that only the most corrupt doctors, the ones keenest to suppress the truth and to fill their wallets, were invited to sit on committees and exercise power. What a conspiracy!

The mass of doctors, the men and women who prescribe and authorise the vaccinations which are given, shut their eyes to the truth because they are well paid to keep silent. And I'd been part of it for too long. I'd known that our practice was making a huge chunk of its income out of force feeding vaccines to children and to the elderly but until Molly forced me to think about what we were doing I had kept my eyes and mind firmly shut. I had never even thought of asking the questions any decent doctor should have asked. I had trusted the government, the medical establishment and the drug industry implicitly. Did that make me a fool or a cheat or a crook? Whatever it made me I was part of the fraud.

As a breed, doctors used to be respected for their noble motives. Individual doctors had bravely fought greed, stupidity and the established way of doing things. John Snow, Ignaz Semmelweiss and Joseph Lister had fought on behalf of patients, and with no thought for their own professional positions. No more. Today, the drug companies have succeeded in controlling the profession and they have driven out all noble motives. Any doctor who dares to question the established way of doing things is regarded as, at best, an iconoclast, a maverick and a renegade and, at worst, a dangerous self-serving lunatic.

The big drug companies play hard ball in a way that the illegal drug dealers from South America can only envy. Thanks to their efforts the medical profession's leaders are a lethal mixture of psychopaths, frauds, thieves and liars. New discoveries are fêted and welcomed only if they are profitable. The mass of doctors are terrified to take a position questioning the wisdom of what they are told; they sit back, content to do as they are told, happy to ignore the unnecessary deaths and the deliberate disabling and crippling of untold thousands, and to count their fat payments as a reward for their silence.

And because Molly rose up as an unexpected, unwelcome nemesis, a deadly opponent to a hubristic profession, she had to be silenced.

They hadn't intended that she should die, of course.

Silencing her would do.

To begin with they had tried with bribery. The absurd scheme to 'buy' the practice through a bizarre sponsorship scheme was a standard drug company ploy. Throw money to doctors and they will beg endlessly for more. Jock and Deidre had swallowed the bait enthusiastically. Jock had a new, expensive house to rebuild and to furnish. Deidre would have succumbed if they'd offered her a half decent pen, or a weekend in a four star hotel. If the scheme had succeeded Molly would have been fired and, without a reference, she would have been unemployable and, therefore, silenced. But I'd had to stick my bloody-minded neck into the scheme. If I hadn't said 'no' the sponsorship scheme would have gone ahead and Molly would probably still be alive.

But I had defended my virtue; gathering my skirts around me like a Victorian maiden. And the sponsorship scheme had been abandoned.

So then, as a result of my squeamishness, the other plot was laid. Molly's crippled and ambitious but hopelessly untalented boyfriend was seduced with an offer of a spot on television so that she would be in the studios at a convenient moment. They knew that she would be with him and that I would be on call. They knew that if I could not remain on duty I would ring her and she would stand in for me. It was all blindingly simple. A few notes to a yob with a doubtless stolen truck. An offer of a contract to an ambitious young director. A spiked drink. Some telephone calls. A young doctor's career, respectability and reputation are ruined.

So very, very simple.

But things had gone even better than planned.

Molly had punched the policeman and as a result the case had become even more serious than the organisers had dared hope. And broken in spirit a young doctor with passion and compassion had killed herself. The nemesis was conveniently, if unexpectedly, silenced. Mission very accomplished.

As dawn broke, I listened to the sound of the waking birds and all became very simple. What I had to do wasn't just about vaccines and vaccination. It wasn't about revenge for Molly. It wasn't just about right or wrong. Mainly it was about self-respect.

It is always the existence of alternatives and choices which creates dilemmas, and suddenly there were no alternatives and no choices. 'Should I stay or should I go?' was no longer a question which was worth asking because there was no choice. I had reached a point where the pleasure in staying (which had, for some time, been reduced to the security of a comfortable sum appearing in my bank account every month) was far outweighed by the cost to my spirit. The upside was far outweighed by the unpleasant consequences of continuing to work with Jock and Deidre in a practice which would forever be run with about as much compassion as the average landmine factory. We didn't treat patients; we processed them. The patients we treated (and injected) were simply a means to an end. They were no longer the reason for our professional existence.

When now becomes then, what will our descendants think of us? We should live in shame.

I wrote my letter of resignation and on the way to the surgery I popped it into a post box.

I didn't care what happened to Jock or Deidre or Jim or Lavinia or Alfred Lunt. I would never be able to find enough evidence to convict any of them of anything. And they were, after all, nothing but foot soldiers fighting a war they didn't even really know they were fighting.

And in a way none of that mattered. Nothing would change the fact that Molly was dead; another casualty in the war to tell the truth.

The only thing that really mattered was the truth.

Chapter 36

Clarice and I went to an Italian restaurant neither of us had ever been to before. They called it a restaurant but on the continent it would have been described as a café. It wasn't very big. There were no more than eight or nine tables. She was wearing a simple, pink and white cotton dress which reminded me of summer days. Her hair lay loose around her shoulders. It was the first time I'd seen it hanging free. I was wearing my faithful sports jacket and the only pair of trousers I could find that weren't covered in blood, ink or food remains. My hair was uncombed and unbrushed because I could not find either a comb or a brush. I had, however, flattened and tidied it with my fingers. The restaurant was almost empty, either because it was unfashionable in that strange way that good eating places sometimes are, or because it was considered too out of the way for the locals, but the salad, the pasta and the baked pears in red wine had all been excellent. They didn't have steak and kidney pudding on the menu but I didn't care. They didn't even make chips.

I'd picked Clarice up at home and we'd decided not to bother with the cinema. The only films showing seemed to both of us to have been made with the sole aim of helping to sell over-priced popcorn and cola to indiscriminating teenagers in search of somewhere warmer, more comfortable and infinitely more private than the front room sofa.

She had a black eye which she had tried to disguise with make-up and she eventually told me how she'd got it.

`My ex-husband turned up. One of the neighbours phoned him and said I was seeing someone.'

`How did they know?'

`Probably because they'd heard I'd booked the babysitter. The neighbours where I live are seriously nosy. They would get prizes for gossiping if any were being given out; they probably moonlight for MI5.'

I told her I was sorry I'd caused her so much trouble.

`It's you I'm worried about,' she said. `If he finds out you're my doctor he'll cause as much trouble for you as he can.'

'He can't cause any trouble for me,' I told her. 'I don't think even the GMC will be interested in the fact that I've bought a meal for a patient.'

'And mended her washing machine.'

'They might be more worried about the washing machine,' I laughed. 'There's probably something in the code of conduct about not servicing domestic appliances which are connected to the mains water.'

'Seriously, could you get into trouble?'

'Not at the moment. It depends…' I left the thought unspoken.

She blushed. It was a charming, unexpected blush. 'If you want to see me again I could change practices. Would that help?'

I nodded. 'I do want to see you again. But you don't have to change practices. I've quit. Resigned.'

She looked surprised. 'Why? I didn't know doctors ever quit. They just always seem to go on for ever in the same place.'

I explained. I told her about Molly, and how and why she'd died, and about Jock and Deidre.

'Were you and Dr Tranter very close?' she asked.

'She was like a daughter,' I said. 'She was very brave. Too brave. Too young and too innocent to realise what she was taking on.'

'You and she weren't…?'

'No, no. Nothing like that. She had a boyfriend. He was disabled. The drug companies used him to help get to her.'

I told Clarice about the accident, Molly's arrest and her death. I told her what I knew and I told her what I suspected.

'Does he know? The boyfriend. Does he know they used him?'

I shook my head.

'What will you do? Will you stay in general practice?'

'Probably. It's the only thing I know how to do. But I'll have to move. There aren't any vacancies round here. Besides, I want to find a small solo practice. I want a job looking after a few hundred people living in a small, isolated community. I want to work too far away from civilisation for bureaucrats and social workers to visit and be a pain in the neck. I want to practice in an old-fashioned way; to be a solo practitioner, without an appointments system and without having to give bloody vaccinations. And because there will only be a few patients I'll have time to do a little research and writing of my own. I can carry on where Molly left off. I'm going to write the book she was planning to write. Or something similar. I'm going to tell the truth she started to tell. Someone has to take on the drug companies and the medical establishment. It pisses me off that they all continue to get away with suppressing the truth and killing patients simply so that they can carry on making vast amounts of money.'

'Do you think you'll be able to make people listen?'

'I don't know. But I have to do something - even if I fail to make a difference. The best any of us can hope for is to be judged by our intentions rather than our accomplishments. The truth is that I've wasted too much of my life. The most valuable commodity any of us has is time; it's the ultimately depreciating and deflationary asset. And I don't want to waste any more of it than I have to. I want to go somewhere quiet and peaceful where the days go by more slowly and where I can live in the past at a more peaceful pace. And while I'm there I'll write the book that may, or may not, change the world a little.'

The life had been squeezed out of me and I had forgotten what life was for. Now, I had a new life with new hopes. I had purpose.

'Are there any places like that?'

'Oh yes. If you travel far enough into the highlands of Scotland there are heaps of places like that. There are even a few islands which need doctors.'

'Aren't places like that swamped with applications from doctors wanting to get away from it all?'

'No. Not at all. Apparently they have a job finding doctors prepared to give up the 21st century dream and go back to living the sort of life that doctors enjoyed half a century or more. I rang someone working for NHS Scotland who is trying to find a GP to work on a small Scottish island with 200 inhabitants. It sounds perfect. The last GP who worked there used to do a morning surgery that sometimes lasted as long as half an hour.' Once or twice a week he visited a patient at home. Most of the rest of the time he painted and fished and knitted sweaters which he sold to a shop in Edinburgh. There's one pub and a tiny church and a boat which goes to the mainland three times a week to collect mail and supplies. In winter they're sometimes cut off for weeks at a time. The woman I spoke to said they'd give the job to the first doctor who applied as long as he was properly licensed and still breathing without external help. She said they'd prefer someone who didn't need an iron lung because of the slightly dodgy electricity supply on the island.'

Clarice looked to her right. We were sitting in an alcove by the window. Outside it was dark and raining lightly. A few cars were hurrying past. There were no pedestrians. `I've always dreamt of somewhere like that,' she said softly. `When I was a little girl I used to dream of living in a cottage miles from anywhere. Somewhere with log fires and a stream outside and lots of green as far as you can see.'

For a few moments neither of us said anything. We both took sips of cold coffee.

`I'll have to move too,' said Clarice at last. `My ex-husband will be back when he wants money. Or when he wants a woman he can beat up. I need to be somewhere else when he does turn up. Doug, my little boy, is terrified of him.'

`Will you be OK tonight?'

`He'll be paralytic by now. He won't come at night.'

Neither of us spoke for a while. One of the waiters was clearing away nearby tables. He was trying not to make too much noise.

`So we're both on the move,' I said.

Somehow, during the latter part of the evening our fingers had somehow become entwined. Very gently I squeezed her hand. She squeezed me back. It's surprising what you can say with a touch of the fingers.

`I'm going to sell everything I own here,' I told her. `Start afresh. Sell the house and send all the furniture to auction. I'll just keep my clothes and a few books. And the papers Molly collected. I want to get rid of everything else.‘

`Except your pipes.'

`I'll keep my pipes,' I agreed. `Wherever I go I want to be able to drive there. I don't want to fly and I don't want to take the train. I want to go there slowly, over a few days. You know how when you go somewhere by plane it's as though you haven't really gone anywhere new? The place looks different and the weather may be different but it's only taken an hour or two to get there and so it feels as if you've not really travelled.'

`I know what you mean. You want to go by car so that it'll seem as though you've travelled further; as though you're making a real break with the past.'

'Exactly. I want to travel a long, long way from here. I think I'll sell the car and buy an estate car. Or maybe a truck. Then I can take all my remaining stuff with me.'

Clarice looked down.

'What's the matter?'

She looked up. There were tears in her eyes.

'What's the matter?'

'It's silly. We've only just met. This is our first date. But it now it looks as though it might be our last.'

I touched her cheek with my free hand and wiped away a tear with my forefinger. 'That isn't the way I was thinking.'

'No?'

'We both want to change our lives. Why we don't we change them together?'

'You hardly know me.'

'It'll be an adventure we can share. We can get to know each other as we find our new lives together.'

'I've got a son.'

'I'd noticed him. I wasn't going to suggest that we left him behind. I'd like a son. And Doug is young enough for me to teach him tons of things about which I know absolutely nothing. A ready-made son is absolutely fine. Straight onto the football and cricket. No nappy rashes and sleepless nights. There's a small school on the island I mentioned. The woman I spoke to was very keen for me to know of all the amenities. They've got a road too. And one vehicle that functions as fire engine, ambulance and delivery truck. The last doctor who worked there did all his calls in a horse drawn buggy. The locals park their cars on the mainland and only use them when they leave the island.'

'Can you handle a horse?'

'I have no idea. I rode a donkey on the sands at Weston-super-Mare when I was six so I expect it'll all come to me quite easily. What do you think about living on an island?'

'I think it sounds idyllic.'

'Maybe not idyllic in the middle of winter when there's three foot of snow on the ground and no boat can reach the island. '

'This is all completely crazy.'

'Absolutely. It's totally crazy. What have we got to lose?'

She shook her head and laughed. She laughed a lot. She'd laughed more since I'd met her than Jock and Deidre had laughed in the years since I'd met them. She'd laughed more than Enid too. A good deal more. `Nothing. I've got nosy neighbours, a violent ex-husband and someone else's broken down kitchen appliances.'

`If we go by car you'll need to junk a lot of stuff.'

`Good. I haven't got much stuff and most of what there is needs junking.' Clarice looked around. `Have you noticed that we're the last people in here.'

`Do you think we should go and let them shut up and go home?'

The two solitary waiters were standing by the door to the kitchen. They had cleared and cleaned all the other tables. I drew a rectangle in the air. The head waiter brought over the bill which he had already prepared. I paid him, adding a generous tip. He smiled and seemed content. Sometimes it's very easy to make people happy. We left. I took Clarice back to the neat semi with the clean kitchen floor and the washing machine which no longer leaked. We stood on her doorstep. The street lights had been switched off long ago but the house and the street were lit by a half moon. We kissed. Although it was the end of an evening it was the beginning of something much more substantial.

It wouldn't be easy. But for the first time in many years I was looking forward to tomorrow.